Creating Inclusive Learning Opportunities in Higher Education

A UNIVERSAL DESIGN TOOLKIT

Sheryl E. Burgstahler

HARVARD EDUCATION PRESS
Cambridge, Massachusetts

Paperback ISBN 978-1-68253-540-0
Library Edition ISBN 978-1-68253-541-7
Library of Congress Cataloging-in-Publication Data

Names: Burgstahler, Sheryl, author.
Title: Creating inclusive learning opportunities in higher education : a universal design toolkit / Sheryl E. Burgstahler.
Description: Cambridge, Massachusetts : Harvard Education Press, [2020] | Includes index. | Summary: "In Creating Inclusive Learning Opportunities in Higher Education, Sheryl Burgstahler provides a practical, step-by-step guide for putting the principles of universal design into action"—Provided by publisher.
Identifiers: LCCN 2020030723 | ISBN 9781682535400 (paperback) | ISBN 9781682535417 (library binding)
Subjects: LCSH: People with disabilities--Education (Higher)—United States. | People with disabilities—Services for—United States. | College students with disabilities—Services for—United States. | Universal design—United States. | Barrier-free design—United States. | Educational equalization—United States. | Learning disabled—Education (Higher)—United States.
Classification: LCC LC4818.38 .B87 2020 | DDC 371.9/04740973—dc23
LC record available at https://lccn.loc.gov/2020030723

Published by Harvard Education Press,
an imprint of the Harvard Education Publishing Group

Harvard Education Press
8 Story Street
Cambridge, MA 02138

Cover Design: Endpaper Studio
Cover Image: iStock.com/HORDIEIEV ROMAN

The typefaces used in this book are Candide and Trade Gothic.

This book is dedicated to people who take actions, large and small, to promote a world that fully includes people who do not look like them, talk like them, think like them, or act like them.

CONTENTS

Foreword vii
Ana Mari Cauce

Preface ix

1 Diversity, Disability, and Civil Rights 1

2 A Framework for Inclusive Practices 27

3 Physical Spaces 57

4 Technology 73

5 Teaching and Learning Activities 109

6 Teaching and Learning Services 151

7 Teaching About UD 163

8 A Model for an Inclusive Campus 177

9 What I Know for Sure 207

Notes 211

About the Author 217

Index 219

FOREWORD

NO INSTITUTION can truly achieve greatness unless it recognizes and welcomes the full spectrum of human diversity—the vast range of identities, perspectives, strengths, and weaknesses, including people with disabilities. Inclusion cannot be an afterthought; it is foundational for excellence. However, all too frequently, the concepts of diversity and inclusion are held up as institutional values without a meaningful understanding or effective framework by which to make them more than mere slogans.

Even the most well-intentioned colleges and universities can struggle with how to adopt and operationalize policies and practices that fully enable everyone to be seen and heard and to participate. In this, the follow-up to her book *Universal Design in Higher Education: From Principles to Practice*, Sheryl Burgstahler offers a practical, step-by-step guide to put the principles of Universal Design in Higher Education (UDHE) into practice, sharing real-world applications that relate to the business of postsecondary teaching and learning in the United States.

Professor Burgstahler has been a pioneer of UDHE. Her simple yet radical approach has been to ask how courses, technologies, physical environments, systems, and whole institutions can be designed from the ground up to be accessible to people who may be blind, deaf, have mobility limitations, or are neurodiverse. Indeed, she has helped the world redefine and expand the definition of diversity to acknowledge that people with disabilities are and always have been a part of our human family. Through the UDHE lens that she presents, we can all begin to ask ourselves what it will take to construct a world that is as accessible as possible for as many people as possible. Through this lens, future advances in technology and design will better serve all of us by creating environments that serve everyone.

Just as UDHE invites us to think broadly about how different people interact with the human-made world, Dr. Burgstahler also invites us to think broadly about who can play a role in creating accessibility and to see how nearly everyone involved in the educational ecosystem can be supportive of inclusive teaching and learning. This includes educators and student service providers, but it also includes IT support staff, parents, peers, and policy makers. In a work that covers everything from basic terminology to comprehensive systemic change, there is something for everyone who cares about inclusivity in higher education.

Through stories, examples, and first-person accounts, Dr. Burgstahler presents a pragmatic picture of how to take specific and realistic steps to make institutions more accessible and inclusive. The stories—especially from the people whose lives are most affected by increased accessibility—are a profound reminder that people with disabilities are not an abstraction. They are our colleagues, classmates, neighbors, friends, and family. They are entitled to share the spaces, systems, and technologies that we all rely on. And when those elements of daily life are not available to them, the result is injustice and a price that, ultimately, we all pay.

As the director of Accessible Technology Services (ATS), which includes the DO-IT (Disabilities, Opportunities, Internetworking, and Technology) Center at the University of Washington, Dr. Burgstahler is a national leader in empowering people with disabilities and promoting a cultural shift toward leveling the playing field for people with disabilities. Through her work, she has educated, advocated, and worked tirelessly to increase access to the classroom and workplace for people with disabilities. By applying the innovative strategies presented in this book, countless others will now have the opportunity to develop more inclusive practices at their own institutions.

Ana Mari Cauce
President, University of Washington
Professor of Psychology

PREFACE

AS A STUDENT at Hazel Valley Elementary School in Seattle in the mid 1950s, when I saw my first Patrol Boy, I was immediately enamored with the "uniform"—a white sash that shouted out that you had an important job to do, and the flag on a stick that gave you the authority to tell other kids when it was safe to cross the street. I decided early on that, when I reached sixth grade to qualify, I would immediately apply—this was the perfect job for me. When I was old enough, however, I was told that the position was only for boys, as clearly indicated by its title. I knew that *boy* was in the title, but I also knew I could do the job. I had been hanging out with my brother, male cousins, and the guys who worked at my dad's used car business; it did not concern me that I would be the only girl in the group. I made a compelling case for inclusion on the Patrol Boy team, but my application was still rejected. *Boy* meant boy! And, besides, as the principal pointed out, girls were not "strong enough" for the position. But wait—had I missed something in the job description? I knew I was strong enough to carry the flag. To add insult to injury, my teacher was encouraging boys to apply to be Patrol Boys because not enough had done so that year. I left the experience disappointed but concluded that people in leadership positions make silly decisions. Since my girlfriends were uninterested, I was certain I was the only girl who wanted to be a Patrol Boy but have since learned that some girls broke through the glass ceiling before I was even born. In 1944, the Canadian Schoolboy Patrol Club, which launched in 1937, admitted Canadian girls to their ranks and changed their name to Safety Patrol.

End of story.

Not quite! But you'll have to wait until chapter 9, "What I Know for Sure," to learn how my dream of becoming a Patrol Boy was eventually realized due to the sensitivity of a young man who learned about my failed pursuit.

So what does the quest of a pushy young girl to become a Patrol Boy have to do with the topic of this book? Well, a commonly reported barrier that people with disabilities face in reaching success in college and careers is the negative attitudes of individuals in gatekeeper positions who label them unqualified without knowing much about them and with little interest in learning more. Some people who impose limits have good intentions or at least claim to. Their attitudes are particularly hard to change in part *because* they are associated with good intentions.

This book provides practical steps you can take to make postsecondary offerings more inclusive, particularly of people with disabilities, and thus contribute to a paradigm shift to a more inclusive campus. I start with a little background information about the experiences of students with disabilities in higher education and the efforts of the DO-IT Center, which I founded in 1992 and continue to lead as part of my responsibilities as the Director of Accessible Technology Services (ATS) at the University of Washington (UW). DO-IT stands for Disabilities, Opportunities, Internetworking, and Technology.

Although there is a significant gap between the accomplishments of students with and without disabilities, the success stories of some individuals with disabilities demonstrate that opportunities do exist for those who can successfully overcome barriers imposed by inaccessible facilities, technology, documents, textbooks and learning activities, student services, and other aspects of colleges and universities. That's what the DO-IT Center is all about. Our projects and programs have helped hundreds of high school and college students with all types of disabilities—including those that affect speech, sight, movement, social interactions, learning, health, and the ability to pay attention—gain access to transformative technology; develop self-determination, academic, and career skills; and learn to advocate for others. Based on a literature review and evaluation data from almost thirty years of practice, the critical junctures model illustrated in figure P.1 presents key steps toward the success of people with disabilities, particularly in science, technology, engineering, and mathematics (STEM) fields.[1] It highlights technology access, mentoring, peer support, and other interventions that are effective in supporting them on their life journeys. Participants continue in our programs to offer support to those who come after them. Project staff are fortunate to be among those who engage with participants as they find their way toward success in college, graduate school, and careers, as well as help others do the same.

FIGURE P.1 DO-IT's *AccessSTEM* inputs lead students with disabilities through critical junctures toward careers

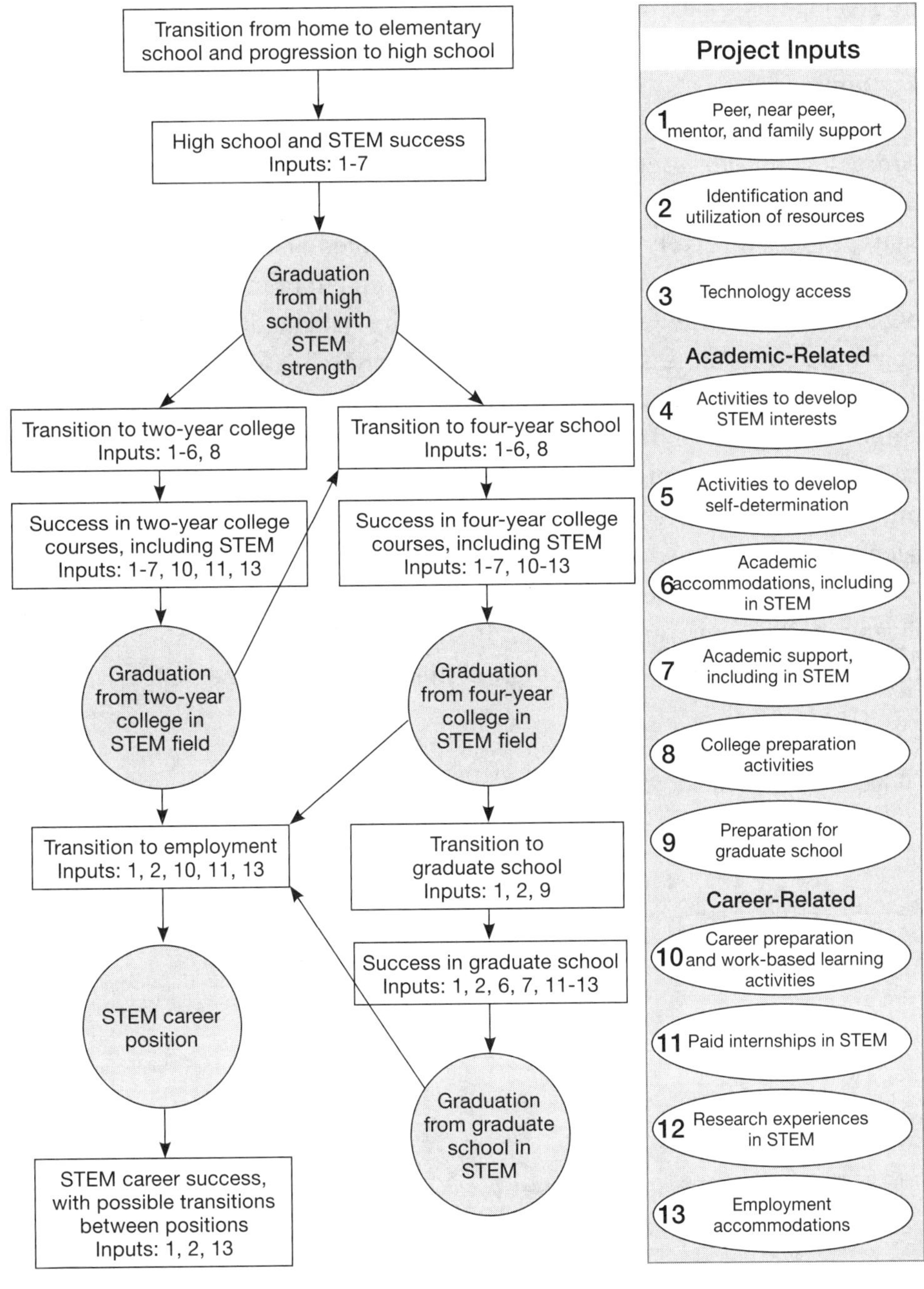

Now all we need to do is replicate programs like DO-IT, as we did with the launch of DO-IT Japan in 2007, for students with disabilities around the globe to develop the social, behavioral, technological, and academic competencies needed to realize their dreams.

Not so fast!

Preparing individuals with disabilities for success, undoubtedly important, addresses only one facet of the problem. Societal changes are also necessary to dismantle institutional inequities and level the playing field for this population, just as is the case for other underrepresented and underserved groups. Systemic changes like these require the involvement of many individuals and organizations. Figure P.2 identifies many of the stakeholders who can impede or promote the success of individuals with disabilities in higher education and careers. They include family members and allies; technology companies; employers; postsecondary administrators, faculty, and staff; legislators and policy makers; peers, near peers, and other individuals with disabilities; community leaders; service providers; K–12 teachers and counselors; and funding agencies. Who was it who said, "It takes a village"?

Institutions of higher education often profess goals to attract students with diverse backgrounds and provide all students with an equitable academic experience. Most relevant to the topic of this book, among their efforts to meet

FIGURE P.2 Stakeholders who can promote the success of people with disabilities

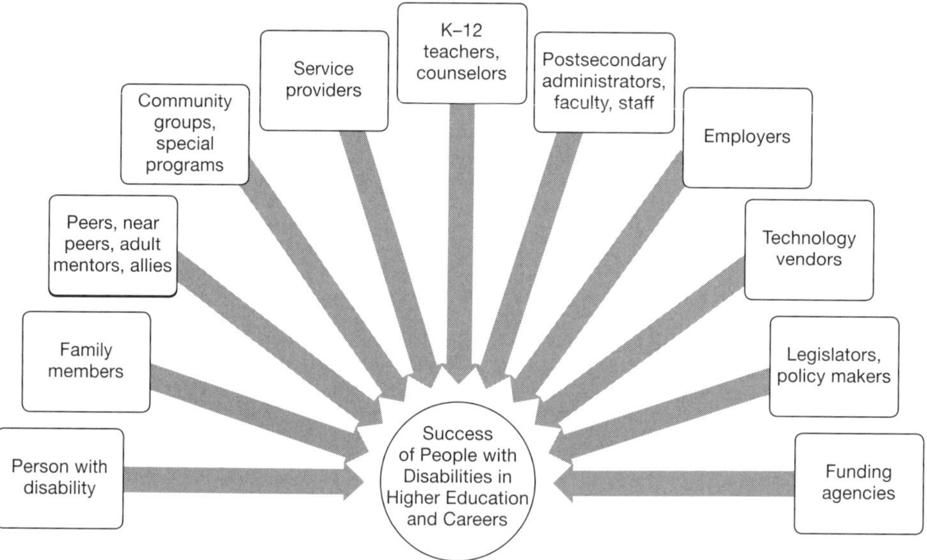

diversity and equity goals, postsecondary institutions can take steps to make physical spaces, technology, courses, and services accessible and otherwise welcoming to everyone, including people with disabilities. Universal design (UD) offers an overall approach for making necessary changes. Broadly speaking, UD challenges society to construct a world in which everyone can fully participate.

UD is consistent with social models of diversity and disability that, rather than looking first at characteristics of an individual, look first to those of products, environments, and social structures to identify and then remove barriers to full inclusion. UD encourages anyone designing a building, a course, a service, an event, a video, a website, or another product or environment to consider in the design process the diverse characteristics of potential users, including those with respect to race, ethnicity, culture, language, gender, sexual orientation, age, and ability. Proactive thinking at the design stage can reduce the need for disability-related accommodations and other adjustments required to include an individual after an inaccessible product or environment is created. In this book I share examples of how looking through a UD lens can lead to making curriculum and instruction better for everyone, physical spaces better for everyone, technology better for everyone, student services better for everyone, just about every design better for everyone. When those of us who teach include UD topics in our curriculum, we can also contribute to a world that is more inclusive of everyone through the future careers of our students.

Much of the content for this book emerged from projects associated with the DO-IT Center. With most funding coming from the US Department of Education and the National Science Foundation (NSF), DO-IT has led dozens of Universal Design in Higher Education (UDHE) initiatives to promote the application of UD to all aspects of postsecondary education. During its UDHE journey, DO-IT has engaged with hundreds of postsecondary institutions nationwide to develop and apply UDHE to the procurement, development, and use of technology, as well as to the design of physical spaces, student services, and learning materials and activities. Early efforts culminated in the formation of the Center for Universal Design in Education on the DO-IT website (uw.edu/doit), which continues to grow as new initiatives unfold. Among CUDE's many resources is the Knowledge Base. Search the Knowledge Base for questions and answers, case studies, and promising practices relevant to UDHE applications in education by selecting "Knowledge Base" and the "CUDE" Program/Area; then refine your search to locate content related to UDHE among the hundreds of articles included in the Knowledge Base.

The DO-IT website also hosts *AccessCollege*, a comprehensive collection of resources tailored to the needs and interests of specific stakeholders. Here, you will find the following "rooms":

- *The Faculty Room*, for instructors and academic leaders
- *The Student Services Conference Room*, for student service administrators and support staff
- *The Board Room*, for college and university administrators
- *The Student Lounge*, for students with disabilities
- *The Veterans Center*, for student veterans and related service providers
- *The Employment Office*, for employers
- *The Science Lab*, for STEM teachers
- The *Center for Universal Design in Education*, for all educators

My passion for inclusion is grounded in personal, academic, and professional experiences. Many ideas coalesced in the late 1970s when I taught a child named Rodney how to use a desktop computer. Rodney, whose hands could not operate a keyboard, used a mouth stick to press the keys. In our journey, we had to discover how to modify the computer so that he could fully operate it with his mouth wand. As I engaged with Rodney, my view came to be that most of the obstacles he faced were not caused by his physical limitations, but rather the limitations of physical products and environments he encountered—the building entrance, the elevator, the floor plan, the computer, the candy machine, and the list goes on and on. Clearly, designers did not routinely expect someone like Rodney to use what they created. But why not? There have always been children with disabilities in the world. Sometimes society chooses not to see them. Sometimes well-meaning people try to protect them from a harsh world. Others write them off as uninterested or incapable of reaching goals typical of their peers who do not have disabilities.

I joined forces with others who asked simple questions like "Why can't a person who is blind use this computer?" We rejected simple answers like "Because she is blind." Instead, we asked, "Why can't this oh-so-smart computer just speak to her?" Over time, the work in ATS, including the DO-IT Center, has increasingly addressed the proactive design of accessible mainstream technologies to minimize the need for, but be compatible with, specialized technologies for individuals with disabilities. It became clear to us that campuses worldwide have erected many other obstacles for people with disabilities that could have been easily avoided through the adoption of inclusive practices throughout all phases of the design process. A UD approach holds promise for moving forward the agenda of advocates for a more inclusive world.

ABOUT THIS BOOK

This book documents applications of UDHE that impact teaching and learning on-site and online. Although differences in UD terminology are presented in the literature, "the goal is profound: we can and should make our human-made world as accessible and usable as possible for as diverse a user population as possible."[2] To control its length, although UDHE is applied worldwide and benefits many people, most examples presented in the book are in the United States and focus on students with disabilities. I share UDHE perspectives and practices gathered throughout my travels, but many specific examples are from my campus, not because they are necessarily best practices, but rather because I know their evolution, challenges we encountered in implementation, and lessons we learned.

This book complements *Universal Design in Higher Education: From Principles to Practice*, for which I am editor and lead author.[3] In that book, more than forty authors and coauthors who are leaders in the field present a comprehensive exploration of research and practice relevant to UDHE. It is appropriate for academic courses in higher education, student services, and diversity studies, and I use it as a text in online courses I teach in disability studies and disability services programs. In this book, I often refer to this earlier work for a deeper dive into the content being discussed and a more comprehensive list of references.

The first book is not a prerequisite for understanding this one. The current publication should be particularly useful for those readers who are ready to undertake actions for making their institution or a specific aspect of it more inclusive. It is particularly well suited for

- disability service providers who want to learn how to move from accommodation-focused services for students with disabilities to an approach that also promotes inclusive practices campuswide to minimize the need for accommodations;
- managers of information technology (IT), facilities, and student services who want to be more proactive in making their on-site and online offerings beneficial to everyone;

- academic instructors and instructional designers who wish to combine UD with evidence-based on-site and online teaching practices to better meet the needs of an increasingly diverse student body;
- professional development trainers who wish to include inclusive practices in their training and make on-site and online training sessions accessible to all learners;
- individuals who are looking for tips to get started in implementing UD in their area of practice; and
- diversity leaders looking for a potential framework to underpin an implementation model that can be tailored to address diversity issues on any campus.

In this book I present a UDHE framework as one that can be fleshed out into a toolkit for the design of physical spaces, technology, teaching, and services that is compatible with any other approaches an institution embraces for becoming more inclusive. I also briefly cover the development and measurement of campus culture, medical diagnoses related to specific impairments and disabilities, reasonable accommodations, commercially available assistive technology, accessible technology design, and legal issues and in each chapter point to more resources to learn more. Following are titles of the nine chapters of this book:

- Chapter 1: Diversity, Disability, and Civil Rights
- Chapter 2: A Framework for Inclusive Practices
- Chapter 3: Physical Spaces
- Chapter 4: Technology
- Chapter 5: Teaching and Learning Activities
- Chapter 6: Teaching and Learning Services
- Chapter 7: Teaching About UD
- Chapter 8: A Model for an Inclusive Campus
- Chapter 9: What I Know for Sure

UD strategies are presented throughout but were also used to create this book. For example, it is available from the publisher in an accessible electronic format for people who face challenges to reading printed materials. This book includes UD features that make it more readable for everyone, including those with disabilities related to sight or learning. Each chapter begins with an abstract summarizing its content followed by an introduction that includes specific learning objectives so you know where you are headed. Chapters are ordered so that new content builds on previous chapters, but all chapters point to earlier foundational material and thus can be read out of the order in which they are presented. I define acronyms when first used in each chapter—so be prepared to see UDHE spelled out nine times! I also make generous use of bulleted lists to make content easy to digest in small chunks. "My Go-To Resources" sections at the end of each chapter list good launch points for further exploration.

Throughout the book you will find content with a shaded background under "TAKE ACTION!" section headings with this image:

Each Take Action! item is labeled as a (LEARN), (REFLECT), or (APPLY) exercise according to its purpose for you to

- REFLECT on how the content in the chapter is relevant to you,
- LEARN about UDHE topics by yourself or within academic and professional development courses or communities of practice, or
- APPLY UDHE to practices in a specific area or institutionwide.

Another feature of the book is periodic sidebars with optional reading labeled as follows:

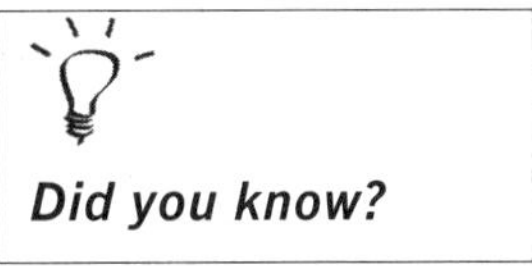

If you want to absorb the content of this book without considering specific actions or reading optional text, simply skip all of the shaded Take Action! items and "Did you know?" sidebars. To locate specific content, consult the table of contents, the index, or table P.1 to discover where answers to specific questions can be found.

Throughout the book you will find many ways you can personally engage in a UDHE initiative. In addition, through the DO-IT Center, you can

- join our UDHE online community of practice (CoP) of individuals interested in sharing UDHE practices and resources; send your request to doit@uw.edu;
- propose questions and answers, case studies, and promising practices to add to DO-IT's Knowledge Base; send a draft to doit@uw.edu; and
- submit articles to an online book in the CUDE, *Universal Design in Higher Education: Promising Practices*, by following the author guidelines in its preface.

TABLE P.1 Questions answered in this book

If this is your question	*Find your answer in chapter:*
What are types of disabilities?	1
What challenges do postsecondary students with disabilities face?	1
What are rights and responsibilities of students with disabilities and institutions regarding access issues?	1
What is the history of UD?	2
How does UD compare with other proactive approaches to design?	2
How are UD, UDHE, UDL, and UDI defined?	2
To what institutional offerings can UDHE be applied?	2
What is a framework for applying UDHE?	2
What are the principles of UDHE and a process for applying it?	2
What would a paradigm shift toward a more inclusive campus look like?	2
Who are beneficiaries of UDHE?	2
What are UDHE principles and guidelines for physical spaces?	2, 3
What is the difference between a space being "ADA compliant" and universally designed?	3
What are UDHE principles and guidelines for IT?	2, 4
What is the difference between assistive technology and accessible technology design?	4
What are key points in the civil rights rulings regarding the inaccessible design of IT?	4
What are UDHE principles and guidelines for teaching and learning activities—the Universal Design of Instruction (UDI)?	2, 5
How does UDI relate to teaching and learning theories and research?	5
How can I apply UDI when I teach online ?	5
How can I apply UDI to an entire academic department or program?	5
What do students with disabilities have to say about UDI?	5
What are UDHE principles and guidelines for campus services offered on-site and online?	2, 6
What types of services can be enhanced by applying principles of UDHE?	6
Why teach about disabilities, accessibility, and UD in courses?	7
How can I integrate disabilities, accessibility, and UD concepts into my courses?	7
What might a model for an inclusive campus look like?	8
How can a model for an inclusive campus be applied to IT?	8
What are roles stakeholders can play in promoting UDHE?	8
What are promoters and inhibitors of change to a UDHE paradigm?	8
How does Oprah Winfrey fit in?	9

CONCLUSION

I have always considered UD to be an old idea with a new name, an ideal more than a fully achievable result, a process more than a set of prescriptive practices, and a journey more than a destination. I look forward to sharing the journey with readers of this book as I have with collaborators in DO-IT's UDHE initiatives. Many thanks to those who have contributed to my ever-growing understanding of how looking at all offerings through a UDHE lens can contribute to making a campus more inclusive. A special thanks also goes to the DO-IT Center for creating line drawings presented in this book; you can use them in your publications or on your websites as well; check out our collection at uw.edu/doit/line-drawings-and-images.

Sheryl E. Burgstahler, PhD
Founder and Director, DO-IT Center
and Accessible Technology Services
University of Washington, Seattle

Acknowledgment

Some of the content of this book is based on work supported by the US Department of Education Office of Postsecondary Education (grant numbers P333A990042, P333A020044, and P333A050064) and the National Science Foundation (grant numbers CNS-1539179, DRL-1824540, DRL-199906147, HRD-0833504, and HRD-1834924). Any opinions, findings, and conclusions or recommendations are those of the author and do not necessarily reflect the policy or views of the federal government. The Principles of Universal Design were conceived and developed by the Center for Universal Design at North Carolina State University. Use or application of the Principles in any form is separate and distinct from the Principles and does not constitute or imply acceptance or endorsement by the Center for Universal Design of the use or application.

CHAPTER 1

Diversity, Disability, and Civil Rights

The secret of getting ahead
is getting started.

—Mark Twain

IN THIS CHAPTER I share a historical perspective on diversity in higher education and touch on topics that include the meaning of *impairment, disability*, and *handicap*; disability awareness; rights and responsibilities of students with disabilities and institutions of higher education; and the accommodation approach to providing access to postsecondary opportunities.

INTRODUCTION

For many years, institutions of higher education in the United States were dominated by white, able-bodied men. Today, more than half of the postsecondary student population is female, and students are diverse with respect to race, ethnicity, cultural background, sexual identity, socioeconomic level, age, religious beliefs, values, marital status, academic interests, work experiences, specific abilities, and myriad other characteristics. Each individual is associated with multiple identity groups, most of which are not obvious to others, and makes choices regarding which identities to disclose, to whom, and when. Diversity is not unusual, but rather the norm, when it comes to the human experience.

In this chapter I introduce diversity issues, especially those related to people with disabilities, as well as institutional efforts to accommodate them. By the end of the chapter, you should be able to

- describe ways students on postsecondary campuses represent a diverse group;
- tell how each ability of any individual can be measured on a continuum;
- compare meanings of *impairment*, *disability*, and *handicap*;
- describe challenges students with disabilities face in transitioning to and succeeding in college;
- discuss differences in services provided to precollege and college students with disabilities;
- define and provide examples of *accommodations*;
- compare challenges to education experienced by students with different types of disabilities; and
- summarize the rights and responsibilities of students with disabilities and institutions of higher education.

DISABILITY BASICS

Most groups are diverse in myriad ways. With respect to a person's level of ability, this diversity can be related to personal characteristics, past experiences, as well as aspects of the environment. For example, a student who does not have a visual impairment sitting in the back row of an auditorium may not be able to see the content of a presentation slide because the text is too small for anyone seated so far from the screen. Given specific conditions, every person could be rated on a scale from "not able" to "able" with respect to the ability to see, hear, move, read print, write with a pen or pencil, communicate verbally, tune out distraction, learn, manage physical/mental health, and perform various tasks, as illustrated in figure 1.1. This approach is consistent with our understanding of variations with respect to other human characteristics such as socioeconomic status and age.

A person with a low level of a specific ability may be labeled as having a disability. His disability may have been diagnosed at birth or later in life and may change over time as a result of an underlying medical condition or as a normal

FIGURE 1.1 Abilities can be measured on a continuum

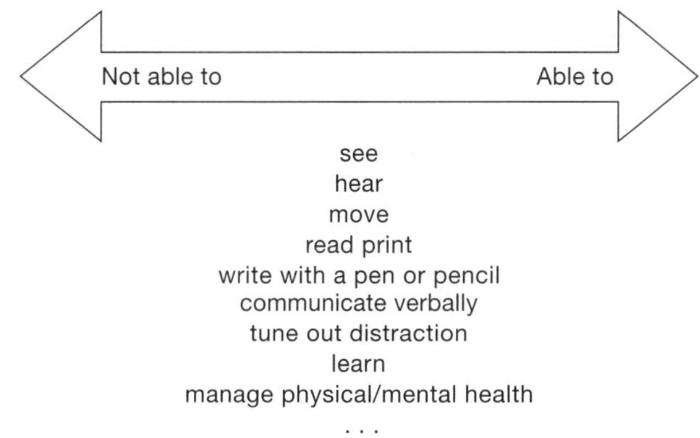

part of the aging process. A great deal of diversity exists within specific disability categories and various levels of disability within those categories. There are, for example, many types of specific learning disabilities and of levels of severity within each type. Typically, students with dyslexia mix up letters in words and find it difficult to read printed materials, people with dysgraphia have trouble forming letters and writing, students with dyscalculia find it difficult to understand certain math concepts and symbols, and those with dyspraxia mix up words and sentences while talking. With so many types and levels of disabilities combined with other types of differences, it is good that most of us do not need to be knowledgeable about the medical diagnosis of a specific individual with a disability. Disability services offices on our campus are charged with dealing with that level of detail. For the rest of us, our time might be most productive by learning to design our offerings to be inclusive of students with diverse characteristics. Good news: That is what this book is all about.

The words *impairment, disability,* and *handicap* are often used interchangeably, and their precise meanings continue to be debated within disability-related communities and the academic field of disability studies. The term *impairment* is often used to refer to a loss of or an atypical capability with respect to a psychological, physiological, or anatomical structure or function, such as having damage to a certain portion of the brain or having only one leg. Consistent with the US Americans with Disabilities Act of 1990 (ADA) and its 2008 amendments, *disability* is considered a physical or mental impairment that substantially limits a major life activity.[1] A major life activity includes caring for oneself, seeing, hearing, eating, sleeping, walking, lifting, speaking, breathing, learning, reading, concentrating, and communicating. When we use terms in these ways, someone may have an impairment but not a disability because the impairment does not substantially limit a major life activity.

The term *handicap* is generally considered an outdated and derogatory term for describing a person with an impairment or disability. It may, however, be appropriately used when referring to a circumstance that makes success at something difficult for a person: a criminal record is a handicap when seeking employment. Considering a handicap in this way focuses attention on the interaction of an environment and a person attempting to reach a specific outcome within it. A person does not *have* a handicap but may *experience* one in a certain situation.

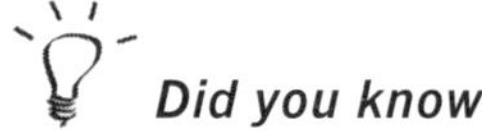

Did you know?

You may wonder why both *Deaf* and *deaf* are used in the literature when referring to people who are deaf or hard of hearing. The lowercase *d* can be used when you are specifically talking about hearing ability. A capital *D* is used when referring to Deaf culture, with which many people who are deaf or hard of hearing identify.

Some individuals have strong opinions about proper terminology to use when referring to people with impairments or disabilities. I'm one of them. Will someone please convene a meeting so that *we*—whoever that might include—can reach consensus on what terms are proper and under what circumstances? Until that happens, it is good to respect preferences of individuals regarding how they wish to be addressed, to use commonly accepted words, and to avoid within-group slang. You can rest assured that if one person says *everyone* in a group of individuals with a specific disability prefers certain terminology, that statement is almost certainly wrong. Even the popular person-first way of describing people with disabilities—that is, "people who are blind"—is challenged by some who prefer identity-first language—that is, "blind people." Stereotyping people in the majority population should be avoided as well; any sentence that begins with "People without disabilities think that . . . " is most likely untrue.

When talking about people with disabilities, it is good to just remove from our vocabularies *afflicted with*, *crippled*, *deformed*, *dim*, *feeble-minded*, *freak*, *lunatic*, *moron*, *retarded*, *stricken*, *suffers from*, *victim*, and other outdated terms with a negative connotation. Simply being descriptive is usually adequate. Saying a person is *confined* to a wheelchair or *wheelchair-bound*, for example, frames the wheelchair and the person using it in a negative light. It is also inaccurate. Someone using a liberating technology like a wheelchair would be *confined* without it. Referring to people with disabilities as *patients* in nonmedical situations is also an inaccurate use of the word.

Even labels that at first glance appear positive can come across as dismissive or patronizing and may be inaccurate. As a young woman who is blind responded to the label *alternatively able*, "There is nothing about being blind that makes me *alternatively able* to do something!" She isn't *alternatively able* to play the piano; she is simply *able* to do so. She wondered out loud, "Doesn't intentionally avoiding the term *disability* suggest that there is something inherently negative about having one?"

Did you know?

Neurodiversity is a viewpoint that brain differences are normal, not abnormal. With this view, people with conditions like attention-deficit hyperactivity, autism, and learning disabilities can be described as neurodivergent or neuroatypical. People without such characteristics are sometimes called neurotypical.

Stereotypes should always be avoided. Even if considered positive, they can be hurtful to those who do not conform to them. I am reminded of a student I caught cheating on a test in a calculus class I taught. Although there was a penalty for his behavior, I have never forgotten his touching confession of the pressures he felt from his family and associates for being an Asian student who was *not* good at math. This student's experience made me reflect on my experiences in feeling the pressure to constantly prove my skills in mathematics because I did not "look like" someone who was good at math. We should remember that people with disabilities experience success at *all* levels, including at the extraordinary level of Stephen Hawking, the famous theoretical physicist and cosmologist who was director of research at the Centre for Theoretical Cosmology at the University of Cambridge at the time of his death in 2018. His image is presented in figure 1.2.

I could fill many pages with terms for medical diagnoses and disabilities, but that is beyond the scope of this book. To locate such details, consult the "My Go-To Resources" section at the end of this chapter.

Did you know?

Increasing numbers of leaders in postsecondary institutions are considering disability a diversity issue and arguing for terminology that is a better reflection of this view. For example, *neurodiversity* is sometimes used to refer to diversity with respect to the neurological characteristics of a student body;[2] a person on the autism spectrum might be referred to as *neuroatypical* while another student might be labeled *neurotypical*.

Accurate statistics regarding people with disabilities are hard to come by because of differences in the way disabilities are defined, lack of systemized processes for collecting data, and inconsistences as a result of relying on self-reports. A further complication in

FIGURE 1.2 Stephen Hawking operates a computer-based communication device

classifying people is that people who have disabilities have other identities as well that impact their performance and engagement in different settings. It is important to consider such intersectionality to avoid misconceptions about a group. The functional abilities of two students who are at the same level on the autism spectrum, for example, may be quite different if one received minimal special education services and engagement of parents in therapy and the other benefited from a rich set of services and significant parental involvement.

Estimates indicate that more than 10 percent of the students in postsecondary education in the United States have disabilities, and most of them are not obvious—for example, learning disabilities, autism spectrum disorders, and attention deficits. Estimates also indicate that fewer than one-third of students who have disabilities report them to the institution in which they enroll. Students may not report disabilities because they don't need accommodations or because they fear potential discrimination, are embarrassed about their disabilities, or don't understand what accommodations are available and how they might benefit them.

One thing we know for sure is that the total number of students who disclose their disabilities and receive accommodations continues to increase at a fast rate. Some schools report the number of students making use of their services for students with disabilities has more than doubled in the past decade. Why is this? There are more students with disabilities? More students are being diagnosed with disabilities? More students with disabilities are being adequately prepared for college studies? Individuals with disabilities are more accepted on a postsecondary campus? Better services are offered on campuses? More information technology (IT) products that benefit individuals with disabilities are born accessible? Better medication and other treatments allow more people with disabilities to engage in postsecondary studies? I think the answer to the "why" question might be a combination of these issues and more. The point is, students with disabilities have an increasing presence on our campuses, and institutions of higher education have typically responded with more accommodations.

CHALLENGES FACED BY STUDENTS

People with disabilities have a long history of less access to information, technology, places, and services than that of other people. The following subsections provide examples of challenges faced by some students with various levels of physical, sensory, learning, attention, and communication abilities. Solutions are detailed in later chapters of this book.

Physical Differences

Spaces that are not wheelchair accessible and do not offer options for furniture arrangement are not usable by some students and instructors. Some furniture in classrooms is uncomfortable for larger students. An individual who uses assistive technology that emulates only functions of a standard keyboard, as illustrated in figure 1.3, cannot navigate campus websites that require the use of a mouse.

Communication Differences

Fast-paced on-site or online discussions, webinars, or audio conferences may limit the participation of students with communication differences that may be related to hearing ability, brain injuries, autism spectrum disorders, native language, culture, or age. Audio content of videos and other multimedia that is not captioned or transcribed may be inaccessible or difficult to process for these individuals.

Visual Differences

Web content that requires the ability to distinguish one color from another may present a barrier to access for people who are color blind. Content on a

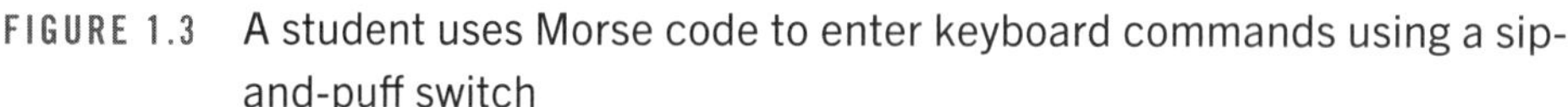

FIGURE 1.3 A student uses Morse code to enter keyboard commands using a sip-and-puff switch

standard computer screen is inaccessible to individuals who are blind unless it is available in a structured text-based format that can be read aloud by screen reading software and a speech synthesizer and converted to braille devices, as illustrated in figure 1.4. Individuals who have limited vision use software to enlarge screen images and often view only a small portion of content at one time; they are handicapped by cluttered web pages and inconsistent page layouts.

Learning Differences

Delivering course content in a single mode, such as by lecture, may create an access challenge for some students with a wide variety of learning strengths and preferences. Websites that change formats from one page to the next, crowd too much content on the screen, or move to new content using timers rather than user-controlled functions erect barriers to students with specific learning disabilities that affect the ability to read, write, or process information. When time provided to complete a test is inadequate, students with disabilities that affect processing speed are placed at a disadvantage. Some students with learning disabilities that affect their ability to interpret written text are at a disadvantage when printed textbooks that cannot be read aloud are the only option.

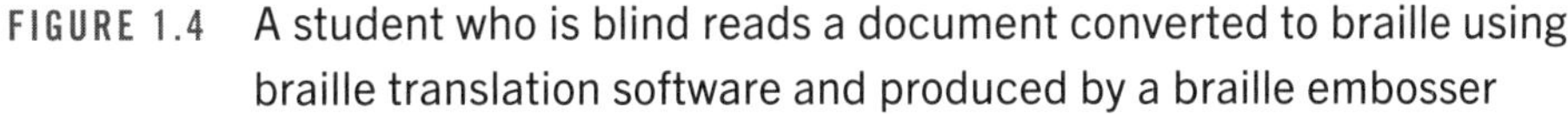

FIGURE 1.4 A student who is blind reads a document converted to braille using braille translation software and produced by a braille embosser

Attention Differences

Some students may find it difficult to pay attention to a lecture, lab, or other activity unless printed outlines or other organizational tools, breaks, or opportunities to move in the room are provided.

DISABILITY AWARENESS

A life with a disability is different from a life without, but perhaps not as different as many people believe. Individuals with disabilities report being frustrated by how others treat them, but feelings about their disabilities do not necessarily dominate their lives. In the online community of teens and young adults with disabilities hosted by our Disabilities, Opportunities, Internetworking, and Technology (DO-IT) Center, occasionally a conversation like this comes up, "If there was a pill that could make your disability go away, would you take it?" Many say they would not take the pill. This response might be a surprise to some people. The view of respondents is often related to being grateful for the insights they have gained from the combination of having disabilities, being happy with their lives now, and wondering if things would have turned out as well if they did not have disabilities.

Communication Tips

Of course, the best way to learn about the experiences of people with disabilities is to engage with them. However, some people tell me they are reluctant to interact with individuals who have disabilities because they fear they will say the wrong thing or because they anticipate communication will be awkward. It is important to respect preferences for communication expressed by individuals, but often we are in a situation where we do not know what they are. Although I did not apply for the position of Miss Manners, since this concern is expressed so often, I reviewed some resources and talked with people with disabilities to collect a few hints that I share in the list that follows. Warning: We are entering treacherous territory here. It is difficult to give hints on how to communicate with a group of people without offending some of them.

- Ask people if they would like help before providing assistance.
- Refer to a person's disability only if it is relevant to the conversation and do not ask intrusive questions about it.
- Use commonly accepted, respectful, and accurate terminology and avoid derogatory, slang, dismissive, patronizing, and negative descriptions when referring to a person's disability. Feel free to use common terms and phrases like "See you later" or "Let's go for a walk."
- Avoid negative phrases that relate to disabilities, like "He's crazy" or "What an insane idea."
- Do not compare people with disabilities to those who are "normal"; if a comparison is needed at all, simply compare them to people without that disability.
- Accept that not everyone communicates using eye contact or desires physical contact, such as handshakes, high-fives, or hugs.
- Provide information in clear, calm, respectful tones and be prepared to provide information in alternate forms (e.g., written or spoken words, diagrams). Offer directions or instructions both orally and in writing and be prepared to read them when asked.
- Avoid interacting with a person's guide dog or service animal or touching assistive devices without the owner's consent.
- Talk directly to a person with a disability, not through a companion or interpreter. If an interpreter is being used, speak directly to the person who is deaf, and if an interpreter voices what a person signs, look at the person who is deaf.

- When interacting with people who are blind or have low vision, be descriptive. Say, "The computer is about three feet to your left" rather than "The computer is over there." Verbally describe key visual content presented in charts, graphs, and pictures, and offer your arm to guide them instead of pushing or grabbing them.
- When carrying on a long conversation with an individual using a wheelchair, consider doing so from a seated position.
- Listen carefully to individuals who have difficulty speaking. Repeat what you think you understand and then ask the person to repeat portions you did not understand.
- Face people who are deaf or hard of hearing and avoid covering your mouth and talking while chewing gum or eating. Speak clearly at a normal volume and talk louder if requested. Use paper and pencil or type comments on a mobile device if the person who is deaf does not read lips and an interpreter is not available.

Panels, Demonstrations, and Simulations

Activities where individuals with disabilities share their experiences with a group of people include panels, demonstrations, simulations, and video presentations. Before including one of these activities in an academic or professional development course, give serious thought to what, specifically, you expect participants to learn through engagement in the activity and how that learning is related to course objectives. In convening a panel, do you just want participants to learn about difficulties associated with certain types of disabilities? This outcome may be of limited value and actually perpetuate misconceptions about what people with disabilities can accomplish. A better approach may be to expect participants to also learn how to avoid the creation of barriers for individuals with particular types of disabilities through the inclusive design of products and environments relevant to the objectives of the course. If convening a panel is impractical, consider searching through YouTube, TED, TEDx, the DO-IT Center, or other collections of videos to locate presentations that feature individuals with disabilities sharing experiences, including both challenges and solutions, that are related to the objectives of the course. Consider showing several videos to ensure that multiple perspectives and types of disabilities are represented.

An example of a demonstration that could be effective in a course on web design is for the instructor to, before teaching accessible web design principles and guidelines, have a person who is blind demonstrate how to access digital content with a screen reader and speech synthesizer, which reads aloud text presented on the screen. Participants will witness how the system reads aloud all of the content presented in a text format, but none of the content embedded within images unless it is also described using alternate text. The focus is not on limitations of an individual, but rather on limitations of a product that make it inaccessible to some people and of how such design flaws might be avoided.

Simulations of experiences of people with disabilities are often used to show learners what it is like to have a disability. Examples include having individuals without disabilities complete tasks while covering their eyes or using a wheelchair or engage in an online experience that simulates differences in visual, learning, or other abilities. Unfortunately, many simulations do not do a good job of simulating common experiences of people with disabilities. Spending a short period of time in a simulation gives participants at best a sense of what it might be like at the moment when a person suddenly acquires an impairment, perhaps when both legs are broken in an automobile accident, long before having a chance to learn to accomplish daily tasks in alternative ways or with assistive technology (AT). A participant using a wheelchair for the first time can be overwhelmed with challenges in maneuvering it, just like people do in their first attempt to ride a bicycle. Why focus on such a rare moment in time? Simulations in this style can also evoke feelings of pity and low expectations of what people with disabilities can do unless facilitators explicitly point out how designers can avoid erecting barriers to products and environments.[3]

In planning a simulation for an academic or professional development course, facilitators should ask themselves, "What could a participant learn by engaging in the simulation that is relevant to the course objectives?" To focus on inclusive design, participants with a simulated disability could be asked to interact with both an accessible and an inaccessible product or environment. For example, a participant using a wheelchair could maneuver within both an inaccessible and accessible library space, share experiences in the two environments, and discuss specific ideas for designing library spaces that are accessible to wheelchair users. Pfeiffer described another type of simulation that reveals how society treats people with and without obvious disabilities.[4] In a team of two, students took turns using a wheelchair while conducting basic tasks such as entering a building, eating in a cafeteria, and using an elevator. Each student recorded observations regarding how other people interacted with them in each of the two roles. Within a lively debriefing session, participants discussed how society treats people with obvious disabilities differently than they treat other people.

Online simulations of disabilities can be used as part of disability awareness activities. For example, in a curriculum, course participants might benefit from accessing an online simulation of dyslexia to gain insight into how this learning disability impacts reading and how text-to-speech software that reads aloud content presented in a text format benefits students with this type of learning disability. As in this example, the best simulations of a disability are often paired with follow-up discussions and activities about how pedagogy, products, and environments can be designed to be most effective for individuals with certain types of disabilities and how ATs and other interventions can contribute to a person's success in specific situations.

I'll conclude this section with a few words of caution about learning about the lives of people with disabilities. One person's experiences never represent those of everyone with a specific type of disability. And important voices to consider besides those who live in the margins are their family members, allies, and others who interact with them.

CIVIL RIGHTS

Now we are getting to the fun stuff—the law! Before legislation made it illegal in the United States, some institutions of higher education adopted discriminatory enrollment policies that excluded individuals with disabilities. In the middle of the last century, veterans injured in World War II and the Korean and Vietnam wars, other people with disabilities, and their families and allies engaged in a barrier-free movement that resulted in the enactment of legislation such as the Architectural Barriers Act of 1968. Inspired by civil rights movements for women and minorities, efforts by people with disabilities and their allies led to civil rights mandates for people with disabilities in Section 504 of the Rehabilitation Act of 1973. Section 504 demands that no qualified individual with a disability be excluded from, be denied the benefits of, or be subjected to discrimination under any program or activity receiving federal funds of any type, which is the case for the vast majority of institutions of higher education. The Americans with Disabilities Act of 1990 (ADA) and its 2008 amendments extend similar requirements to all public entities. Similar to Section 504, according to the ADA, no otherwise qualified individual with a disability shall, solely by reason of that disability, be excluded from, denied the benefits of, or subjected to discrimination under programs of a covered entity. A student with a disability protected under this legislation

- has a physical or mental impairment that substantially limits one or more major life activities,
- has a record of such an impairment, or
- is regarded as having such an impairment.

To be considered "qualified," a student with a disability—with or without reasonable modifications to rules, policies, or practices; the removal of architectural, communication, or transportation barriers; or the provision of auxiliary aids and services—meets the eligibility requirements for enrollment in the institution, program, or activity. When he signed the ADA, President George H. W. Bush said:

> With today's signing of the landmark Americans with Disabilities Act, every man, woman, and child with a disability can now pass through once-closed doors into a bright new era of equality, independence, and freedom.[5]

The United Nations' Preamble of the Convention on the Rights of Persons with Disabilities, which has been adopted by more than one hundred countries, specifically recognizes "the importance of accessibility to the physical, social, and economic and cultural environment, to health and education, and to information and communication, in enabling persons with disabilities to fully enjoy all human rights and fundamental freedoms."[6] Governments around the world have enacted similar laws to protect the rights of citizens with disabilities. Although progress is slower than desired by many advocates, legislation has resulted in worldwide protections from discrimination for individuals with disabilities, including students at all levels of education.

Research and practice in the fields of civil rights, social justice, and multicultural education with respect to diverse groups shed light on issues relevant to individuals with disabilities. For example, the ruling of the US Supreme Court in the 1954 *Brown v. Board of Education of Topeka* case on racial segregation established the principle that separate education is not equal education. This principle helped fuel a movement toward the inclusion of the vast majority of students with disabilities in mainstream programs rather than in segregated schools and programs.

Differences in legislation have contributed to different services for students with disabilities at K–12 and postsecondary institutions. Section 504 and the ADA apply to both levels of education. K–12 schools, however, are also guided by the Individuals with Disabilities Education Act (IDEA), which ensures that children with disabilities are granted a free appropriate public education in the

TABLE 1.1 Typical practices in K–12 education and postsecondary institutions

K–12 education	*Postsecondary*
School identifies disability and provides assessment.	Student self-identifies and provides documentation.
School pays for services for all students with disabilities.	School pays for reasonable accommodations for otherwise qualified student with a disability.
School provides specially designed instruction, modifications, and accommodations.	School does not change essential requirements of curricula and programs.
School provides personal assistant.	School does not provide personal assistant.
Parents are involved.	Parents are not involved, unless the student with a disability approves their involvement.

least restrictive environment. In contrast, in higher education, students with disabilities must meet entrance, course, and graduation requirements with or without reasonable accommodations for which they must request and seek approval from the institution in which they are enrolled. Table 1.1 shares some of the implications of legislation for services at these two educational levels.

Why is this content relevant to the focus of this book? I think it is important for faculty and administrators to know that some students with disabilities have difficulty adjusting to major differences in services between high school and college. They may not know how to effectively advocate for themselves and what accommodations are considered "reasonable" at the postsecondary level. In response, some schools and organizations offer programs for students with disabilities to support them in their transition to higher education—for example, the DO-IT Scholars program at the University of Washington. Such programs are similar to those offered to other groups that have been under-represented and underserved in higher education, including first-generation college students, women, and racial and ethnic minorities.

Even today, aspects of many courses, facilities, technologies, and services are inaccessible to individuals with some types of disabilities. So what are reasonable accommodations that allow them to participate? Simply put, reasonable accommodations are modifications or

Did you know?

Inclusive design is often used synonymously with *universal design*. But, be careful not to confuse *inclusive design* in higher education with how *inclusion* is defined in K–12 education, where any modification, regardless of how it impacts academic standards, is used to make instruction appropriate for a child with a disability.

adjustments to existing products or environments that give students with disabilities opportunities to fully participate in and benefit from activities offered by an institution. The goal is for these students to have learning and other opportunities and communications that are as effective as they are for other students. Accommodations commonly provided to students with disabilities in postsecondary education include

- adjusting the application process to ensure an equal opportunity to apply for enrollment;
- moving a class to a room that is physically accessible to a student enrolled in a course;
- arranging for a sign language interpreter or note taker;
- providing captions on a video for a student who is deaf;
- giving a student extra time to complete an exam or allowing that student to take it in a location with fewer distractions;
- extending the length of time for completion of an assignment or program;
- substituting an alternative course for one that is typically required;
- modifying an assignment or giving a student an alternative one; and
- converting digital documents, textbooks, and other materials into accessible formats for a student.

The purpose of a reasonable accommodation is not to fundamentally alter the nature of a program or to give someone an advantage, but rather to create a level playing field for all students. Still, some faculty members express concern that in some cases an accommodation for a student with a disability gives that student an unfair advantage. Even though this is not the intent of an accommodation, it is understandable for a faculty member to expect fairness. Therefore, open communication between faculty and the disability services office is important.

In much of this book, I share strategies that instructors can offer to *all* students in a class to avoid access barriers, thus reducing the need for accommodations. To gain ideas for practices in this regard, every time instructors are directed to provide a student with an accommodation, they can ask themselves, "What could I do in the future to make this accommodation unnecessary?" Sometimes the answer may be "nothing," but other times it may be "something"—for example, routinely caption videos and adopt course materials that are available in accessible formats—that they can incorporate into the design of future courses.

LIMITATIONS OF THE ACCOMMODATION APPROACH TO ACCESS

An accommodation process for addressing the inaccessible design of physical spaces, technology, courses, and services is deeply rooted in the culture of most postsecondary institutions, to a large degree because of the legislation that requires it. This approach takes a "medical" or "deficit" view of disability, in which a professional identifies an individual's medical condition and functional deficits and prescribes adjustments that allow this person to engage in an offering that is not accessible to him. The idea of an accommodation rests on the assumption that the difficulties people with disabilities experience are a direct result of their impairments and the major task of professionals is to adjust the individual (e.g., through surgery, medication, rehabilitation) or provide accommodations.

Securing approved accommodations at postsecondary institutions typically requires that a student with a disability takes the first step. The student presents documentation of a disability to and requests accommodations from a disability services office. Personnel in this office determine reasonable accommodations and, with the student's approval, communicate the approved accommodations to faculty and staff who will ensure that they are implemented. In other words, the school determines that characteristics of a course, service, physical space, or technology are inaccessible to a specific person, identifies the individual's deficit as the problem, and offers an accommodation to solve that problem.

Negative qualities of the accommodations approach for making courses and campus offerings accessible to students with disabilities include the following.

Did you know?

There are many views regarding what a "disability" is. Search on the internet for the following terms to get a sense of the wide variety of approaches people have taken to express what it means to have a disability:

- tragedy/charity model
- moral/ethical model
- expert/professional model
- medical model
- deficit model
- social model
- economic model
- consumer model

- The process for securing accommodations marginalizes students with disabilities by requiring a segregated process for gaining access to what the institution routinely offers to other students.
- An accommodation does not always result in the student receiving content and experiences equitable to and at the same time as those received by other students.

- Accommodations benefit only students with documented disabilities they have self-disclosed, not students with disabilities they have not disclosed.
- Accommodations (e.g., remediation of documents offered in inaccessible formats) can create a dependency on a disability services office for routine, predictable academic needs that could be systematically eliminated (e.g., by making the use of accessibly designed materials a standard practice).
- Accommodations (e.g., captions on videos) are not available to other members of a class who might benefit from them (e.g., English language learners).
- The work in developing an accommodation for one student does not in and of itself make a course or other campus offering more accessible to future students.

Accessibility efforts that primarily rely on accommodations in postsecondary institutions have been criticized for their focus on the perceived "deficit" of an individual with much less attention given to remediating deficits in the designs of educational products and environments. Although most people recognize the need to provide some accommodations (e.g., sign language interpreters for students who are deaf), proponents of proactive, inclusive design practices suggest that institutions reflect on their role in creating systemic barriers and commit to eliminating or at least reducing them.

Thinking about the ideal roles for accommodations and proactive design practices reminds me of a situation that occurred in one of our DO-IT Scholars summer programs for teenagers with disabilities. On the first day of a three-summer program, a first-year participant who had mobility, speech, and learning challenges as a result of a brain injury reported that the women's restroom was accessible to her, with one exception. When seated in her wheelchair, she could not reach the handle of the swing-in door required to exit the restroom. On the spot we negotiated with her an accommodation where she would inform a female staff member or intern when she wanted to use a restroom; that person would stand inside the main door and open it when it was time for her to leave. But we did not stop there. I asked if she would be willing to report this accessibility barrier to the building manager. She agreed. The two of them agreed that installing a second handle below the one already present would solve the problem. He thanked her for bringing up the issue so that he could correct the situation but also for people who may have encountered the barrier but did not speak up. He pulled out a work order and said he would submit a request for installation of a second handle on all of the restroom doors in the building. Reporting that it would likely be a month or more before the work was completed, he gave her his business card so that she could, if she wished, contact him to confirm that the work was done before she returned the next summer (and it was!).

This example illustrates how an accommodation can be provided to an individual and *also* contribute to continuous movement toward a more inclusive institution.

1. The accommodation is provided as an immediate response to an exceptional situation where an unanticipated accessibility barrier is revealed by a person with a disability.
2. The institution then explores possibilities for eliminating the barrier for future users.

Compare this process with what often happens in remediating inaccessible digital documents for a student with a disability on many campuses: a student is given reformatted documents as an accommodation through a disability services office, but the instructor is not engaged enough to ensure that accessible documents will be used in future offerings of the course. Hmmm . . . what is wrong with this picture and how can we fix it?

Do accommodations on your campus inspire inclusive practices that are reducing the need for future accommodations? Read on. . . .

MY GO-TO RESOURCES

Following are some good places to start in your exploration of topics covered in this chapter.

- *Disability and Health Overview* of the *Centers for Disease Control and Prevention (CDC)*
  cdc.gov/ncbddd/disabilityandhealth/disability.html
- *Association for Higher Education and Disability*
  www.ahead.org
- *National Center for College Students with Disabilities*
  nccsdonline.org
- *Students with Disabilities Preparing for Postsecondary Education: Know Your Rights and Responsibilities*
  www2.ed.gov/about/offices/list/ocr/transition.html

- *Knowledge Base*
  uw.edu/doit/knowledge-base
- *TED* and *TEDx*
  ted.com and tedx.com (use *disability*, *diversity*, and related search terms)
- *YouTube*
  youtube.com (use *disability*, *diversity*, and related search terms)

CONCLUSION

In this chapter I touched on issues related to diversity, terminology, legislation, disability awareness, rights and responsibilities of students and institutions, and the accommodation approach to providing access to postsecondary opportunities. In the next chapter I propose a framework that you can flesh out to create a toolkit for addressing diversity issues that avoids the limitations of an accommodations-only approach.

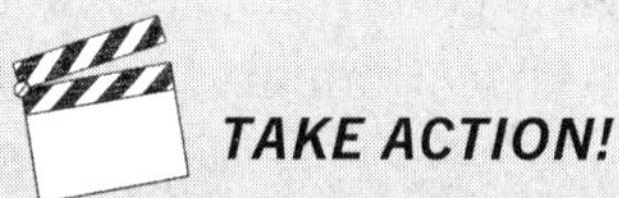

TAKE ACTION!

(REFLECT) Consider your context

Reflect on these questions:

- What challenges did you face in transitioning from high school to college? What factors made your transition easier? harder? How could institutional practices ease the transition for students?
- What experiences and perspectives might some students at your institution bring that are different from your own? How might students with diverse characteristics benefit the institution?
- What are your experiences with students with disabilities?

(LEARN) Test the myth of average

In an awareness-building training session or community of practice, view Todd Rose's TEDx talk, "The Myth of Average," which can be located at youtube.com/watch?v=4eBmyttcfU4&t=12s. Sit back and enjoy exploring what it means to be an "average" fighter pilot with respect to physical characteristics. Ask participants to submit their height and eye color on a slip of paper. Compute (before the next class session) the average height and determine the most common eye color. Is there anyone in the group who is average height and has the most common eye color?

Most likely, all or the majority of the participants are not "average." Discuss how this exercise makes the case for design approaches that address the characteristics of a diverse group rather than those of a person with average characteristics.

(LEARN) Communicate with students who have disabilities

In an academic or professional development course or a community of practice, present a short list of tips for communicating with postsecondary individuals who have disabilities (perhaps DO-IT's list at uw.edu/doit/programs/accesscollege/student-services-conference-room/resources/helpful-communication-hints). Have participants discuss suggestions in the list and share other effective strategies. Encourage participants to disagree with the suggestions and explain why.

(LEARN) Convene a panel

Within an academic or professional development course or disability awareness event, convene a panel of students with a variety of disabilities. Ask them to introduce themselves and share some of their interests or experiences related to the topic of the course or activity. For example, if a student panel is part of professional development for faculty, each panelist might be directed to take the following steps.

- Introduce yourself; share what you would like to about your disability and any accommodations you have received in courses.
- Share an example of a challenge you have faced in a course and how the challenge was overcome.
- Tell what you would like your instructors to know about you, especially as it relates to your disability.
- Share an experience where the way an instructor interacted with the class or you personally was of benefit to you. Then tell about an experience where the faculty member's behavior was not helpful to you.
- Share advice you have for instructors about how to effectively work with students who have disabilities similar to yours.
- Follow with questions from the audience, stating that participants can ask any question they wish, but individual panelists will answer only questions they wish to address.

(LEARN) Gain perspectives through videos

Numerous videos on the internet feature individuals with disabilities sharing their perspectives and experiences; many are relevant to postsecondary education. Watching some of these presentations can lead to a greater understanding of the lives of people with a wide variety of disabilities; watching several of them can drive home the point that the perspectives and experiences of one individual do not represent those of a whole group.

Individual viewing is of value, but video presentations can also be effective learning tools within an academic or professional development course. The instructor can find titles that are particularly relevant to people with disabilities in college, graduate school, and careers in many places, but here are my three favorites:

- On the DO-IT website (uw.edu/doit), select "Videos" to find a collection of video presentations about students with disabilities using technology and pursuing college and careers.
- On the TED (ted.com) and TEDx (tedx.com) websites, search *disability* and *accessible design* to find short, high-quality titles that include one of my favorite TED Talks, "I'm Not Your Inspiration, Thank You Very Much."
- The YouTube website (youtube.com) hosts a huge and diverse collection of videos with respect to content and quality. Begin with search terms *disability* and *accessible*.

Tie videos presented in an online or on-site course or training to specific objectives. If a video reveals barriers facing people with disabilities, be sure you discuss how these barriers can be eliminated or reduced. Also, make sure the videos have accurate captions, keeping in mind that it is a bad idea to use inaccessible products to make points about accessibility unless the point is that even videos about disability are often inaccessible and how this situation might be corrected (e.g., encouraging video owners to edit the computer-generated draft captions that YouTube provides).

(LEARN) Gain perspectives through a demonstration

As the instructor in an academic or professional development course for IT staff, ask personnel in the disability services office if they are willing to send a message to students engaged with that office to recruit a student who is blind and willing to demonstrate the use of a screen reader in the class or workshop (ideally, offering a small honorarium). In the presentation ask the screen reader user to

- give a short demonstration of the functional capabilities of a screen reader;
- demonstrate how the screen reader clearly reads aloud text presented on an accessibly designed website;
- demonstrate how the screen reader cannot read aloud text presented on an accessibly designed website where content is not presented in a text format; and
- engage in a discussion with the class on accessible design features of IT that make it accessible to individuals who are blind.

Conduct a similar activity with a person who has dyslexia and uses text-to-speech technology to read aloud text content. What the audience will learn is that the challenges that people who are blind and people with learning disabilities face with respect to reading printed text are quite different, but both groups benefit from the availability of materials in text formats that can be read by their AT.

(LEARN) Use simulations to motivate the development of solutions

In an academic course, discuss various types of simulations that have been used to increase awareness of disability-related issues, some of their unintended negative outcomes, and how these negative outcomes might be avoided through the careful design of a simulation and the discussion that follows. As an assignment, have each student design and present to the class (1) the objectives for the exercise, (2) a description of the simulation, (3) questions to be addressed in the follow-up discussion, and (4) evaluation of the simulation with respect to its objectives.

(LEARN) Engage in online simulations

In an academic or professional development course, have participants gain a better understanding of challenges faced by students with some types of disabilities through engagement in online simulations.

- Simulation of Vision Condition at perkinselearning.org/scout/blog/simulation-vision-conditions
- Color Blindness Simulator at perkinselearning.org/technology/blog/color-blindness-simulator
- Dyslexia Simulator at geon.github.io/programming/2016/03/03/dsxyliea

After viewing a simulation, engage participants in a discussion of implications with respect to inclusive design. For example, after students, faculty, web developers, or online learning designers engage in a dyslexia simulation, ask how this experience reveals the importance of designing technology so that it allows text-to-speech systems to read aloud text to increase reading speed and comprehension for individuals with dyslexia. After engaging in a vision condition or color blindness simulator, ask participants what they learned that could inform the design of signage, websites, brochures, and other materials.

(LEARN) Compare challenges for different diversity groups

In an academic or professional development course, have participants select a disability and another diversity category (e.g., students with learning disabilities and English language learners) and identify at least one challenge to on-site or online course access that is similar and one that is different for the two groups.

(LEARN) Identify similar access challenges and solutions

In an academic or professional development course, have participants select two types of disabilities. Then identify at least one challenge to participation in an academic course that is similar for members of these two groups as well as a solution to that challenge for each group.

(LEARN) Explore disability as a difference

Some individuals with conditions labeled as a "disability" consider themselves as just having a different language, way of thinking, or approach to doing things. As an individual or in an academic or professional development course, view the TEDx Talk "ADHD as a Difference in Cognition, Not a Disorder" at youtube.com/watch?v=uU6o2_UFSEY.

On the TED (ted.com) or TEDx (tedx.com) website, search for *disability* to find other stories about the experiences of people with disabilities. What can you learn from these speakers about the many ways people experience disability in their lives? How can some of the challenges revealed be eliminated or avoided?

(LEARN) Consider inclusion and exclusion

In a course or professional development offering, provide small groups with large images of spaces (e.g., a library) and products (e.g., a toaster). Have each group answer these questions and at the end of the activity share their answers with the group.

- What abilities are necessary to gain access to the intended functions of this product or environment?
- What are characteristics of individuals who cannot fully access the features or functions of this product or environment?
- Brainstorm how you could modify the design to create a product or environment that is accessible to a more diverse audience.

(APPLY) Discuss value of diversity knowledge

After discussing diversity issues in a professional development course or community of practice, ask participants to tell how an understanding of diversity issues could inform their work. Be specific.

(APPLY) Promote "Nothing About Us Without Us"

"Nothing About Us Without Us!" is a slogan, with origins in central European political traditions, used to communicate the idea that no policy should be decided by any representative without the full and direct participation of members of the group affected by that policy. It came into widespread use in disability activism during the 1990s.

In an academic or professional development course, have students search the internet for historical highlights and an image commonly used with the slogan as part of disability advocacy. Why is this message important, and what might its embrace mean for academic studies, research, policies, and practices at a postsecondary institution?

(APPLY) Offer transition support for new students with disabilities

Consider employing evidence-based practices to help students with disabilities adjust to college life. Content can include tips for securing accommodations, for developing time management and other skills, for making use of on-campus and online resources, for advocating for other students with disabilities, and for making all aspects of college life inclusive.

CHAPTER 2

A Framework for Inclusive Practices

[I]f you judge a fish by its ability to climb a tree, it will live its whole life believing that it is stupid.

—Albert Einstein

UNIVERSAL DESIGN (UD), Universal Design for Learning (UDL), Universal Design of Instruction (UDI), and other proactive approaches to design have been employed to create inclusive technology, physical spaces, services, teaching and learning activities, and resources in higher education. In this chapter I share historical highlights, definitions, principles, guidelines, practices, and processes that come together to create a framework for Universal Design in Higher Education (UDHE) that can be fleshed out to create a toolkit for making a postsecondary institution more inclusive.

INTRODUCTION

Consider the "Coffeepot for Masochists" presented in figure 2.1. This image depicts an item included in the *Catalogue D'objets Introuvables* by the French painter, illustrator, and designer Jacques Carelman.[1] Carelman's whimsical catalog, first published in 1969, is a parody of a mail order catalog featuring

FIGURE 2.1
The Coffeepot for Masochists

designs of tools, furniture, toys, clothing, and other everyday things that are intentionally unworkable. It would certainly be difficult to efficiently *and safely* serve coffee from the Coffeepot for Masochists. I doubt that many people presented with it would just adjust their approach for serving coffee to make it work. (How about taking the lid off and pouring coffee out the top? Or, if you're an engineer, I'm sure you could integrate a pump of some sort.) Can we agree that the product is poorly designed for serving coffee?

So what does a poorly designed coffeepot have to do with the topic of this book, other than being an absurd product idea the author is particularly fond of? When a student does poorly in our course, shouldn't we routinely consider that the poor performance may not be due solely to the student's limitations, but rather at least in part to limitations of the design of the course itself? And, once we recognize that possibility, shouldn't we consider how to make the course more usable? Universal design practices appeal to people like me who recommend that initial attention be paid to the inclusive design of a product or environment, rather than waiting to provide an accommodation to someone who cannot effectively use it. That is what UD is all about.

By the end of this chapter, you should be able to

- compare UD with other proactive approaches to design, including design for all, barrier-free design, accessible design, and usable design;
- explain differences between an accommodations approach and the UDHE Framework for ensuring access to postsecondary offerings for students with disabilities;
- describe components of a UDHE Framework—definition, principles, guidelines, practices, and process;
- name the three sets of principles that underpin the UDHE Framework;
- explain how the UDHE Framework can be adapted to specific application areas;
- suggest motivations individuals might have for applying UDHE;
- describe how stakeholder roles might change if the UDHE Framework is adopted; and

- apply UDHE practices to physical spaces, teaching and learning activities, information technology (IT), and student services.

WHY UNIVERSAL DESIGN IN HIGHER EDUCATION?

I learned from my mathematics curriculum and instruction professor "teach each math concept three different ways using three different senses." We practiced this approach to the point where I could *not* not think of it when I was teaching middle school—and took the strategy along with me when I moved on to teaching college mathematics and computer programming. I have observed how students benefit when they hear it, see it, touch it—and talk about it too. Spoiler alert: that is an application of UD to an instructional practice!

The successful design of any educational product or environment involves myriad factors—among them, purpose, aesthetics, safety, industry standards, usability, and cost. Traditional design practices often focus on the average user—for example, the "typical" student in a class. In contrast, UD strives to make products, environments, and social structures useful to individuals who are diverse with respect to gender, sexual identity, race, ethnicity, age, socioeconomic status, ability, disability, veteran status, learning preferences, primary language, and other characteristics. Originally applied to physical spaces and consumer products and later to IT, UD has more recently been used to guide the design of on-site and online instruction and student services.

Traditional efforts on campuses nationwide embrace a medical or deficit view of disability, where the focus is on medical diagnoses of individuals, their functional limitations, and how accommodations can help them participate in an established environment (e.g., an online course) or use an existing product (e.g., a website) that is not designed to make it accessible to them. Proponents of universal design suggest that every step in the design process address all types of diversity to

Did you know?

In the book *Disguised: A True Story*, Patricia Moore, an industrial designer and gerontologist, reported her experiences undertaking everyday activities while disguised as an elderly woman with limited physical and sensory abilities. Barriers she encountered included lights that could not be controlled, directions on signs that could not be read, steps that could not be negotiated, knobs that could not be turned, and doors too heavy to push. Moore's book, her appearances on television talk shows, and articles published in magazines and newspapers increased public awareness of the need for the built environment to be made more suitable for people of all ages and abilities.[2]

create products and environments that are accessible to, usable by, and inclusive of a diverse audience and minimize the need for accommodations. The UD approach has been promoted by educators (like me) worldwide to reduce negative aspects of the accommodations approach by eliminating deficits in products and environments that make them inaccessible to some people. Such approaches align with a social view of disability that accessibility barriers often stem from the failure of designers to take into account the needs of individuals with a wide range of characteristics, including those classified as disabilities. Embracing UDHE holds promise for reducing systemic barriers and exclusionary practices to create more inclusive spaces, technology, instruction, and services.

A number of proactive approaches discussed in the literature consider a broad audience in design practices. Besides universal design, they include accessible design, barrier-free design, usable design, inclusive design, and design for all. These terms are related but not interchangeable, and there are tons of definitions from which to choose. *Accessible design* is often used to describe design considerations for making it possible for individuals with disabilities to operate products and engage within physical environments. *Barrier-free design* often refers to practices to make physical spaces more accessible. *Usable design* focuses on the extent to which a product can be effectively operated by specified users to accomplish tasks for which the product was created. Usability engineers study the performance of tasks by individuals with specific characteristics; some test designs with people with disabilities, but many do not. *Inclusive design* ensures a diversity of ways people can participate and have a sense of belonging. A related approach is called *participatory design*, which is an approach to design that attempts to actively involve all stakeholders (e.g., employees, partners, customers, citizens, end users), including those with disabilities, in the design process to help ensure the result meets their needs and is usable for a diverse audience.

Of the proactive design approaches, there is no approach that addresses greater user diversity than universal design, which is also called *design for all*. The term *universal design* was coined late in the twentieth century by Ronald Mace, an internationally recognized architect, product designer, educator, and wheelchair user. He defined UD as "the design of products and environments to be usable by all people, to the greatest extent possible, without the need for adaptation or specialized design."[3] Mace challenged traditional conventions in his view that all designs should contribute to a more accessible, usable, and inclusive world *for everyone*. Figure 2.2 illustrates three distinctive

FIGURE 2.2 Characteristics of a UD practice: It is accessible, usable, and inclusive

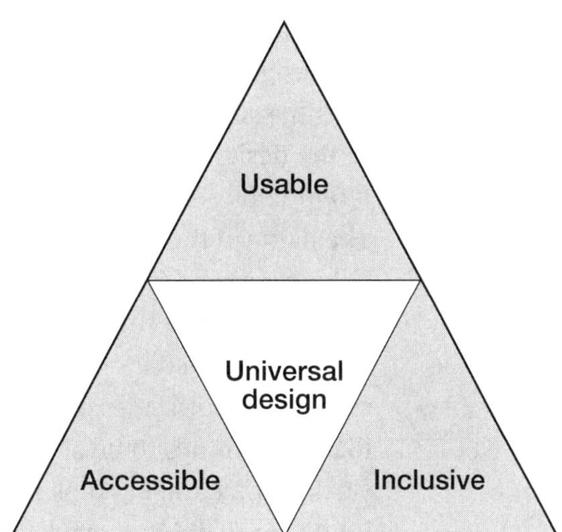

Source: Sheryl Burgstahler, "Universal Design in Higher Education," in *Universal Design in Higher Education: From Principles to Practice*, 2nd ed., ed. Sheryl Burgstahler (Cambridge, MA: Harvard Education Press, 2015), 15.

characteristics of universal designs: they are *accessible* to and *usable* by people with a wide range of characteristics and can be offered in an *inclusive* setting. UD characteristics can be integrated into any design approach.

If you have ever been involved in hosting a large conference, you know that people have strong opinions about nametag design. As far as nametags with clear vinyl holders, there are three primary preferences: clips on the top, safety pins on the back, and lanyards. Have you ever wondered how you might universally design a nametag? Never? The fact that I have attests to my obsession with UD and my enthusiasm in sharing how my staff applied UD to address the nametag preference issue. We considered that individuals might want a different style of nametag from one day to another (e.g., if they have a collar on which to clip a nametag on one day but not the next) as well as the limitations of each of these designs (like the tendency for nametags on lanyards to flip around to a blank side, making attendees wonder whether they should flip them over). Fast forward, our universally designed nametag is illustrated in figure 2.3.

The design of the nametag illustrates the three characteristics of a universally designed product. It has a clear vinyl nametag holder with a clip and added feature of a safety pin attached to the clip; also included is a lanyard to

FIGURE 2.3
Image of the back side of a universally designed nametag, featuring large print and clip, pin, and lanyard options

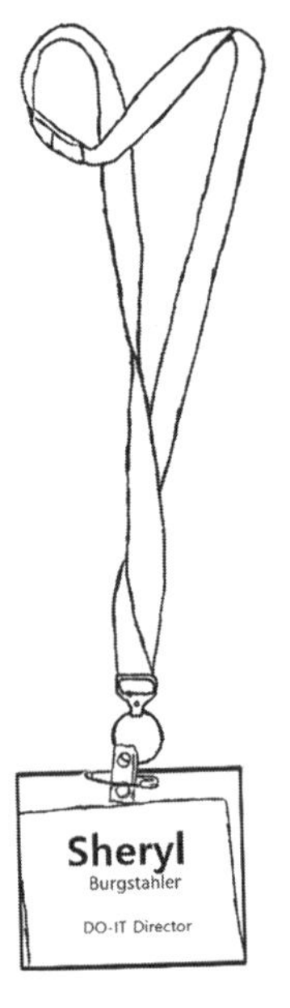

which the nametag can be clipped. Thus, the design is more *inclusive* than a one-size-fits-all approach because it builds flexibility into the design by offering user-controlled options within a single product; an important quality in the design is that the user can make a different choice for each day of the conference. The name of the attendee is printed in a large, bold, sans serif font on a high-contrast plain background, thus making it more *accessible* to and *usable* by a diverse audience. Printing the content on both sides of the nametag ensures that it continues to be accessible when a lanyard user's nametag flips to the back side. Is it fully accessible to *everybody*? No. For example, people who are blind can effectively use the nametag to share their names with others, but we have not found a *practical* way to make the design useful for accessing the names of others. In the interest of continuous product improvement, we welcome suggestions for improving our design.

Universal design is a good design approach to embrace in higher education because it can be applied to any type of product or environment and results in making them beneficial to diverse populations of students, faculty, and staff. The Centre for Excellence in Universal Design in Dublin does a good job of correcting some misconceptions about UD in its list of "10 things to know about UD."[4] Essentially, Centre assertions include the following.

- UD is much more than just a new design trend.
- UD strives to improve an original design concept by making it more inclusive.
- UD benefits are not limited to older people and people with disabilities.
- UD is not about "one size fits all."
- UD is not a synonym for compliance with accessible design standards.
- UD should be integrated throughout the design process.
- Universally designed products can have high aesthetic value.
- A universally designed product is the goal; UD is the process.

- UD does not aim to replace the design of products targeted at specific markets.
- UD can be undertaken by any designer, not just by specialists.

So, when all is said and done, who on a postsecondary campus benefits from the systematic practice of UDHE? Among the beneficiaries are individuals who disclose their disabilities, those who have disabilities but do not disclose, learners with various learning preferences and technological expertise, those whose native language is not English, people who are older than the average student or employee, members of specific racial and ethnic groups, and everybody else! In other words, UDHE can be applied to all offerings to address the interests and needs of a diverse postsecondary student body, workforce, and greater community.

Images in figures 2.4 and 2.5 illustrate a subtle but important difference between an environment that is accessible and usable and one that is inclusive as well. Figure 2.4 shows a ramp next to steps to the main entrance of a campus building. This design is accessible, usable, and probably "ADA compliant" (see *The ADA Checklist for Readily Achievable Barrier Removal* in the "My Go-To

FIGURE 2.4 An entrance that is accessible and usable

FIGURE 2.5 An entrance that is accessible, usable, and inclusive, i.e., universally designed

Resources" list at the end of this chapter), but it is not *inclusive* because people reach the entrance in different ways. If I walked up to this building with someone who uses a wheelchair or walker, I would likely use the steps to avoid the awkward situation of walking in front of or behind my companion using the ramp. In contrast, the wide, sloping ramp to the main entrance shown in figure 2.5 would allow us to approach and enter the building side by side, thus meeting all three characteristics of a space that is universally designed.

In the case of a universally designed entrance to a building, the primary entrance is the one that is most accessible, but individuals are not denied a choice to use steps. In DO-IT's universally designed nametag example, three user-controlled choices are integrated into the basic design of a single product. Combining the UD approach and the capabilities of digital technology allows users to customize a product to make it almost unrecognizable with another user's configuration. A universally designed smartphone, for example, gives users myriad choices (including text size, background color, speech output) for tailoring an environment to their unique preferences. Unfortunately, most technology developers today do not apply UD and continue to create products that are inaccessible to some users with disabilities.

The bottom line is that universally designed products are *born* accessible, usable, and inclusive. Infusing UDHE into all aspects of higher education is an important step toward destigmatizing disability and ensuring equity for all groups. In summary, UDHE

- is a goal to make all campus offerings accessible and usable for faculty, staff, students, and visitors with diverse characteristics;
- values access, equity, and inclusion;
- considers differences in ability, as with other diversity characteristics, to be part of the normal human experience;
- is a process for developing flexible educational products and environments that are welcoming to, accessible to, and usable by everyone;
- improves any design by making it more inclusive;
- provides a foundation for the development of strategies for the design of all on-site and online products and environments found in higher education; and
- reduces the need for disability-related accommodations.

THE UDHE FRAMEWORK

Are you sold on UDHE yet? Whether you are or aren't, I hope you will keep reading to learn more about how to make it happen for a course, program, service, and campus and why you might choose to do so. To help you fully understand what it means to embrace UDHE, I unpack aspects of UDHE into a framework that addresses the scope, definition, principles, guidelines, exemplary practices, and process of UDHE. The UDHE Framework is illustrated in figure 2.6.

In the sections that follow, I begin to flesh out content for each component of the UDHE Framework to create a toolkit you can use as you apply UDHE to all offerings of a postsecondary institution or to a specific area of focus.

FIGURE 2.6 Components of the UDHE Framework

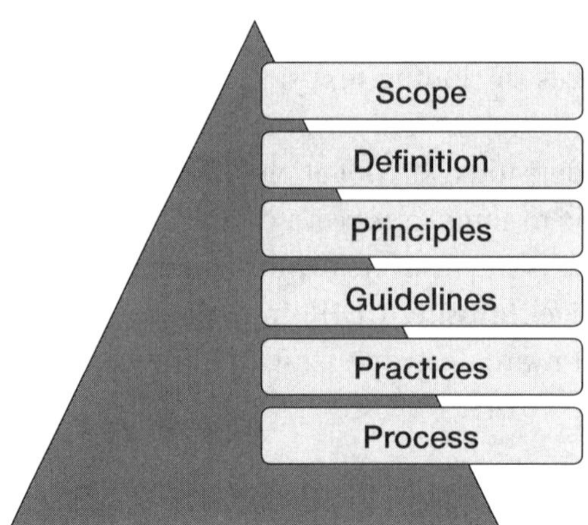

SCOPE

The scope of UDHE applications covered in this book comprises all products and environments that directly or indirectly support teaching and learning in higher education.

DEFINITION

Although much attention is given to how UD benefits individuals with disabilities, its definition requires consideration of all characteristics of a diverse population. Adding "in higher education" to the definition of UD developed by Ron Mace reinforces its applicability to this domain. Thus, UDHE is just the application of UD to postsecondary education—the design of products and environments *in higher education* to be usable by all people, to the greatest extent possible, without the need for adaptation or specialized design.

PRINCIPLES AND GUIDELINES

UD has a rich history in applications to the physical environment, to commercial products, and to IT. Our Disabilities, Opportunities, Internetworking, and Technology (DO-IT) Center at the University of Washington (UW), along with its collaborators from postsecondary institutions nationwide, have engaged in multiple UDHE initiatives funded by the US Department of Education and the National Science Foundation. These initiatives resulted in the establishment of the online Center for Universal Design in Education at the turn of the twenty-first century.[5] Although some collaborators in DO-IT's UDHE initiatives considered the basic UD definition and related principles adequate for addressing all postsecondary products and environments, many saw the value of the Universal Design for Learning principles when designing teaching practices and of the Web Content Accessibility Guidelines (WCAG) when designing technology. Applying all three sets of principles for the UDHE Framework ensures that all campus offerings—including facilities, curriculum and pedagogy, technology, and services—are accessible, usable, and inclusive. The contribution of each set of principles and corresponding guidelines to the UDHE Framework is discussed in the following three subsections.

The Contribution of UD to the UDHE Principles and Guidelines

Ronald Mace helped create the first building code for accessibility in the United States and contributed to the passage of the Architectural Barriers Act of 1968, which mandates that facilities designed, constructed, or altered with federal funds or leased by a federal agency comply with standards for physical accessibility. In 1989, Mace established a center now known as the Center for Universal Design (CUD) at North Carolina State University. Building on the definition of UD, a group of CUD product developers, architects, and engineers established seven principles of UD and corresponding guidelines to consider in the design of any product or environment. The principles can be used to evaluate existing designs; guide the design process; educate designers and consumers about the characteristics of more accessible, usable, and inclusive products and environments; and provide a foundation on which practitioners can develop design practices, standards, and compliance tests in specific fields.

Did you know?

Marc Harrison, a professor of industrial engineering at the Rhode Island School of Design, was a pioneer in creating products with characteristics that would come to be called *universal design*. He suggested that design approaches that focus on individuals of average size and ability should be replaced by one that addresses the needs of people of all abilities.

The seven design principles and related guidelines for UD follow.

1. *Equitable use.* The design is useful and marketable to people with diverse abilities. Guidelines for this principle are as follows:
   - Provide the same means of use for all users: identical whenever possible; equivalent when not.

- Avoid segregating or stigmatizing any users.
- Provisions for privacy, security, and safety should be equally available to all users.
- Make the design appealing to all users.

2. *Flexibility in use.* The design accommodates a wide range of individual preferences and abilities. Guidelines for this principle are as follows:
   - Provide choice in methods of use.
   - Accommodate right- or left-handed access and use.
   - Facilitate the user's accuracy and precision.
   - Provide adaptability to the user's pace.

3. *Simple and intuitive use.* Use of the design is easy to understand, regardless of the user's experience, knowledge, language skills, or current concentration level. Guidelines for this principle are as follows:
   - Eliminate unnecessary complexity.
   - Be consistent with user expectations and intuition.
   - Accommodate a wide range of literacy and language skills.
   - Arrange information to be consistent with its importance.
   - Provide effective prompting and feedback during and after task completion.

4. *Perceptible information.* The design communicates necessary information effectively to the user, regardless of ambient conditions or the user's sensory abilities. Guidelines for this principle are as follows:
   - Use different modes (pictorial, verbal, tactile) for redundant presentation of essential information.
   - Provide adequate contrast between essential information and its surroundings.
   - Maximize "legibility" of essential information.
   - Differentiate elements in ways that can be described (i.e., make it easy to give instructions or directions).
   - Provide compatibility with a variety of techniques or devices used by people with sensory limitations.

5. *Tolerance for error.* The design minimizes hazards and the adverse consequences of accidental or unintended actions. Guidelines for this principle are as follows:
   - Arrange elements to minimize hazards and errors: most used elements, most accessible; hazardous elements eliminated, isolated, or shielded.

- Provide warnings of hazards and errors.
- Provide fail-safe features.
- Discourage unconscious action in tasks that require vigilance.

6. *Low physical effort.* The design can be used efficiently, comfortably, and with a minimum of fatigue. Guidelines for this principle are as follows:
   - Allow user to maintain a neutral body position.
   - Use reasonable operating forces.
   - Minimize repetitive actions.
   - Minimize sustained physical effort.

7. *Size and space for approach and use.* Appropriate size and space is provided for approach, reach, manipulation, and use regardless of the user's body size, posture, or mobility. Guidelines for this principle are as follows:
   - Provide a clear line of sight to important elements for any seated or standing user.
   - Make reach to all components comfortable for any seated or standing user.
   - Accommodate variations in hand and grip size.
   - Provide adequate space for the use of assistive devices or personal assistance.[6]

Mace emphasized that universal designs consider the characteristics of all people, not just people with disabilities, and promoted the idea that UD can be applied to the design—of just about everything. These UD principles have stood the test of time. For example, instructors can apply Principle 5, "Tolerance for error," to the design of online courses—by providing feedback to guide students when they make a selection error—even though courses were not offered online until many years after the principle was established.

Did you know?

Some predict that demand for accessible products and environments will grow because of a demographic bulge in which senior citizens comprise the fastest-growing segment of the population worldwide. This trend may contribute to the promotion of universally designed products and environments. As a Canadian social critic explains, "Greed is a far more reliable and universal agent of change than is the urge to do good for your fellow man. The future of any great idea is always made more bright when it's found to be profitable."[7]

The application often pointed to as the first widely adopted UD practice is the provision of curb cuts in sidewalks. This feature allows a person using a wheelchair to go from sidewalk to street level without negotiating a curb. Figure 2.7 is a sketch of an article that appeared in the UW *Daily* student newspaper in 1970, along with a picture of a student with a sign affixed to the back of his wheelchair: "Ramp the curbs. Keep me off the street." In 1970, many people thought this was an interesting goal that would never be realized on the UW's hilly campus. They were wrong. And who benefits from curb cuts? Not just people with disabilities. Parents pushing baby strollers or walking with young

FIGURE 2.7 A UW student posts a sign on his wheelchair that reads "Ramp the curbs. Keep me off the street."

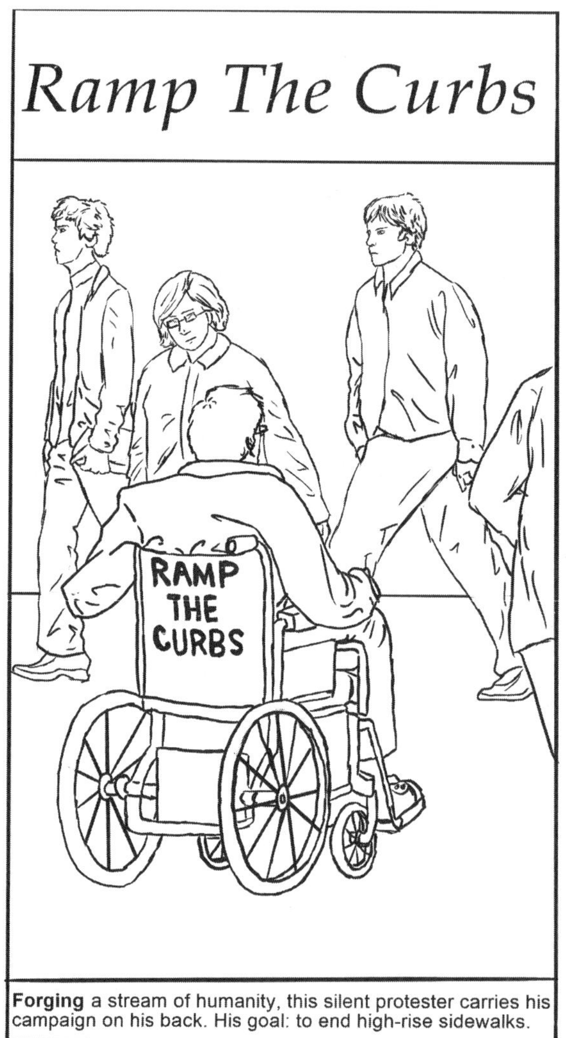

Forging a stream of humanity, this silent protester carries his campaign on his back. His goal: to end high-rise sidewalks.

children, delivery personnel with carts, travelers with rolling bags, and (perhaps unfortunately) skateboarders. And, as with other universal designs, adding the curb cut as a UD feature of a sidewalk does not *deny* people the choice to step directly from the sidewalk to street level. Today, many curb cuts have the additional UD feature of tactile bumps to alert people who are blind that they are moving from the sidewalk to the street level.

My first-hand experiences with access issues include those that occurred at the UW during the three years before my first husband died in his early twenties. He became a paraplegic as a result of a treatment for Hodgkin's lymphoma that involved high doses of radiation to slow down the progress of the cancer but, unintentionally, caused irreversible damage as it penetrated his spine. Both students at the time, we experienced a physical environment that was clearly not designed with wheelchair users in mind. By comparison, the accessibility of physical spaces at the UW today is impressive. However, more work needs to be done before going beyond ADA compliance to embrace UD of the built environment becomes common practice. I am encouraged by interactions such as a recent one with faculty and student leaders who want to improve the physical accessibility of the very old building in which their department is housed. They made clear their desire to go beyond minimum compliance so that their department is more welcoming to prospective students, faculty, and staff with disabilities.

The Contribution of WCAG to the UDHE Principles and Guidelines

In the early years of the internet, UD practices began to be applied to the design of hardware and software to ensure accessibility to individuals with disabilities, English language learners, and other groups. These efforts led to the Web Accessibility Initiative of the World Wide Web Consortium.[8] The WCAG and related practices are underpinned by four guiding principles. Together, they require IT components to be

1. *Perceivable.* Users must be able to perceive the content, regardless of the device or configuration they are using.
2. *Operable.* Users must be able to operate the controls, buttons, sliders, menus, etc., regardless of the device they are using.
3. *Understandable.* Users must be able to understand the content and interface.
4. *Robust.* Content must be coded in compliance with relevant coding standards to ensure it is accurately and meaningfully interpreted by devices, browsers, and assistive technologies.

The guidelines presented in the WCAG are organized into three levels of compliance—Levels I, II, and III, where III represents the highest level of accessibility. Most postsecondary institutions required to address civil rights complaints over the inaccessibility of their IT have adopted the latest version of WCAG Level II as their standard going forward.

The Contribution of UDL to the UDHE Principles and Guidelines

Applications of UD to create inclusive teaching and learning opportunities have led to an alphabet soup of terms—among them, UDL, UDI, UID (Universal Instructional Design), UDT (Universal Design of Teaching), UCD (Universal Course Design), IDL (Inclusive Design for Learning). Several different approaches have been taken in adopting principles to underpin guidelines and practices for applying the UD approach to teaching and learning products and environments. Some leaders in these efforts have simply applied the seven principles of UD and their respective guidelines.[9] The Center on Postsecondary Education and Disability at the University of Connecticut added two new principles to the UD list because the staff considered them necessary for making them more relevant to postsecondary instruction.[10] The Center for Applied Special Technology (CAST) created a new set of principles with roots in cognitive neuroscience to underpin practices for the Universal Design for Learning (UDL).[11] The UDL principles follow.

1. *Provide multiple means of representation.* Three UDL guidelines under this principle promote the development of curriculum and instruction that includes multiple options for perception; language, mathematical expressions, and symbols; and comprehension.
2. *Provide multiple means of action and expression.* Three UDL guidelines under this principle promote the development of curriculum and instruction that includes multiple options for physical action, expression and communication, and executive functions.

Did you know?

The Center on Postsecondary Education and Disability at the University of Connecticut embraced CUD's seven principles of UD and added two more, described here, to make them more relevant to postsecondary teaching practices.

- *A community of learners.* The instructional environment promotes interaction and communication among students and between students and faculty.
- *Instructional climate.* Instruction is designed to be welcoming and inclusive. High expectations are espoused for all students.[12]

3. *Provide multiple means of engagement.* Three UDL guidelines under this principle promote the development of curriculum and instruction that includes multiple options for recruiting interest, sustaining effort and persistence, and self-regulation.

From the guidelines, the UDL team developed a total of thirty-two specific checkpoints that share specific practices and their research base. For example, checkpoint 2.5 argues that it is important to "illustrate through multiple media" as described here.

> Classroom materials are often dominated by information in text. But text is a weak format for presenting many concepts and for explicating most processes. Providing alternatives—especially illustrations, simulations, images or interactive graphics—can make the information in text more comprehensible for any learner and accessible for some who would find it completely inaccessible in text.[13]

UDL is embraced as part of the UDI, and more general UDHE, Framework because of its specific contribution to the design of teaching and learning activities, which is critical to what postsecondary schools are all about.

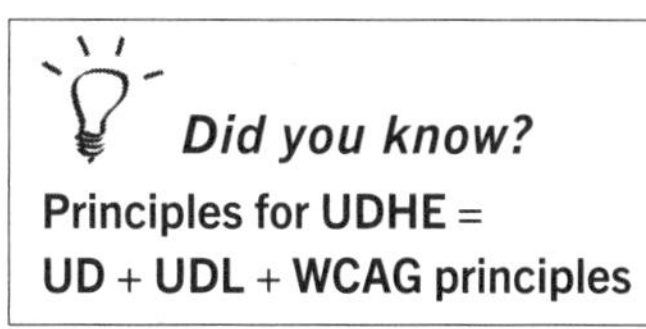

I conclude this discussion by listing the complete set of principles that support UDHE practices discussed in the next section of this chapter and presented throughout the remaining chapters of this book.

UD 1 Equitable use
UD 2 Flexibility in use
UD 3 Simple and intuitive
UD 4 Perceptible information
UD 5 Tolerance for error
UD 6 Low physical effort
UD 7 Size and space for approach and use
UDL 1 Multiple means of engagement
UDL 2 Multiple means of representation
UDL 3 Multiple means of action and expression
WCAG 1 Perceivable
WCAG 2 Operable
WCAG 3 Understandable
WCAG 4 Robust

PRACTICES

Collaborators in DO-IT's UDHE initiatives developed, tested, and refined UDHE practices for four types of products and environments relevant to higher education: instruction (both on-site and online), IT (including videos, websites, digital documents), physical spaces (such as science labs, classrooms), and services (including career services, counseling centers, teaching and learning centers, libraries). Figure 2.8 highlights aspects of these four broad areas to which UDHE can be applied.[14] Note that, although the need is minimized with the UDHE approach, reasonable accommodations in some cases are still necessary to ensure full access and engagement for a particular individual. For example, a student with a learning disability engaging in a universally designed course may still require extra time on an examination as determined by a postsecondary disability services office. Students who are deaf will still employ the accommodation process to secure interpreters. Students who are easily distracted may still need to take tests in an environment where distractions are minimized.

FIGURE 2.8 Application areas for UDHE

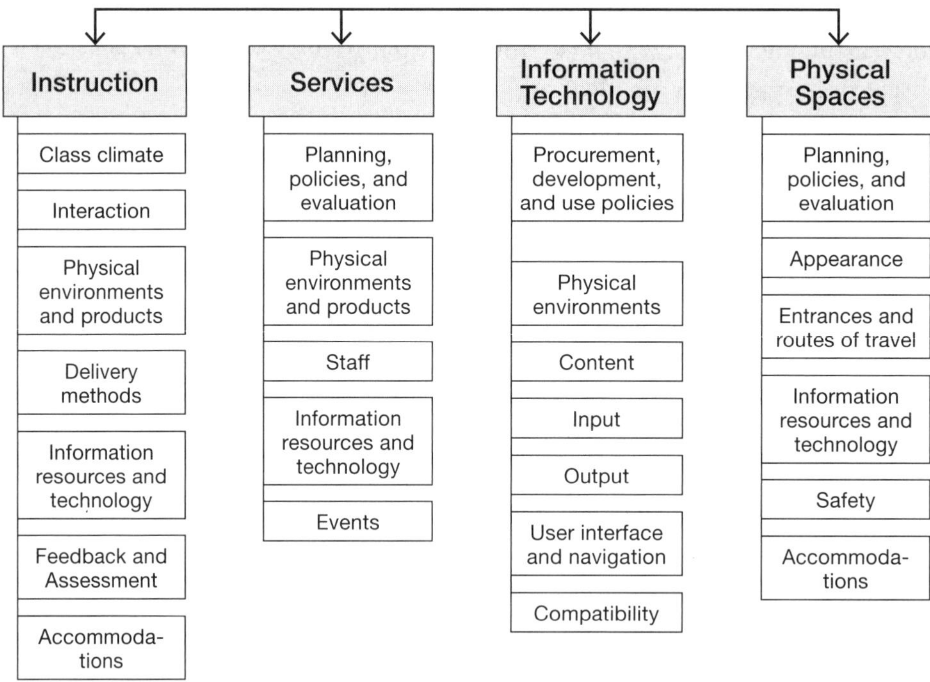

Source: Sheryl Burgstahler, "Universal Design in Higher Education," in *Universal Design in Higher Education: From Principles to Practice*, 2nd ed., ed. Sheryl Burgstahler (Cambridge, MA: Harvard Education Press, 2015), 1.

Specific practices developed as part of DO-IT's UDHE initiatives apply UDHE principles to particular aspects of postsecondary offerings. Examples are presented in table 2.1.

TABLE 2.1 Examples of UDHE principles applied to higher education practices

UDHE principle	*Example of UDHE practice*
UD 1. Equitable use	*Career services*. Job postings are in formats accessible to people with a great variety of abilities, disabilities, ages, racial/ethnic backgrounds, and technologies.
UD 2. Flexibility in use	*Campus museum*. An exhibit design allows a visitor to choose to read or listen to descriptions of the contents of display cases.
UD 3. Simple and intuitive	*Assessment*. Testing is conducted in a predictable, straightforward manner.
UD 4. Perceptible information	*Dormitory*. An emergency alarm system has visual, aural, and kinesthetic characteristics.
UD 5. Tolerance for error	*Instructional software*. An application provides guidance when a student makes an inappropriate selection.
UD 6. Low physical effort	*Curriculum*. Software includes on-screen control buttons that are large enough for students with limited fine motor skills to select.
UD 7. Size and space for approach and use	*Science lab*. An adjustable table and flexible work area are usable by students who are right- or left-handed and have a wide range of physical characteristics.
UDL 1. Multiple means of engagement	*Courses*. Multiple examples ensure relevance to a diverse student group.
UDL 2. Multiple means of representation	*Promote services*. Multiple forms of accessibly designed media are used to communicate services provided.
UDL 3. Multiple means of action and expression	*Course project*. An assigned project optimizes individual choice and autonomy.
WCAG 1. Perceivable	*Student service website*. A person who is blind and using a screen reader can access the content in images because text descriptions are provided.
WCAG 2. Operable	*Learning management system (LMS)*. A person who cannot operate a mouse can navigate all content and operate all functions by using a keyboard (or device that emulates a keyboard) alone.
WCAG 3. Understandable	*Instructional materials*. Definitions are provided for unusual words, phrases, idioms, and abbreviations.
WCAG 4. Robust	*Application forms*. Electronic forms can be completed using a wide range of devices, including assistive technologies.

In the next four chapters I elaborate on UDHE practices in physical spaces, technology, instruction, and services, respectively. As a preview of coming attractions, in figure 2.9 I share examples of UDHE practices in these four areas.[15] Reflection on these examples reveals that many UDHE practices are easy to implement and can benefit people other than those with disabilities. These examples make me wonder: if variation in abilities is a natural part of the human experience, why do so many postsecondary institutions wait until

FIGURE 2.9 Examples of universal design practices in higher education

In Instruction

- Multiple delivery methods
- Multiple assessment options
- Multiple means of interaction
- Captioned videos
- Accessibly designed curriculum, documents, and web pages
- Examples that appeal to students with a variety of backgrounds and interests
- Content outlines and other organizational tools
- Instructor awareness of processes and resources for making disability-related accommodations

In Services

- Service counters that are at heights accessible from both a seated and standing position
- Pictures in publications and on websites that include people with diverse characteristics
- A statement in publications and on websites that tells how to request disability-related accommodations and other assistance
- Printed materials that are easy to reach from a variety of heights and without furniture blocking access
- Computers, publications, and online resources that adhere to accessibility standards
- Captioned videos
- Staff awareness of processes and resources for making disability-related accommodations

In Information Technology

- Captioned videos
- Computers, documents, and online resources that adhere to accessibility standards
- Procurement policies and procedures that promote the purchase of accessible products
- On-site computers that are compatible with assistive technologies, comfortable for right- and left-handed users to operate, and located in adjustable-height tables in an uncluttered area

In Physical Spaces

- Clear directional signs that have large, high-contrast print
- Restrooms, classrooms, and other facilities that are physically accessible to individuals who use wheelchairs or walkers
- Furniture and fixtures in classrooms that are adjustable in height and allow arrangements for different learning activities and student groupings
- Emergency instructions that are clear and visible and address the needs of individuals with sensory and mobility impairments
- Nonslip walking surfaces

Source: Sheryl Burgstahler, "Universal Design in Higher Education," in *Universal Design in Higher Education: From Principles to Practice*, 2nd ed., ed. Sheryl Burgstahler (Cambridge, MA: Harvard Education Press, 2015), 22.

students with disabilities experience barriers to a course, space, service, or digital resource rather than prepare for their arrival? I know for sure that paying more attention to applying UDHE principles to all campus offerings has the potential to reduce the need for accommodations.

It is helpful to understand how UDHE principles build on established principles for UD, UDL, and WCAG. You do not need to memorize them, however, to effectively practice UDHE. Take time to intentionally look at institutional practices through a UDHE lens and develop a habit of asking, "Does our approach give individuals multiple ways to interact within courses, services, technological environments, or physical spaces?" "Is each practice *accessible* to, *usable* by, and *inclusive* of a diverse population?" and "Does our approach minimize the need for accommodations for individual students?" Aim for "yes," "yes," and "yes."

PROCESS

When used as a noun, the *design* in UD refers to a desired end state. The *design* in UD, however, can also be used as a verb. Rather than focusing on the typical user, in applying UDHE it is important to consider the diverse characteristics of potential users—for example, with respect to gender, age, ethnicity, race, native language, learning preferences, size, abilities—and the challenges they might encounter when attempting to engage with the product or environment. You can gain perspectives through publications and videos, consultation with diversity and disability programs, and engagement with people who have diverse characteristics. Ideally, include people with disabilities in the development, implementation, and evaluation of the application.

The following list of steps for the *process* of applying UDHE, summarized in figure 2.10, was informed by a review of the literature and the experiences of collaborators in DO-IT's UDHE initiatives. Note that this process suggests that the best designs for products and environments integrate *both* UDHE practices and best practices within the field of application. Putting captions on a movie of poor quality (a UDHE practice) will simply make a poor movie accessible to more people, including those who are deaf.

1. *Identify the application and best practices in the field.* Specify the product or environment to which you wish to apply UDHE. Identify best practices within the field of the application (e.g., evidence-based teaching practices, technology standards, architectural design specifications).

FIGURE 2.10 A process for applying UDHE to a product or environment

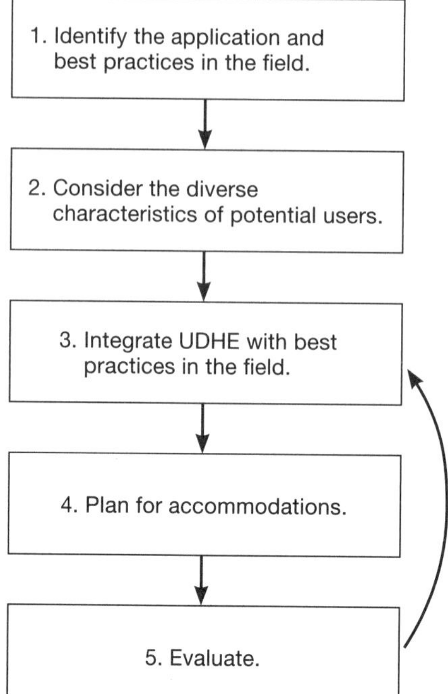

2. *Consider the diverse characteristics of potential users.* Describe diverse characteristics of potential users for which the application is designed—for example, with respect to gender; age; ethnicity; race; native language; learning preferences; size; abilities to see, hear, walk, manipulate objects, read, speak—and the challenges they might encounter when attempting to engage with the product or environment.
3. *Integrate UDHE with best practices in the field.* Integrate UDHE practices (underpinned by relevant UD, UDL, and WCAG principles) with best practices within the field of application to maximize the benefits of the application to individuals with a wide variety of characteristics.
4. *Plan for accommodations.* Develop processes for the provision of accommodations for individuals for whom the design does not automatically provide access (e.g., with assistive technology or sign language interpreters). Make these processes known through signage, syllabi, publications, or websites.
5. *Evaluate.* After implementing the product or environment, collect feedback from individuals with diverse characteristics who use it (e.g., through online surveys, focus groups). Make modifications based on the results.

Return to step 3 if evidence from your evaluation suggests that improvements should be made to your design.

UDHE

On many campuses today, embracing UDHE requires a shift from a medical to a social view of disability, from a view of disability as a deficit to a view of disability as a diversity characteristic, from considering inaccessibility as a problem caused by a person's impairment to a problem that may be the result of design flaws in a product or environment, from a focus on the average person to a focus on individuals with diverse characteristics, and from a reactive accommodation approach to proactive design practices that minimize the need for accommodations. The images in figure 2.11 illustrate how ramping up UDHE practices reduces the need for accommodations.

Applying UDHE enhances the quality of campus offerings but may impact the roles of faculty, staff, and disability services personnel when it comes to serving students with disabilities. In an accommodation approach, a disability services unit is the focus of efforts for ensuring access to students with disabilities; typically, the student presents documentation to a disability services staff member who approves reasonable accommodations and tells faculty and staff members to implement them.

FIGURE 2.11 Comparing campuses that embrace an accommodation approach and those that embrace a UDHE Framework in providing access to people with disabilities

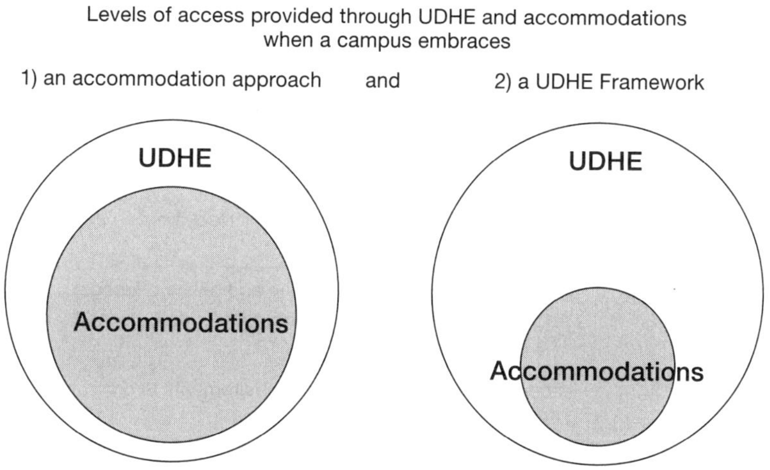

With a UDHE Framework, faculty, staff, and disability services personnel share responsibilities for creating accessible, usable, and inclusive products and environments. In this approach, staff offering disability, facility, IT, procurement, teaching, online learning, library, and other specialized services may perform UDHE consulting roles to help faculty and staff design their physical spaces, IT, and online and on-site courses and services to be accessible, usable, and inclusive. Table 2.2 articulates the potential roles of students with disabilities, disability services staff, faculty, and student service administrators when a UDHE Framework is embraced.

How the postsecondary community discusses access issues reveals attitudes about disability issues and areas of responsibility. For example, a professor might say, "My course videos are not accessible to Kylie because she is deaf." A professor who embraces the UDHE Framework might instead say, "Kylie cannot access the content presented in a course video because the video is not captioned." A fully UDHE-enlightened professor might say, "Kylie can access the content in course videos because I provide captions to benefit students who

TABLE 2.2 Examples of possible stakeholder roles on a campus that embraces a UDHE Framework

Stakeholders	*Potential roles*
Person with a disability	■ Apply self-advocacy and other self-determination skills to address access issues. ■ Individually or in an advocacy group, encourage the application of UDHE in all campus offerings.
Disability services staff	■ Authorize and arrange for reasonable accommodations. ■ Promote the application of UDHE campuswide.
Faculty member	■ Implement UDHE practices in online and on-site courses and other department resources, events, and other offerings. ■ Implement reasonable accommodations determined by disability services staff.
IT staff	■ Ensure that IT procured and developed at the institution is accessible to people with disabilities. ■ Consult on the accessible design of documents, videos, websites, and other IT.
Campus services staff	■ Apply UDHE practices to on-site and online offerings. ■ Implement reasonable accommodations determined by disability services staff.
Procurement staff	■ Incorporate accessible design requirements in contracts and other procurement processes. ■ Encourage campus units to procure products that employ accessible/universal design practices.

are deaf or hard of hearing, whose native language is English, who wish to search through the content for specific topics, or who want to know the spelling of technical terms used in the presentation." Rather than viewing disability as an individual's problem to be dealt with by a disability services office, a UDHE-enlightened educator recognizes accessibility barriers that reside in a product or environment and takes proactive steps to avoid them.

A Model for an Inclusive Campus

Systematically implementing UDHE practices can contribute to making a paradigm shift toward a broadly defined inclusive campus. By *paradigm*, I am referring to "a theory or a group of ideas about how something should be done, made, or thought about."[16] The dominant paradigm is the collection of values or a system of thought in a society or organization that is widely held at a given time. For the group that has adopted the paradigm, it provides an almost unconscious, internalized framework that affects the way they think things should work and often goes without question.

Paradigm shifts—when the collection of values or the dominant system of thought changes—are slow in coming and require adjustments to many moving parts. Some paradigm shifts are accomplished in the next generation if they become part of early education programs, which is what happened, at least in part, in the movement to get people to routinely recycle. My kindergartener would pull paper out of the garbage when I misbehaved in this regard, chastising me with "Mom, you're killing the trees!" Imagine if all children learned about disabilities? I am encouraged when I hear about day-care programs that teach a little sign language simply as an interesting way some people communicate, right along with learning phrases in Spanish, Japanese, and other languages. We all interact with children in some way and so can potentially all play a role in encouraging young children to think inclusively.

Did you know?

Frank Bowe, a professor who was deaf, argued that society handicaps people with disabilities through inaccessible facilities, equipment, instruction, and services, and advocated for wide application of inclusive design practices to eliminate or at least reduce these barriers. Coining the term *universally designed teaching*, Bowe encouraged educators to plan for the full inclusion of students from various ethnic, racial, and cultural backgrounds and with different learning preferences. He affirmed: "[t]he principles of universal design place responsibility for making curricula, materials, and environments accessible to and usable by all students upon the teacher and the school."[17]

What might a road map leading to a paradigm shift to a more inclusive campus look like? Well, it could involve embracing a vision for an inclusive campus; identifying campus values that support the shift; embracing the UDHE Framework to create a toolkit for achieving the shift; identifying relevant current practices; modifying existing practices or creating new ones that are more in line with the campus vision, values, and adopted UDHE Framework; measuring and analyzing outputs, outcomes, and impacts; and applying results to further improve practices to be more in line with the desired paradigm shift.

Hold everything! There is a lot more to learn before completing a campus road map.

Whew! That is good news for me. Otherwise, this book would be *way* too short!

As a preview of coming attractions, figure 2.12 presents the Inclusive Campus Model that is underpinned by the UDHE Framework. When fleshed out with details, this flexible model can be used as a tool to guide the creation of a road map for making your campus more inclusive.

MY GO-TO RESOURCES

Following are some good places to start in your exploration of topics covered in this chapter.

- *The ADA Checklist for Readily Achievable Barrier Removal*
  www.ada.gov/checkweb.htm
- *The Center for Universal Design in Education (CUDE)*
  uw.edu/doit/programs/center-universal-design-education
- *UDL on Campus*
  udloncampus.cast.org/home
- *Knowledge Base*
  uw.edu/doit/knowledge-base
- *TED Talks*
  ted.com (use *universal design* as a search term)
- *YouTube*
  youtube.com (use *universal design* as search term)
- *Published Books and Articles About Universal Design in Higher Education*
  uw.edu/doit/programs/center-universal-design-education/resources/published-books-and-articles-about-universal
- *Universal Design in Higher Education*[18]

FIGURE 2.12 Inclusive Campus Model underpinned by the UDHE Framework

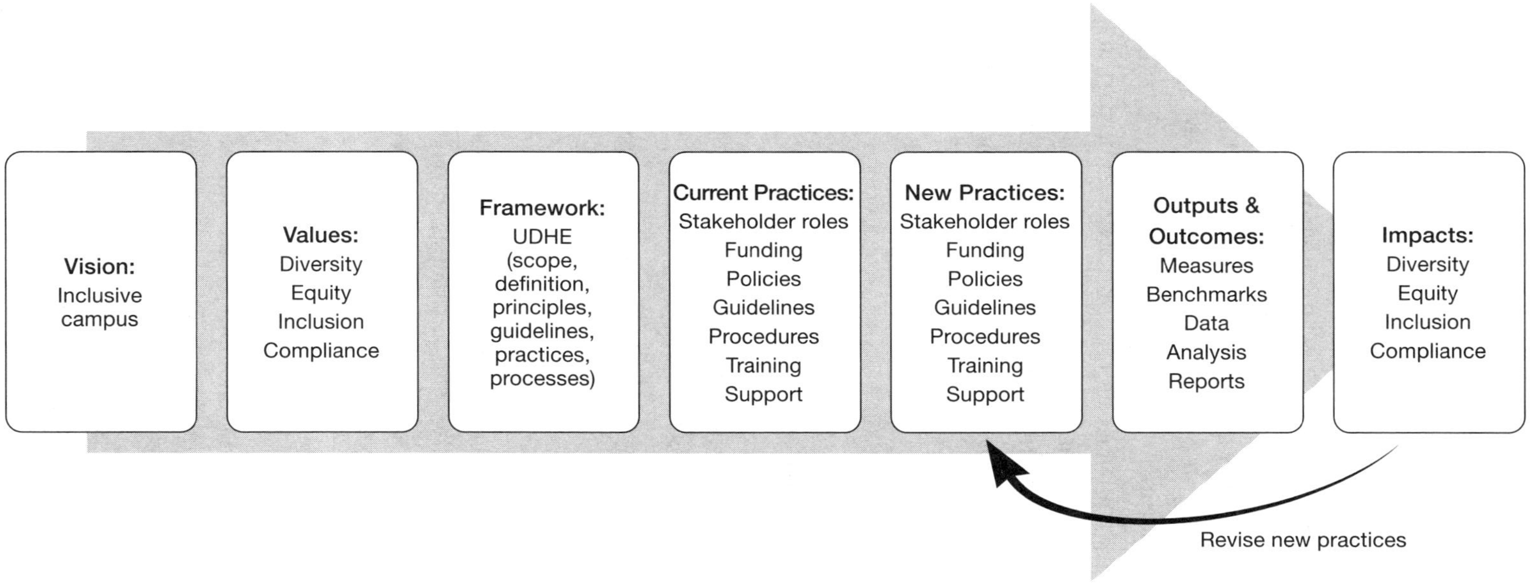

Vision:
Inclusive campus

Values:
Diversity
Equity
Inclusion
Compliance

Framework:
UDHE (scope, definition, principles, guidelines, practices, processes)

Current Practices:
Stakeholder roles
Funding
Policies
Guidelines
Procedures
Training
Support

New Practices:
Stakeholder roles
Funding
Policies
Guidelines
Procedures
Training
Support

Outputs & Outcomes:
Measures
Benchmarks
Data
Analysis
Reports

Impacts:
Diversity
Equity
Inclusion
Compliance

Revise new practices

CONCLUSION

In an era of rapidly changing demographics and increasing sensitivity to diversity and civil rights, it may be more effective and efficient for postsecondary institutions to consider the great diversity within the student body rather than focus on developing products and environments for the average student and providing accommodations for students with disabilities. In this chapter I shared a UDHE Framework that can be fleshed out to create a toolkit that can be used to make all institutional offerings more accessible, usable, and inclusive. Although much work remains to be done, particularly with respect to technology and course design, I'm honored to be part of a loosely defined group of people with disabilities and their coconspirators that keeps the UW moving in the right direction. In the next four chapters, respectively, I elaborate on UDHE practices for physical spaces, technology, teaching and learning activities, and campus services.

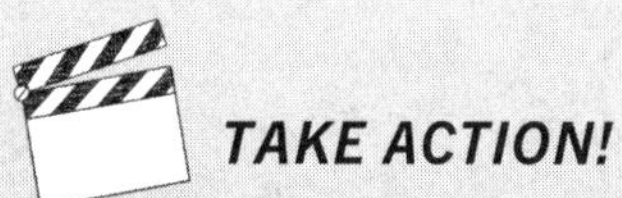

TAKE ACTION!

(REFLECT) Consider your context

Reflect on these questions:

- In what ways do you try to make everyone feel welcome in an academic or professional development course, a service, or employment?
- What UDHE practices do you already apply? What are additional ones you could apply now?
- How can you contribute to changes toward a more inclusive campus?
- How can leaders promote inclusive practices on your campus?
- How might you convince senior leaders at your institution to engage in a campuswide UDHE initiative?

(LEARN) Find UD in the news

In an academic class or community of practice, have students conduct an internet search to locate and read news articles about UD. In small groups, have each person describe an article, its source, and how it is relevant to the focus of the course.

(LEARN) Explore legal issues

Within an academic or professional development course, have students make an argument regarding how Section 504 of the Rehabilitation Act of 1973 and the

Americans with Disabilities Act of 1990 and its 2008 amendments could be used to promote UDHE on a postsecondary campus. What are potential positive and negative outcomes of making a legal argument for applying UDHE?

(LEARN) Ask, "Why not UD?"

Campuses typically use an accommodation approach in their efforts to provide access for individuals with disabilities rather than a proactive, inclusive approach like UDHE. In an academic or professional development course, have students share why they think that UDHE is not routinely applied in higher education.

(LEARN) Teach about the history and definition of UD

In an academic course, talk about the history and definition of UD—"the design of products and environments to be usable by all people, to the greatest extent possible, without the need for adaptation or specialized design"—and how it can be applied to products, environments, and social structures in the fields of study and practice relevant to the course.[19]

(LEARN) Explore characteristics of UD

In an academic course, discuss examples of products or environments related to the course content that meet none, some, or all of the three characteristics of universal designs—that they are accessible, usable, and inclusive of everyone who might potentially use them.

(APPLY) Brainstorm UD impact on accommodation services

In a task force or community of practice, share examples of specific campus practices that could potentially reduce the accommodation needs of students with disabilities. Brainstorm how positive changes to practices could be made.

(APPLY) Create a community of practice

Create a community of practice of stakeholders interested in how UDHE can be applied to all of your college or university offerings. Give your group a name such as the UDHE Community of Practice or UDHE Advocates. Meet in person each month and communicate within an online forum to share access problems and UDHE solutions. Formulate plans, host activities, write articles, and invite others to join your group.

(APPLY) Teach UD in an engineering course

In an engineering course, require that students apply UD principles, guidelines, and practices in their design projects.

(APPLY) Explore the UD of products, environments, or social structures

In an academic course, have students in small groups choose a product, environment, or social structure relevant to your course and brainstorm challenges that individuals with specific disabilities might face if it is designed to meet the needs of only the average user. Be sure they consider differences with respect to physical, visual, hearing, learning, attention, cognitive, and communication abilities. Ask them to brainstorm potential solutions and report to the class their conclusions and lessons learned.

(APPLY) Uncover applications of UD

In a professional development workshop, have participants explore central websites such as those hosted by the president, disability services, diversity units, human resources, and other high-level offices at your institution. Discuss content on campus websites that reflects a priority for what could be called universal design practices and what changes could be made to better promote such practices.

CHAPTER 3

Physical Spaces

Do what you can, with what you have, where you are.

—Theodore Roosevelt

WHEN UNIVERSAL DESIGN in Higher Education (UDHE) principles, along with other design considerations, are applied, physical spaces become more inclusive of students, faculty, staff, and visitors with diverse characteristics, including those related to disabilities. In this chapter I describe how the UDHE Framework can be applied to campus facilities and outdoor spaces.

INTRODUCTION

My husband, Dave, and I have a beach house on Hood Canal, a natural waterway that extends for about fifty miles and separates the Kitsap Peninsula from the Olympic Peninsula in Washington state; it is actually *not* a canal but rather a fjord connected to Puget Sound. Years ago, we rebuilt our deck at the beach house and added a simple ramp that wraps around one side of the house, connecting the deck with the sidewalk below. The reactions of our neighbors who visited the house during construction were remarkably consistent with respect to the ramp. With concern expressed through body language and tone of voice, and sometimes in roundabout ways, they asked which of our elderly relatives or friends could no longer walk. They seemed surprised when I said we had no particular person in mind who would use the ramp. In fact, the primary beneficiaries of the ramp over the years have been children and adults moving toys and other items from the garage to the deck; everyone uses it.

Our deck project is an example of the application of universal design (UD)—proactively designing a space to meet the needs and interests of potential users with a wide range of abilities and interests. We hope our ramp sends the message to anyone who requires its use, "We expected you to come to our home. You are welcome here."

By the end of this chapter, you should be able to

- describe components of a UDHE Framework—definition, principles, guidelines, practices, and process—with respect to the design of physical spaces;
- name the three sets of principles that underpin the UDHE Framework;
- give examples of physical barriers and related access solutions for individuals with specific types of disabilities;
- list UDHE practices that make physical learning spaces accessible to, usable by, and inclusive of individuals with diverse characteristics, including disabilities;
- describe the process for applying the UDHE Framework to physical spaces;
- apply UDHE practices to classrooms, makerspaces, engineering labs, and other specific spaces.

Over the past decade, makerspaces have popped up on campuses around the world. Although they come in multiple forms and include a wide variety of high-tech and low-tech tools, at their core they are collaborative workspaces for making, learning, exploring, and sharing. Imagine a prospective engineering student who uses a wheelchair attends an open house in a new makerspace on a postsecondary campus. Pleasantly surprised, he can easily maneuver into and within the space, reach equipment controls, and imagine himself engaging with other students there. The message seems to be "We expected you to come to our makerspace. You are welcome here." Is this your school? Yes? Then, good for you. No? Then, no worries; it is not too late to apply UDHE to make it a more inclusive place.

Designers who apply UDHE to physical spaces anticipate the wide variety of abilities and other characteristics potential users might have, and make design decisions that both serve the needs of the broadest audience and are reasonable under the given circumstances. When an existing space is not suitable for a specific user, UD advocates consider how the environment might be improved so that, even if an accommodation must be provided to address an immediate access barrier, efforts will be made to remove the barrier for future users of the space. Applying the UDHE Framework to physical environments that support learning can contribute to the success of all students who engage within them.

FRAMEWORK, SCOPE, DEFINITION, PRINCIPLES, AND GUIDELINES

Components of the UDHE Framework are scope, definition, principles, guidelines, practices, and process. The scope of applications in this chapter comprises physical spaces, particularly those that support teaching and learning, on a postsecondary campus. These framework categories can be fleshed out to create a toolkit for applying UDHE to any physical space on campus.

A definition that can be used for the application of the UDHE to physical spaces, modified from the basic definition of UD, is the design of *physical spaces in higher education* to be usable by all people, to the greatest extent possible, without the need for adaptation or specialized design. Principles for the design of physical spaces are the combination of the seven principles of UD, the three principles of Universal Design for Learning (UDL), and the four principles that underpin the Web Content Accessibility Guidelines (WCAG). Combining these three sets of principles ensures that all issues regarding the design and use of a physical construction are adequately addressed. Principles of UD guide the design of an accessible space and products within it; UDL principles contribute to making learning activities occurring within the space inclusive of everyone; and principles that underpin WCAG steer the accessible design of technology used within or accessed from the space. Guidelines for spaces build on relevant principles, as do the process and practices for their implementation detailed in the following two sections of the chapter.

Did you know?

Article 20 of the international Convention on the Rights of Persons with Disabilities requires that countries identify and remove barriers to ensure that people with disabilities can access the environment, transportation, and public facilities.

PRACTICES

In developing inclusive practices for campus spaces, you do not need to memorize UDHE principles and guidelines. Instead, simply focus on

- the basic definition of UDHE;
- the importance of offering multiple ways to access and engage within the environment; and
- the three basic characteristics of each UD strategy—that it is accessible, usable, and inclusive.

Postsecondary campuses have many types of spaces—among them, classrooms, auditoriums, seminar rooms, learning commons, museums, theaters, computing spaces, science and engineering labs, makerspaces, libraries, student union buildings, athletic facilities, and dormitories. They can all be made more inclusive through the application of UDHE. In designing a space, keep in mind that individuals using the space may have a range of abilities with respect to vision, hearing, speech, and mobility/dexterity; also consider the needs and preferences of those who are short and tall, are right- and left-handed, come from a wide variety of cultures, have different gender identities, and have a range of English language skill levels. Make sure everyone feels welcome and can get to the facility and maneuver within it, communicate effectively with staff and fellow users, access printed materials and electronic resources, and operate equipment and software in the space.

FIGURE 3.1
A button to open a door makes it accessible to more people

A push button to open a door, such as that presented in figure 3.1, makes opening the door possible for more individuals but is still inaccessible to people without the ability to push the button. The push-button approach is not as inclusive as what we have grown to expect at supermarkets—that the door opens automatically for *everyone* who approaches it. All customers are beneficiaries of this UD feature. Although not always affordable, wouldn't it be ideal if entrances to all buildings were universally changed? If not *all*, at least the more prominent ones.

Flexibility with respect to the design of furniture and the ability to arrange it in multiple ways is ideal. Figure 3.2 presents an image of a simple design

FIGURE 3.2 Alternate rows of swivel chairs facilitate student interactions

feature for an auditorium: chairs in alternate rows can spin around, making it more flexible for conducting "Turn and Talk," "Think. Pair. Share," and other small group discussions in a course.

From the basic UD definition, principles, and guidelines, the Center for Universal Design (CUD) and other entities developed recommendations for applying UD to homes, public facilities, landscapes, and other spaces. For example, checklists for the design of aspects of residential spaces were developed by the American Association of Retired Persons (AARP).[1] Included are suggestions that a home include an entry with no steps, main rooms on the ground level, thresholds that are flush with the floor, wide doorways, non-slip surfaces, lever door handles, grab bars, controls labeled with large print, wheelchair-accessible bathrooms, kitchens that can be used from a seated position, and adequate lighting for walkways and work areas. Other checklists for inclusive practices created by researchers and practitioners are those for architectural studios, student housing, museums, science and engineering labs, and makerspaces.

Practices for All Spaces

I reviewed existing guidelines and checklists for accessible and universal design to identify practices that applied UD principles to physical spaces on postsecondary campuses. The strategies were updated with formative feedback from members of a nationwide leadership team—representing a diverse set of institutions of higher education nationwide—who engaged in the Disabilities, Opportunities, Internetworking, and Technology (DO-IT) Center's UDHE initiatives. The practices are organized around seven areas of consideration when designing or updating a campus space: planning, policies, and evaluation; appearance; entrances and routes of travel; fixtures, furniture, and equipment; information resources and technology; safety; and accommodations. The last category, accommodations, is included as a reminder that even a universally designed space may not work for everyone; therefore, it is important to establish and publicize a system whereby individuals can request accommodations. Examples of practices included in the checklist are presented in table 3.1.[2]

With respect to the practice to "Prioritize UD features when selecting equipment and other products used in the facility," you might be surprised to learn about the availability of some *very cool* products that are accessible to people with disabilities—pipette-filling devices with textured and hand-neutral grips; measuring cups with large print and braille labels; beakers with handles and made of plastic rather than glass; tactile models and 3D graphs; extended eyepieces for microscope viewing for wheelchair users; surgical gloves for handling slippery items; equipment that enlarges microscope images; talking weight scales, thermometers, calculators, and color identifiers; and remote-controlled microscopes for people with limited use of their hands. Purchasing specialized products for the inventory in a lab sends the message that it is expected that individuals with disabilities will use the space.

Practices for Specific Spaces

DO-IT projects have developed checklists for specific facilities that include computer labs, engineering labs, engineering research centers, informal science learning facilities, and makerspaces funded by the National Science Foundation. Our most recent effort was motivated by reports from faculty and students that many makerspaces were not fully accessible to students with some types of disabilities. Developing design strategies for this application is complicated by the great variety of equipment involved (such as 3-D printers, electrical tools, and sewing machines) and innovative workspaces used by students, faculty, staff, and sometimes even the broader community that gather together in makerspaces to share knowledge, work on projects, network, and undertake innovative products. An early step was for a group of students with a variety of disabilities to review a makerspace and brainstorm accessibility issues and UD solutions. Then they engaged with project staff to develop guidelines for the

TABLE 3.1 Universal design of physical spaces in higher education

Guidelines	*Examples of UDHE practices in a physical space*
Planning, policies, and evaluation. Consider diversity issues as you plan and evaluate the space.	▪ Include people with diverse characteristics, including various types of disabilities, in planning processes. ▪ Integrate accessibility issues into procurement processes. ▪ Adopt a procedure to ensure a timely response to requests for disability-related accommodations. ▪ Address disability-related issues in evaluation methods.
Appearance. Design the space to foster a campus climate that is inclusive of all students, staff, faculty, and visitors.	▪ Create an environment that appeals to people with a variety of cultural backgrounds, ages, abilities, and other characteristics.
Entrances, routes of travel. Make physical access welcoming and accessible to people with a variety of abilities, body sizes, and ages.	▪ Ensure convenient, wheelchair-accessible parking spaces and routes of travel to and within facilities. ▪ Integrate gently sloping walks into the design so that everyone can travel the same route. ▪ Shelter entryways. ▪ Install outdoor lights with motion sensors near entrances. ▪ Provide sensors to automatically open exterior doors. ▪ Install lever handles rather than knobs on doors that do not automatically open. ▪ Mount ample high-contrast, large-print directional signs throughout the space. ▪ Include wide aisles that are clear of obstructions. ▪ Position electrical outlets and light switches so that they can be reached from both standing and sitting positions. ▪ Make lighting for individual work areas adjustable by facility users.
Fixtures, furniture, and equipment. Provide fixtures, furniture, and equipment that can be used by potential facility users with diverse characteristics.	▪ Install lever handles instead of knobs for cabinets. ▪ Use front-mounted, easy-to-operate controls on other equipment, with instruction labels in large, high-contrast print. ▪ Install work surfaces that are adjustable in height and allow flexible arrangements for different learning activities and student groupings. ▪ Mount mirrors above locations where demonstrations are typically given. ▪ Prioritize UD features when selecting equipment and other products used in the facility.
Information resources and technology. Ensure that information and technology are accessible to everyone.	▪ Position publications to be reachable from standing and sitting positions. ▪ Ensure that information technology (IT) used within or associated with the facility is accessibly designed. ▪ Offer online resources, tools, and communication methods that are accessible to a diverse audience.
Safety. Design the space to minimize the risk of injury.	▪ Use nonslip walking surfaces. ▪ Install emergency systems that incorporate audio and visual warnings.
Accommodations. Develop a system for staff to address accommodation requests by individuals for whom the space design does not automatically provide access.	▪ Include procedures for requesting disability-related accommodations in signage, publications and websites. ▪ Ensure that faculty and staff members know how to respond to requests for disability-related accommodations.*

*Sheryl Burgstahler, *Equal Access: Universal Design of Physical Spaces* (Seattle: University of Washington, 2020), http://uw.edu/doit/equal-access-universal-design-physical-spaces.

universal design of makerspaces that are available on the DO-IT website. Here's what students with disabilities reported regarding the value of efforts to design makerspaces that are accessible to a diverse audience and the importance of engaging people with disabilities in design processes.

- "Makerspaces are about community. We need to ensure everyone from the community can participate."
- "Makerspaces are often used to help build new assistive technology and increase accessibility; however, many of these spaces and tools remain inaccessible. We need to make sure disabled people can access these spaces and create the products and designs that they actually want."
- "With a visual impairment, I create mental maps to navigate spaces. I love that all of the furniture is on wheels to create flexibility, but I also like that a lot of the tools are in fixed spots. I will always know the location of the 3-D printer and laser cutter, even if the space in between changes from day to day."
- "Don't underestimate abilities. Ask if someone needs assistance, but don't assume they cannot do it themselves."[3]

The guidelines and practices developed in this project are organized into seven broad areas:

- *Planning and Policies.* For example, do websites and other materials include pictures of users from diverse backgrounds?
- *Space.* For example, are power cords and work surfaces clearly marked and accessible for individuals with mobility or visual impairments?
- *Furniture.* For example, are adjustable-height tables available?
- *Ideation, Team, and Meeting Space.* For example, do groups have the freedom and flexibility to make the space work for their team?
- *Tools and Equipment.* For example, are training materials and instructions available in multiple formats?
- *Staff, Safety, and Training.* For example, is there a quiet space that groups can use for meeting space?
- *Focus Groups and User Testing.* For example, have we received feedback from individuals with a variety of disabilities about our space?

Figure 3.3 illustrates the importance of including adjustable-height work surfaces and equipment as a UD feature of a makerspace or lab. In a recent online discussion, I learned of a campus that developed a timeline for placing

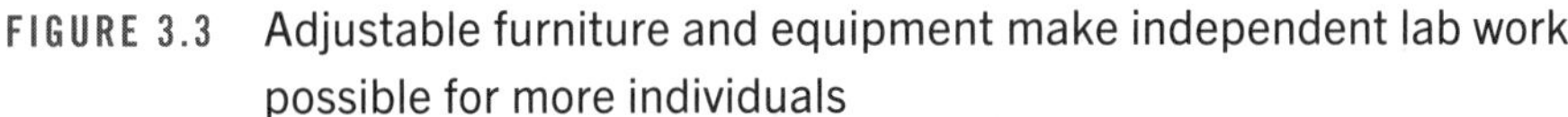

FIGURE 3.3 Adjustable furniture and equipment make independent lab work possible for more individuals

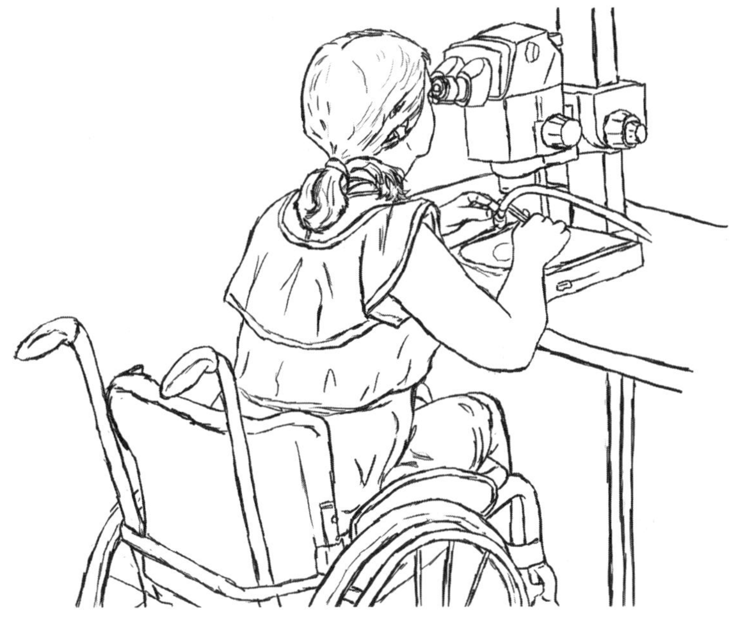

one adjustable-height work surface in each learning space to ultimately eliminate the practice of providing one only in response to an individual request for an accommodation. What a great example of planning for diversity rather than waiting to react to it, of creating an enabling space for learning rather than designing a disabling one.

PROCESS

Although many inaccessible spaces exist, some processes employed on postsecondary campuses have led to the creation of inclusive spaces. For example, in the design of a recreation center at Missouri State University, one objective was that the center "be designed, using universal design concepts, to be accessible to all individuals of the University community."[4] Stakeholders in project committees included the architect, staff members associated with center activities, disability services professionals, and students with disabilities. When systematically and broadly applied, engaging people with disabilities along with other stakeholders in a UD project has the potential to contribute to a campus-wide paradigm of equity and inclusion rather than mere compliance.

When you are applying the UDHE Framework to a physical space on a campus, it is important to plan ahead, to keep in mind the diversity of the campus community, and to engage individuals with diverse characteristics in all stages of development. The following steps, adapted from the more general process of applying UDHE, can be used when designing a new space or making an upgrade to an existing space. The steps are summarized in figure 3.4.

1. *Identify the space and best practices in the field.* Specify the space to which you wish to apply UDHE (e.g., a student union building). Review research and practices to identify best practices within the field of the application (e.g., the design of student service buildings).
2. *Consider the diverse characteristics of potential users.* Describe the potential faculty, students, staff, and visitors who might use the space and the diverse characteristics of the population (e.g., with respect to gender; age; size; ethnicity and race; native language; learning preferences; and abilities to see, hear, manipulate objects, read, and communicate).
3. *Integrate UDHE with best practices in the field of space design.* Integrate UDHE practices (underpinned by relevant UD, UDL, and WCAG

FIGURE 3.4 A process for applying UDHE to a campus space

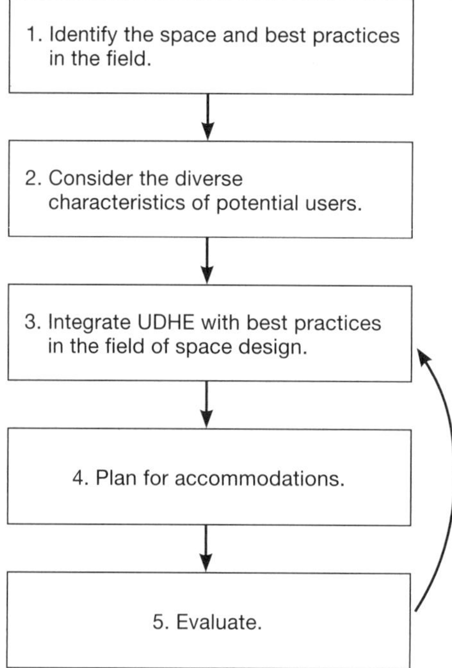

principles) with best practices within the field of design of the type of space (e.g., design practices for student union buildings) to maximize the benefit of the space to individuals with the wide variety of characteristics.

4. *Plan for accommodations.* Develop processes to address accommodations for individuals for whom the design of the space does not automatically provide access (e.g., ensuring that cafeteria staff know how to assist customers with disabilities). Tell potential users of the space how to request accommodations within signage, websites, and publications.
5. *Evaluate.* Once the space is completed, collect feedback from individuals with diverse characteristics who use the space (e.g., through online surveys, focus groups). Make modifications based on the results. Return to step 3 if evidence from your evaluation suggests that improvements should be made to your design.

Did you know?

The increasing size of the aging population and the desire of senior citizens to live in single-family housing as long as possible have kindled interest in accessible design. According to the former chair of the US Architectural and Transportation Barriers Compliance Board, "Universal design is an approach to design that acknowledges the changes . . . everyone [undergoes] during his or her lifetime. It considers children, the elderly, people who are tall or short, and those with various disabilities. It addresses the lifespan of human beings beyond the mythical 'average' person."[5]

Two impediments to broad application of UD to physical spaces are the misconception that it reduces its visual appeal and an all-or-none attitude. You may recognize George Pocock as the name of the Yoda-like inspirational figure and legendary racing shell builder prominent in Daniel James Brown's best-selling book, *The Boys in the Boat,* in which he tells the story of how an unlikely group of Depression-era men became the University of Washington crew team that won a gold medal at the 1936 Olympics. My family's life intersected with Pocock's over thirty years ago when we purchased his family home. Without spoiling its beauty and even though full implementation of UD was not reasonable, in our renovations we integrated a few UD features (e.g., a wheelchair-accessible home entrance and patio, a shower stall with two options for the height of the shower head). Similarly, even employing a few UD features in a physical space at an educational institution does not need to diminish its visual appeal but does make its beauty available to more people.

So is there evidence that our campuses are creating spaces that are universally designed, rather than simply "ADA compliant"? Sometimes I feel as though we are standing still; other times I am uplifted by things like a recent job posting that said a postsecondary institution was "pleased to announce a new position supporting students who are disabled by inaccessible environments." What I know for sure is that isolated efforts can play a role in dismantling institutional inequities.

MY GO-TO RESOURCES

Following are some good places to start in your exploration of topics covered in this chapter.

- *The ADA Checklist for Readily Achievable Barrier Removal*
  www.ada.gov/checkweb.htm
- *Universal Design of Physical Spaces*
  uw.edu/doit/programs/center-universal-design-education
- *The STEM Lab*
  uw.edu/doit/programs/accesscollege/stem-lab/overview
- *Published Books and Articles About Universal Design of Physical Spaces*
  uw.edu/doit/programs/center-universal-design-education/resources/published-books-and-articles-about-universal
- *Knowledge Base*
  uw.edu/doit/knowledge-base
- *Universal Design of Student Services and Physical Spaces in Higher Education*[6]

CONCLUSION

The developers of the UD approach envisioned a world in which products and environments are designed to be accessible to, usable by, and inclusive of everyone. Civil rights movements and legislation throughout the world have contributed to the removal of many physical barriers in public spaces. Curb cuts, elevators, bus lifts, and ramps are commonplace. Most institutions of higher education understand their legal obligations to provide accessible parking and physical spaces overall. Much work remains to be done, however, to make everyone feel welcome to all campus facilities. In the next chapter I elaborate on the UD of technology used in higher education.

TAKE ACTION!

(REFLECT) Consider your context

Reflect on these questions:

- What message is sent to students using wheelchairs when events are held in spaces that are not accessible to them?
- What characteristics make a physical space rigid for teaching or hosting events? What design characteristics make a space more flexible in use?
- How easily can a person using a wheelchair maneuver in the facility where you work? How could access be improved?

(LEARN) Compare ADA compliant versus universally designed spaces

In an academic course or professional development offering, have participants describe the difference between a space being "ADA compliant" and being universally designed. Review the "Americans with Disabilities Act Checklist for Readily Achievable Barrier Removal" at ada.gov/checkweb.htm. Share an example of a UD feature that is likely not required by the ADA.

(LEARN) Find a space that can be made more inclusive with UDHE

In an activity for an academic or professional development course, have participants search online for an image of a physical space at a postsecondary institution or describe one they have experienced that could be more inclusive with the application of UDHE. Share results and discuss how this approach might be used to improve a space on a postsecondary campus.

(LEARN) Identify applications of UD, UDL, and WCAG to a space

In a discussion or assignment in an academic course, ask students to share examples of UDHE practices for a space that apply specific principles of UD, UDL, and WCAG. Have students articulate the importance of all three sets of principles when designing a space, particularly at an educational institution.

(APPLY) Brainstorm the design of a campus space

Before or while a new campus facility is being created or updated, pull together a group of students with disabilities to meet with the architects and campus coordinators of the construction. Share plans for the space and ask participants to identify potential access barriers and suggest solutions that eliminate them.

(APPLY) Universally design a campus space

In a task force or course, have participants access the following or other guidelines or checklists for a facility.

- "Making a Makerspace? Guidelines for Accessibility and Universal Design" at uw.edu/doit/making-makerspace-guidelines-accessibility-and-universal-design
- "Equal Access: Universal Design of Computer Labs" at uw.edu/doit/equal-access-universal-design-computer-labs
- "Access Equal Access: Universal Design of Engineering Labs" at uw.edu/doit/equal-access-universal-design-engineering-labs
- "Equal Access: Universal Design of Your Engineering Research Center (ERC)" at uw.edu/doit/equal-access-universal-design-your-engineering-research-center-erc
- "Facilitating Accessibility Reviews of Informal Science Education Facilities and Programs" at uw.edu/doit/facilitating-accessibility-reviews-informal-science-education-facilities-and-programs
- "Equal Access: Universal Design of Physical Spaces" at uw.edu/doit/equal-access-universal-design-physical-spaces

Eliminate checklist items that are not relevant to your space. Check off those items that are already in place. Put a date on tasks you wish to accomplish. Add other UDHE issues you would like to address. From this exercise create a planning document that lists specific tasks in order by targeted implementation date, followed by a section of completed items (for positive reinforcement as you see how far you have come). Review the document periodically, revising implementation dates and moving items from the plans section to the accomplishments section. The document could be formatted something like this:

UDHE Plans for [name of space]
    Month, year   UDHE task #1
    Month, year   UDHE task #2 . . .
UDHE Accomplishments
    UDHE task accomplishment #1
    UDHE task accomplishment #2 . . .

(Apply) Consider UDHE of a campus space

In subgroups in a task force or in an academic or professional development course, ask participants to choose a specific campus space (e.g., classroom, cafeteria, science lab, dormitory, museum, sport facility), brainstorm how it can be more universally designed, take notes, prioritize practices (considering factors such as likely beneficiaries and costs), and report back to the larger group.

(APPLY) Apply a UDHE checklist in an architecture class

Share with students in an architecture class how the UD of physical spaces goes beyond "ADA compliance." Have each student evaluate the accessibility of a campus facility using a checklist presented in the "Physical spaces" section of the

Center for Universal Design in Education at uw.edu/doit/cude. Discuss how this experience can inform practices in the field of architecture.

(APPLY) Create a new UDHE checklist for a campus space

Ask participants in an academic or professional development course to choose a type of space for which UDHE guidelines or a checklist has not yet been created. Draft a UDHE checklist that could be used to guide the development of an inclusive space of this type. Consider beginning to build your checklist by adapting an existing general checklist for physical space such as "Equal Access: Universal Design of Physical Spaces" at uw.edu/doit/equal-access-universal-design-physical-spaces.

CHAPTER 4

Technology

The nice thing about standards is that you have so many to choose from.

—Computer scientist Andrew S. Tanenbaum[1]

PRINCIPLES OF UNIVERSAL DESIGN in Higher Education (UDHE) can be applied to make information technology (IT)—sometimes called electronic and information technology (EIT) or digital technology—accessible, usable, and inclusive. In this chapter I share highlights of the history of accessible IT as well as strategies for ensuring that everyone—including faculty, staff, students, and visitors with disabilities—can benefit from all digital learning opportunities offered by a postsecondary institution.

INTRODUCTION

Since 1995, I have used four different learning management systems (LMSs) in teaching online courses. With every LMS, I get stuck at some point. I know what I want to do and that the LMS is capable of doing it, but I can't figure out how to make it happen. A younger me blamed the situation on myself: I didn't know enough about the product, I couldn't understand the error messages, I should have read the manual, I just don't know enough about computers. In contrast, my UD-enlightened self *first* wonders why the LMS is not more intuitive, why it does not present useful error messages along with hints on how I can correct my mistakes, and why existing support documents and web resources are inadequate with respect to their content and ease of use. I know, I know—that attitude in and of itself doesn't solve the problem at hand. However, I do feel better when I can, at least for a moment, blame something other than myself for it. In the spirit of UD, look to flaws in the design of a product *first*!

Depending on how it is implemented, IT can serve to level the playing field or to widen gaps in educational opportunities and attainment for students with and without disabilities. Although the availability of technology puts many people on the right side of the "digital divide,"[2] some members of this group continue to find themselves on the wrong side of the "second digital divide":

> This line separates people who can make full use of today's technological tools, services and resources from those who cannot. . . . People with disabilities who are on the right side of the first digital divide too often find themselves on the wrong side of the second digital divide. They have technology but do not have full access to all of the benefits it delivers to others.[3]

A medical or deficit view of disability focuses on the functional limitations of individuals and how these people can be rehabilitated so that they can use existing products and environments. The application of UDHE to digital learning tools and activities offers students flexible ways to access content, engage with other students and the instructor, and demonstrate what they have learned. Applying UDHE principles also ensures that each resource and learning activity is accessible to, usable by, and inclusive of individuals with a wide variety of characteristics and thus minimizes the need for accommodations. Accessible design features include customization options within an operating system, web browser, or software product that allow users to create ideal environments for themselves with respect to displays (e.g., font style, color and size, image size, screen colors) and operations (e.g., timing of events).

In this chapter I give an overview of issues related to the inclusive design of digital tools, activities, and resources that, in some cases, are part of a fully online or blended/hybrid (e.g., partially online and partially on-site) academic or professional development course. This topic is particularly important because of myriad types of ITs—among them, handheld computing devices, websites, social networking, multimedia, LMSs—that profoundly impact the way faculty members teach, students learn, and campus units offer information and services. If applied broadly, inclusive practices ensure that individuals with disabilities are on the right side of the second digital divide!

Pretty simple, right? Yep. Easier said than done? Yes. Impossible to achieve? No. Worth the effort? Yes. In this chapter I sort out much of this. By the end of the chapter, you should be able to

- describe challenges individuals—including those with disabilities related to vision, hearing, mobility, dexterity, mental health, communication, and learning—face in making use of IT and how these challenges can be reduced or eliminated;
- give examples of assistive technology (AT) for making computers more accessible to people with disabilities;
- describe components of a UDHE Framework—definition, principles, guidelines, practices, and process—with respect to the design of IT and related services;
- outline the principles that underpin the Web Content Accessibility Guidelines (WCAG);
- explain basic strategies for creating websites, documents, videos, and online courses that are accessible, usable, and inclusive;
- tell how people without disabilities benefit from universally designed IT;
- summarize results of civil rights complaints and resolutions about the inaccessibility of IT on postsecondary campuses and implications for other institutions;
- apply UDHE to IT products and services.

ASSISTIVE TECHNOLOGY

In 1982, I learned about a local six-year-old, Rodney, unable to use his hands because of a condition called arthrogryposis, who was learning to type on an electric typewriter using a stick in his mouth, called a mouth wand. I met his special education teacher who wondered if Rodney could operate a computer. I didn't know for sure but invited her, Rodney, and his family to come to our Microcomputer Resource Center at Saint Martin's College, where I taught mathematics, computer science, and education courses. Before I met him, his teacher shared with me a copy of the first letter Rodney wrote on a typewriter. In part, he said:

May 3. 1982,

Dear President Reagan,

I want to tell you my name. My name is Rodney and I Am 6 years old . . . I am handicapped bebecause I can't use my legs or my hands because I have little muscles and dbones.

I go to Skyline Exceptional School . . . I get to learn to type with my special mouth wand. Someday I will get to use a computer because I am smart even tho handicapped.

This is my first letter L typed. I Worked hard typing. TThank you for being nice . . .

Rodney

Who *wouldn't* want to get to know this kid? In our first meeting, we quickly realized that Rodney could perform all of the functions available through an Apple II computer keyboard using his mouth wand *except* for those requiring him to press two keys simultaneously. The inability of the Shift, Control, and Repeat keys to be locked presented a barrier to him. So, I embarked on a journey to find a way to fix this computer limitation. First, contacting Apple Inc. and then passing through a chain of technology leaders with no luck, I finally found Gregg Vanderheiden and his colleagues at the Trace Center at the University of Wisconsin. One phone conversation led to the delivery in postal mail of a hand-drawn diagram showing how to build a switch box to lock the Shift, Control, and Repeat keys. I hired an engineering student at the college to build it. Included as figure 4.1 is an image of me with Rodney as he controls a computer using his mouth wand, computer keyboard, and the "magic" switch box.

This was my first experience in a field of research and practice—assistive technology—that was opening a world of digital opportunities for individuals with disabilities. I met with Rodney once a week for many years to teach him programming, word processing, and other applications. By the time he was eight years old, Rodney was sharing programming tips with my college students.

Word about Rodney spread. St. Martin's became a magnet for people exploring computer access issues for individuals with disabilities. I recruited as many experts as I could find (there were only a few nearby) to teach Saturday

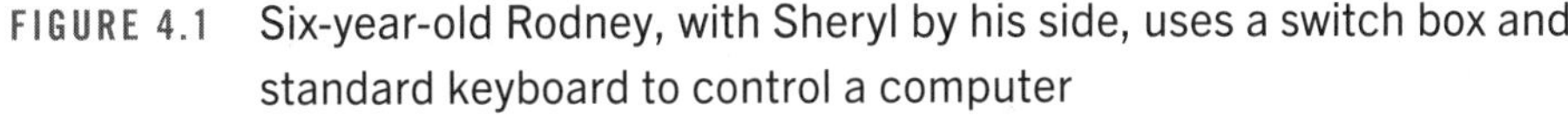

FIGURE 4.1 Six-year-old Rodney, with Sheryl by his side, uses a switch box and standard keyboard to control a computer

workshops on computer use by people with physical disabilities and, later, sensory differences and, later still, learning disabilities. I had a lot to learn.

Because of these experiences, when I was hired to lead the new Microcomputer Support Group (MSG) at the University of Washington (UW) in 1984, I immediately added making IT accessible to faculty, students, and staff with disabilities to the MSG mission statement. In those days, Rodney and I could not have imagined that by today there would be thousands of commercially available AT products, let alone the many features that benefit individuals with disabilities that are integrated into mainstream IT. The locking functions we achieved with Rodney's switch box are now routinely built into operating systems as "sticky keys."

Users today interact with technology in many ways. If you assume everyone uses a standard keyboard and mouse for input and a monitor and printer for output, you are wrong! Some users

- *have low vision* and use magnification software that allows them to enlarge all or specific content presented on the screen;
- *use a mobile device* and, because of the small screen, face accessibility barriers much like individuals with low vision using a standard computer screen unless magnification options are available;
- *have no vision* and use screen readers that work closely with the computer's operating system to provide information—about icons,

FIGURE 4.2 A student retrieves a document created with a Braille embosser

menus, dialog boxes, files, folders, and digital text—that is made available using synthesized speech, equipment that produces tactile graphics, refreshable braille displays (where plastic pins rise up in braille configurations to present screen content one line at a time), and braille embossers, as illustrated in figure 4.2;

- *experience a slow internet connection* and thus prefer to avoid content, such as videos and images, that does not load quickly;
- *have limited time* to watch videos and, instead, prefer to quickly read content provided in a transcript;
- *experience hearing challenges* that prevent them from benefiting from audio content when captions or transcripts are not included;
- *have dyslexia or other reading-related disabilities* and use software to highlight words and phrases as they appear on the screen, as well as to read them aloud using text-to-speech software and synthesized speech;
- *are color blind*, with particular difficulty in distinguishing between red and green;
- *have an impairment* that inhibits dexterity or range of motion, making it impossible to use a standard mouse, and rely exclusively on a standard keyboard (perhaps with a mouth stick for suppressing keys) or an alternative keyboard (e.g., expanded or mini keyboard, speech

FIGURE 4.3 A student uses assistive technology to operate a computer

recognition software, eye-gaze tracking system with onscreen keyboard), as illustrated in figure 4.3;

- *have difficulty typing content into the computer* because of a specific physical or learning disability and use AT that translates their speech to text, as illustrated in figure 4.4;
- *are English language learners* and benefit from seeing words spelled out along with hearing them spoken.

FIGURE 4.4 A student uses speech-to-text AT to enter content into a laptop

Some of these individuals use standard computer configurations, and others use AT to operate mainstream IT and access digital content. ATs enhance or replace standard input and output devices as described later. Morse code systems, alternative keyboards, keyboard guards, joysticks, speech recognition, and hundreds of other input alternatives allow access to functions of a standard keyboard and mouse for individuals who cannot use these devices. Alternatives to access content that is typically presented on a computer screen or printer include systems that read electronic text aloud, enlarge it, or present it in braille.

Besides ATs that interact with mainstream IT, stand-alone ATs are available for specific applications; among them is the speaking watch my elderly mother wears on a wristband because she is no longer able to read the digital screen of a clock, even with enlarged text. Special-purpose ATs particularly useful in higher education include handheld scanning devices that read aloud text from printed materials. These devices are powerful tools for people who have reading-related disabilities, people whose first language is not English, and others who benefit from simultaneously seeing and hearing words presented in printed documents.

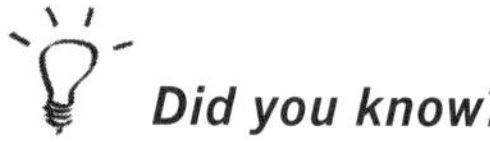

Did you know?

For hands-on and other learning opportunities regarding AT, a good conference to attend is the CSUN Assistive Technology Conference. For details, consult csun.edu/cod/conference.

Section 508 of the Rehabilitation Act of 1973 mandates that IT developed, maintained, procured, or used by federal agencies must be accessible to people with disabilities. Thousands of amazing ATs make it possible for everyone to benefit from all that technology has to offer today—except when they don't. As is often the case with good news, some bad news tags along. (I hate it when that happens.) Unfortunately, much of what technology offers is not designed to be accessible to people with disabilities, even if they are using state-of-the-art AT. Keep reading to learn why this is true and how this situation could be changed so that everyone can "benefit from all technology has to offer today," thus positioning them on the right side of the second digital divide.

ACCESSIBLE IT

Many schools have adopted an accommodations approach for addressing IT access needs. When a person self-identifies a disability and makes a request for an accommodation, someone within a disability services unit makes AT available, reformats inaccessible documents, captions videos, provides an assistant, or otherwise makes the content or functionality of IT available to that person. However, it has become clear to many campus leaders (including me) that an accommodations approach does not address accessibility problems within the IT infrastructure, is inefficient, and often results in an experience for a person with a disability that is not even close to that of others.

In the 1980s, cooperation between leaders in the IT industry, consumers, researchers, educators, government employees, and other stakeholders led to the development of guidelines for the design of IT that is accessible to people who have disabilities related to sensory, physical, cognitive, and language abilities, as well as those with seizure disorders.[4] As the World Wide Web emerged, its creator, Tim Berners-Lee, made clear that "[t]he power of the Web is in its universality. Access by everyone regardless of disability is an essential aspect."[5] In the mid '90s, publications promoting the accessible design of websites began to appear. The World Wide Web Consortium (W3C), the main international standards organization for the internet, supports the goal of making the web available to everyone (e.g., regardless of culture, language, disability status), on everything (e.g., on all computers and mobile devices), from everywhere (worldwide), and through diverse modes of interaction (e.g., using AT). The W3C Web Accessibility Initiative (WAI) promotes accessible design for individuals with disabilities. However, its leaders are quick to point out that web accessibility also benefits people *without* disabilities, including those who use mobile phones and other handheld devices; have "temporary disabilities" due to a broken arm or lost glasses; experience "situational limitations" due to bright sunlight or a noisy environment; have changing levels of abilities due to age; and use a slow Internet connection.

In 1999 the WAI published the first version of its Web Content Accessibility Guidelines, which were developed through a worldwide collaboration. The WCAG (the current version being 2.1 at the time this book was published) are widely regarded as international standards for web accessibility and the design of other IT as well. For each guideline, WCAG provides testable success criteria. To meet the needs of different organizations, three levels of WCAG conformance are defined: A (lowest), AA, and AAA (highest).

Many postsecondary institutions have adopted the current WCAG Level AA as a minimum standard for IT procured, developed, and used on campus. The guidelines and related practices of WCAG rest on four basic principles. For everyone to be able to effectively use it, web content must be

- *Perceivable*—Information and user interface components must be presentable to users in ways they can perceive. For example,
  - Provide text alternatives for any non-text content so that it can be changed into other forms people need, such as large print, braille, speech, symbols or simpler language.
  - Provide alternatives for time-based media.
  - Create content that can be presented in different ways (for example simpler layout) without losing information or structure.
  - Make it easier for users to see and hear content including separating foreground from background.
- *Operable*—User interface components and navigation must be operable. For example,
  - Make all functionality available from a keyboard.
  - Provide users enough time to read and use content.
  - Do not design content in a way that is known to cause seizures or physical reactions.
  - Provide ways to help users navigate, find content, and determine where they are.
  - Make it easier for users to operate functionality through various inputs beyond keyboard.
- *Understandable*—Information and the operation of user interface must be understandable. For example,
  - Make text content readable and understandable.
  - Make Web pages appear and operate in predictable ways.
  - Help users avoid and correct mistakes.
- *Robust*—Content must be robust enough so that it can be interpreted by a wide variety of user agents, including assistive technologies. For example,
  - Maximize compatibility with current and future user agents, including assistive technologies.[6]

The WCAG collection is one of several WAI accessibility guidelines. The series also includes the Authoring Tool Accessibility Guidelines (ATAG) that address issues related to authoring tools, the User Agent Accessibility Guidelines (UAAG) that cover web browsers and media players, and the Accessible Rich Internet Applications Suite (ARIA) that defines ways for making web applications more accessible to people with disabilities.

FRAMEWORK, SCOPE, DEFINITION, PRINCIPLES, AND GUIDELINES

Let's take a quick look at how the UDHE Framework—scope, definition, principles, guidelines, practices, and process—can be used to build a toolkit for guiding accessible IT practices on campus. The scope of applications covered in this chapter comprises teaching and learning activities and online resources supported by IT in higher education. A definition that can be used for the application of the UDHE to IT, modified from the basic definition of UD, is the design of *IT* products and environments *in higher education* to be usable by all people, to the greatest extent possible, without the need for adaptation or specialized design.

A set of principles that can be used to guide the design of IT products and services is a combination of the three sets of principles that underpin UDHE. It may be obvious that including the four principles that support the WCAG is important. You may wonder how the seven principles of UD established by the Center for Universal Design and the three principles of Universal Design for Learning (UDL) established by the Center for Applied Special Technology apply to IT. The answer is that combining the three sets of principles ensures that all issues relevant to IT on a campus are addressed. Applying principles that underpin WCAG steers the accessible design of websites and other technology. The principles of UD provide additional guidance in the design of accessible spaces that include IT. Applying UDL principles ensures that learning activities supported by IT benefit all students.

IT that is technically accessible may not be readily usable by people with disabilities. Some software companies, for example, make a product accessible to people who are blind and using screen readers by providing them with a long list of shortcut commands for performing functions designed in an inaccessible manner. This approach may result in a product that is technically "accessible" but not readily usable since a person who is blind needs to memorize or have close at hand the list of special commands to be able to operate the software. Other products require screen reader users to navigate a separate user interface altogether, resulting in a product that is not inclusive and not likely updated as often as the version intended for general use.

Rather than memorizing principles and guidelines, consider focusing more on the definition of UD of IT in higher education, the importance of offering multiple ways to access and interact with digital content and engage with other people, and the basic characteristics of any UD strategy: it is *accessible, usable,* and *inclusive.*

PROCESS

The process for applying UDHE to IT can be procured, developed, and used on a postsecondary campus. It is described here and illustrated in figure 4.5.

1. *Identify the IT and best practices in the field.* Specify the IT to which you wish to apply UDHE (e.g., a website). Identify best practices within the field of the application (e.g., Hypertext Markup Language [HTML] standards).
2. *Consider the diverse characteristics of potential users.* Describe the potential faculty, students, staff, and visitors who might use the IT and the diverse characteristics of the population (e.g., with respect to gender; age; size; ethnicity and race; native language; learning preferences; and abilities to see, hear, manipulate objects, read, and communicate).
3. *Integrate UDHE with best practices in the field of IT design.* Apply UDHE strategies in concert with other best practices to the design of the IT (e.g., a website) to maximize its benefit to individuals with the wide variety of characteristics.
4. *Plan for accommodations.* Make available appropriate AT and other accommodations for individuals for whom the design of the IT does not

FIGURE 4.5 A process for applying UDHE to IT

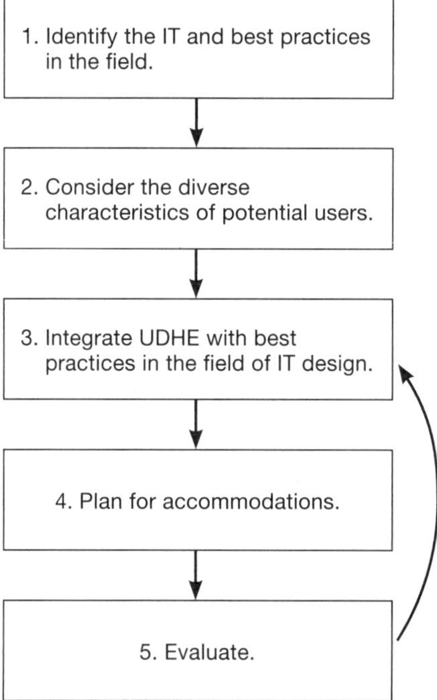

automatically provide access. Make the processes for reporting IT accessibility issues and requesting accommodations known (e.g., on a prominent website).

5. *Evaluate.* After the IT is deployed, collect feedback from individuals with diverse characteristics who use the IT (e.g., through online surveys). Make modifications based on the results. Return to step 3 if evidence from your evaluation suggests improvements for your design.

PRACTICES

Design practices for creating mainstream IT products that are fully accessible to and usable by everyone must address issues related to the diverse characteristics of potential users and of the AT they may employ. Let's first look at IT design implications related to the capabilities of AT. A complicating factor for IT designers is that just because users have access to IT and AT does not mean they know how to use them very well. It is important for IT developers to make their products usable by novices as well as power users. Table 4.1 presents a few of the capabilities and limitations of AT (especially screen readers and keyboard alternatives) that can provide insights into how mainstream IT can be universally designed.

When universally designing IT, consider challenges faced by individuals who may or may not be using AT as well as practices that can eliminate or at least minimize the need for AT. Not all practices that eliminate or minimize user challenges with respect to IT, however, are related to the capabilities and limitations of AT. For example, simply using "plain language" can improve access to websites for many readers. Not long ago I ran into the US government's *Federal Plain Language Guidelines* that were published in 2011 by the Plain Language Action and Information Network (PLAIN) that represents many federal agencies in response to the Plain Writing Act of 2010.[7] The guidelines suggest that agencies write clearly so their readers can find what they need, understand what they find, and use what they find to meet their needs. Great, I thought; rather than share my thoughts on the matter, I planned to simply post the guidelines as a table in this book—until I discovered that the document is 118 pages long, even though one of the guidelines is to "be concise." I'll follow *that* rule by providing one paragraph of suggestions most relevant to the UD of accessible digital content.

The guidelines suggest that you think about your audience (and diversity within it) before you start writing. Then, organize the information to best meet

TABLE 4.1 IT accessibility practices that are informed by typical limitations and other characteristics of assistive technology

Assistive technology	*Therefore:*
emulates the keyboard but may not emulate the mouse.	▪ Design IT to operate with the keyboard alone.
cannot read content presented in images.	▪ Provide text descriptions of content presented within images.
can tab from link to link.	▪ Use hyperlink text that is descriptive of the destination.
can skip from heading to heading.	▪ Structure headings using the formatting tool of the application used to present the content.
cannot accurately convert audio to text.	▪ Caption videos and transcribe audio content.
cannot decipher colors.	▪ Make sure that color is not the only way to understand an image or indicate a choice. ▪ Use high-contrast color combinations. ▪ Avoid color combinations that are often difficult for people with color blindness to distinguish, such as green and red.
cannot give a user guidance for navigating cluttered, unorganized content presented on the screen.	▪ Use large sans serif fonts on uncluttered pages with plain backgrounds that have high contrast with text. ▪ Maintain consistency in format from page to page. ▪ Avoid the addition of extraneous facts along with critical content. ▪ Define terms; spell out acronyms; avoid or explain figures of speech, idioms, and jargon.
can be difficult to operate, especially for new users.	▪ Design for individuals with a wide range of IT and AT skills.

the needs of your audience. The guidelines share writing principles, starting at the word level and moving up through paragraphs and sections. Organizational guidelines include that you make content easy to follow, with useful headings and subheadings, transition sentences to guide the reader, and lists to emphasize key points. Choose simple words and phrases—not to be mistaken with the perverse rule of grammar by author William Safire to "Never use a long word when a diminutive one will do." Avoid jargon; minimize abbreviations; be consistent in your use of terminology; keep sentences, paragraphs, and sections short; and use a conversational style with active voice and pronouns to speak directly to the reader. As far as sentences, keep subject, verb, and object close together and present the main idea before exceptions and conditions. For each paragraph, include a topic sentence, use transition words, and cover only one topic. To enhance clarity, use examples and illustrations. In talking specifically about web content, the guidelines recommend hyperlink text that concisely describes the destination. Most of this sounds familiar to me; as I read the guidelines, I swear I can hear my high school English teacher's voice speaking them aloud. Maybe she *did* know what she was talking about! My exercise in reading the guidelines reminded me once again: most of what can be called UD is simply good design.

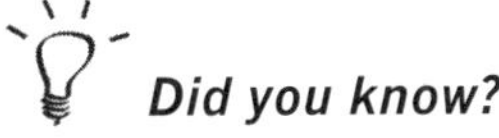

Did you know?

The US Department of Justice states that accessible IT "can be operated in a variety of ways and does not rely on a single sense or ability of the user."[8]

Some accessibility practices particularly beneficial to one group of computer users will likely benefit other users as well. In table 4.2 I share examples of potential IT access barriers and relevant practices for avoiding or minimizing them for individuals with specific types of characteristics. Be sure to keep in mind, however, that access challenges and solutions for many people may not be relevant to everyone within a specific group. As you look through the practices, you will also notice repetition with those listed for addressing AT capabilities and limitations presented in table 4.1.

In the following section, I consider practices from tables 4.1 and 4.2 to create the beginning of a list of UD practices for IT. Some practices are commonly applied, most can be easily built into an IT developer's workflow, and few take significantly more time to implement than inaccessible design practices.

- Present content in multiple ways that are each designed in an accessible manner (e.g., a combination of text, video, audio, or image).
- Use large sans serif fonts on uncluttered pages with plain backgrounds that have high contrast with text.
- Use plain language; define terms and spell out acronyms; and avoid or explain figures of speech, idioms, and jargon.
- Use clear, consistent layouts and organization schemes and break up content with formatted subheadings and bulleted lists.
- Provide text descriptions of content presented within images.
- Use hyperlink text descriptive of the destination.
- Give reminders and prompts when referring to content previously presented.
- With respect to color, use high-contrast combinations; avoid color combinations that are often difficult for people with color blindness to distinguish, such as green and red; and make sure color is not the only way to understand an image or indicate a choice.
- Design IT to operate with the keyboard alone.

- Caption video and transcribe audio content; offer real-time captioning for audio conferences.
- Offer options for communicating and collaborating that are accessible to individuals with a variety of disabilities.
- Design for individuals with a wide range of IT and AT skills.

TABLE 4.2 Examples of IT features that benefit individuals with specific characteristics

IT access issues for some who	*Practices that may especially benefit this group*
are deaf or hard of hearing ■ Content presented in audio clips and video presentations ■ Interactive audio and video conferences ■ Content that requires a high level of reading skills ■ Synchronous communication	■ Caption videos and transcribe audio content. ■ Offer real-time captioning for audio conferences. ■ Use images and diagrams to support content presented in text. ■ Define terms; spell out acronyms; avoid or explain figures of speech, idioms, and jargon. ■ Use clear, consistent layouts and organization schemes. ■ Use plain language. ■ Use asynchronous communication (e.g., email).
have low vision ■ Low-resolution graphics ■ Complicated page layout and design ■ Poor contrast between text and background ■ Small font size	■ Make sure color is not the only way to understand an image or indicate a choice. ■ Provide good contrast between text and background. ■ Use large sans serif fonts on uncluttered pages with plain backgrounds that have high contrast with text. ■ Make sure text flows and the user is not forced to scroll horizontally when text is enlarged. ■ Use clear, consistent layouts and organization schemes.
are blind ■ Images, tables ■ Videos ■ Complicated page layout and design ■ Complex tables	■ Present content in text format. ■ Provide text descriptions of content presented within images. ■ Integrate audio to describe visual content in a video design. Provide additional audio description when this is not possible or reasonable. ■ Structure headings using the formatting tool of the application used to present the content. ■ Use accessible design techniques for tables and avoid complicated ones. ■ Use hyperlink text descriptive of the destination. ■ Design IT to operate with the keyboard alone.
are color blind ■ Certain color combinations are not distinguishable	■ Use color combinations that are high contrast and avoid color combinations that are often difficult for people with color blindness to distinguish, such as green and red. ■ Make sure color is not the only way to understand an image or indicate a choice.

(*continued*)

TABLE 4.2 Examples of IT features that benefit individuals with specific characteristics (*continued*)

IT access issues for some who	*Practices that may especially benefit this group*
have mobility or dexterity impairments ■ Small objects on the screen ■ Synchronous communication ■ Navigation and selection when mouse is required	■ Use asynchronous communication (e.g., email). ■ Provide larger images and text for links. ■ Ensure operations can be made and resources accessed with the keyboard alone. ■ Use clear, consistent layouts and organization schemes. ■ Design IT to operate with the keyboard alone.
have dyslexia or other reading-related learning disabilities ■ Specific reading speed required ■ Content that requires a high level of reading skills ■ Synchronous communication	■ Use images and diagrams to support content presented in text. ■ Define terms; spell out acronyms; avoid or explain figures of speech, idioms, and jargon. ■ Present content in text format. ■ Use large sans serif fonts on uncluttered pages with plain backgrounds that have high contrast with text. ■ Use clear, consistent layouts and organization schemes. ■ Break up content with formatted subheadings and bulleted lists. ■ Make sure the reader controls the timing of presentations of text content. ■ Give reminders and prompts when referring to content previously presented. ■ Use plain language. ■ Use asynchronous communication (e.g., email).
have seizures ■ Blinking content	■ Do not make content blink.
are English language learners ■ Content presented in audio clips and video presentations ■ Interactive audio and video conferences ■ Content that requires a high level of reading skills ■ Synchronous communication	■ Caption videos and transcribe audio content. ■ Offer real-time captioning for audio conferences. ■ Use images and diagrams to support content presented in text. ■ Define terms; spell out acronyms; avoid or explain figures of speech, idioms, and jargon. ■ Use clear, consistent layouts and organization schemes. ■ Use large sans serif fonts on uncluttered pages with plain backgrounds that have high contrast with text. ■ Give reminders and prompts when referring to content previously presented. ■ Use plain language. ■ Use asynchronous communication (e.g., email).
Have a wide range of skills with respect to AT and IT	■ Design for individuals with a wide range of IT and AT skills.

UD of Digital Content

In this section I zero in on content presented as a document using Portable Document Format (PDF) or Microsoft products, or as a web page or within an

LMS content page using HTML. Whichever format you choose, you can follow a few general guidelines to avoid erecting accessibility barriers to individuals with disabilities. Although these general guidelines apply to all digital content, specific steps to apply them depend on the application you are using. Products for creating documents and delivering online learning often provide built-in accessibility checkers and guidelines as well as document templates in accessible formats.

If you design digital content to be accessible to people who are blind and use screen readers, the content will be more accessible to other people as well. For example, documents accessible to this group will also be accessible to individuals using text-to-speech software because of a learning disability or because they are English language learners. That is why in the paragraphs that follow I often mention accessibility to screen readers to justify the following accessibility recommendations.

- Use a text-based format.
- Include alternate text for images.
- Structure headings.
- Format lists.
- Use meaningful hyperlink titles.

Next, I elaborate on each of these five guidelines while avoiding myriad technical details you will encounter when applying them to a specific product.

Use a text format. The default format for Microsoft documents is text, which makes the content accessible to a screen reader or text-to-speech software. PDF documents can be formatted in text but are often presented as scanned images. How can you tell one from the other? Try to perform a cut-and-paste sequence. If you are unable to select text to cut, the document only looks like text; it is actually an image of text. The bottom line is to present digital content in a text format.

Include alternate text for images. Screen readers cannot interpret content in images; therefore, designers or instructors must provide alternate text descriptions, known as "alt text," for content presented within graphic images on web pages and in documents. Screen readers, combined with a speech synthesizer, will read aloud alt text. Each application provides a process for inserting alternate text, and some even present prompts to remind you to do so. For example, when using an LMS to deliver a course, if you upload an image to a content page, you may be prompted to enter alt text for the image. Alt text will not be visible to sighted users, but a screen reader along with a speech synthesizer will read it aloud at the time the image is presented. But what words do you use to describe the image? I suggest that you imagine you are talking by phone to a person who does not have access to the image. What aspects of the image would you describe to this person? That is what the alternate description of the image should include. Make it precise, brief, and not exactly the same as surrounding text already included in the document.

FIGURE 4.6
The Coffeepot for Masochists

When I use a depiction of the "Coffeepot for Masochists" presented in figure 4.6 as an extreme example of poor design, reasonable alternate text for the image is "coffeepot with spout above the handle on the same side of the pot." This text is short and conveys the essential content needed for the reader who cannot see the image to understand why this it presents an example of poor design. As another example, on our Disabilities, Opportunities, Internetworking, and Technology (DO-IT) website, we include an image of our logo. "DO-IT logo" is an adequate alternate description in this case and illustrates an important point: don't overexplain. Years ago a visitor to our website sent me an email message something like this: "I am blind and use a screen reader. Thank you for including alternate text for your image to let me know it is a logo. And thank you for not giving me details about something I will never see." Conduct an online search to locate resources for writing alternate text, including for complex images.[9]

Structure headings. Simply choosing text and making it larger, bold, or italic may make it look like a heading, but it will not be recognized as such by a screen reader. A hierarchical heading structure within a document or web page allows people who are blind and using screen readers to understand how the content is organized. When you format headings, a screen reader can read aloud the heading level and text so the user can skim through the heading titles and levels and quickly locate content of interest. Headings and subheadings can be easily labeled using the built-in heading features of HTML, Microsoft Word or PowerPoint, and PDF. And, consistent with UD principles, a well-thought-out heading structure will make your content more understandable to *all* users.

Format lists. When content items on a web page or in a document are organized with bullets or numbers entered one at a time, they do not form a collection recognized as a list by a screen reader. To make this content accessible, format a bulleted or numbered list using list format controls within the application being used. When lists are explicitly created in this way, screen readers can inform their users that they have encountered a list along with how many items are on it.

Use meaningful hyperlink titles. Screen readers can skip from link title to link title and read them to the user. Therefore, it is critical that a link title conveys clear information about the destination for the link. For example, if a link leads to the DO-IT website, title it "DO-IT website." If every link on a page or in a document is titled "click here," screen reader users will hear "click here," "click here," etc. and thus gain no information about the pages to which the web page links. The user will need to read the entire document to hear the surrounding text that describes the destination of each link.

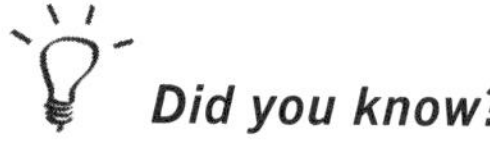

Did you know?

A good way to learn more about the accessible design of websites, documents, and videos as well as related legal and policy issues in higher education is to attend the Accessing Higher Ground Conference. For details, consult accessinghigherground.org.

The suggestions in the previous paragraphs provide a good place to start in understanding document and web page accessibility. Even those without a depth of technical expertise can develop habits to create documents that use a text-based format, include alternate text for images, format headings and lists, and use meaningful hyperlink titles. However, there are many more document types to consider and complex issues to address; they include designing tables to maximize accessibility by keeping them simple; dividing larger tables into several smaller ones; and formatting them to explicitly communicate relationships between column headers, row headers, and cell data. The good news is, everything you do to make content accessible reduces the need for accommodations for people with disabilities attempting to use your material.

The million-dollar question. What format does Sheryl prefer to use? Please don't say, "Who cares?" My feelings are easily hurt.

Are HTML pages accessible? It depends. Are Microsoft Word and PowerPoint files accessible? They can be but may not be. Are PDF documents accessible? Some are, but most that I encounter are not. Can you develop accessible HTML, Word, PowerPoint, and PDF documents? Absolutely. Is it easy or difficult? Yes, no, or it depends. The bottom line is that the accessibility of the content depends on how the creator formatted it. Can you remediate inaccessible documents yourself? That depends on the complexity of the document and your technical skills or interest in gaining them. I argue, however, that of these four formats, you will run into the fewest accessibility issues with HTML and the most with PDF. Can you expect web pages and documents you find on the internet to be designed to be accessible to individuals with disabilities? Not so much. How difficult is it to remediate inaccessible content? As a group, PDFs pose the greatest challenges. In this case, remediation is best accomplished with the purchase of software specializing in PDF remediation. In contrast, remediation of HTML and Microsoft products does not require the purchase of additional products. Another complication in remediating inaccessible content is that what you can remediate and how you do so are likely different—surprise, surprise—for a PC and a Macintosh. Considering all of these issues, HTML is my favorite format. However, I use PowerPoint for presentations and Word for printed documents.

In my online courses I enter instructional content in HTML within the LMS content pages, in part to save students the step of opening an attached document. I use built-in LMS features to provide alt text for images and format lists and hierarchical headings and then insert descriptive hyperlink text. I insert the content of the syllabus within an LMS content page but also offer a version accessibly formatted in Word for students who want to print it or tailor it for their own use by removing content they do need and adding personal notes. With all written content designed to be accessible and videos captioned, no student in my online courses has needed an accommodation for media remediation. Applying UDHE is not difficult when it is baked into all aspects of the course design.

My Accessible Technology Services (ATS) unit practices what we preach by always posting accessible content. Written content shared on DO-IT websites is typically presented in at least two formats—HTML and a printer-friendly PDF—to address the needs and interests of all potential web visitors. You may have guessed that I am not a big fan of PDFs, but they are popular and provide a good option if you want to print a document. Consequently, although we link to an accessible PDF version of our publications, an accessible HTML version is presented as the default format. Our practices illustrate a UDHE approach because it gives individuals multiple options for accessing content, makes *each* option accessible and usable, and presents the most accessible version as the default view.

One particularly disappointing situation regarding the accessibility of instructional content is that many textbooks and online educational materials, especially those in mathematics and science fields, are not accessibly designed. Clearly, these content developers do not consider accessibility an important consideration in the development of a product. Open educational resource (OER) repositories also contribute to the proliferation of inaccessible learning content. This is especially troubling since OERs are popular all over the world because they can be freely used, edited, and redistributed.

IT Accessibility Testers

To test the accessibility of an IT product, it is good to combine the use of electronic tools and human testers. You can do simple checking on your own to learn if some aspects of IT are accessibly designed. For example, a sighted person can turn off the graphics-loading feature of a web browser to see content that is available for a screen reader to read aloud to a person who is blind. Does it make sense? Is it equivalent to the content presented in the visual presentation? As another check, set aside your mouse. Can you navigate the website by using the arrow keys instead of a mouse? Also, try to copy and paste some text presented on the screen; if you cannot, the content is not accessible to screen reader users.

Many software tools, some integrated into specific applications, have been developed for checking web pages, documents, and other IT for accessibility. They are all limited regarding what they can test. For example, digital tools can tell you if an image is accompanied by a text description but not if the text description is accurate, complete, and useful. Consult the "My Go-To Resources" section at the end of this chapter to explore the ever-growing availability of accessibility checkers.

In addition to a technical review, a functional review is of value as well. In a functional review, determine the key functions of the product, prioritize them, test to see if these functions can be accomplished by individuals with specific disabilities, including those who use AT, and measure the user impact regarding inaccessibility to these functions. Note that a product can be technically accessible but not very usable, and a product can be highly usable even if there are some accessibility errors, as long as those errors have little impact on the use of the product.

As far as commercial products, you can make a guess about whether the company employs accessible design practices by looking at its website: can you locate a page about accessibility? Also, has the company completed a Voluntary Product Accessibility Template (VPAT) required by the federal government to sell IT to government agencies? If the answer is "no" to both of these questions, I would be surprised if that company is committed to accessible design practices. If it were, wouldn't it be bragging about this fact?

UD of Video Presentations

Captions provide a great example of applying UD to IT. Although often considered a feature for people who are deaf or hard of hearing, captions benefit many others, including individuals who

- are working in a noisy environment,
- are located in a quiet space (where having their computer's sound turned on is inappropriate),
- are English language learners who understand English better when it is presented in text as well as spoken,
- have dyslexia or another reading-related disability and benefit from viewing the spelling of words as they are spoken,
- want to know the spelling of words spoken in the video, and
- wish to search the content for a specific word.

To maximize benefits, captions should be synchronized with the content (so that corresponding text appears when words are spoken), equivalent to the content delivered with audio, and accessible to everyone (e.g., provided in a text-based format that can be accessed with screen readers).

Most media players and video hosting services today support captions. For example, if you post a video on YouTube, it automatically creates computer-generated captions. These initial captions should be considered a draft that can be edited using YouTube's caption editor. The silliness of captions on many YouTube videos makes clear that this editing feature and other websites and downloadable software for captioning videos are not routinely used.

Access Technology Services at the UW has produced dozens of videos on a wide range of topics related to individuals with disabilities accessing curriculum, using technology, and pursuing challenging academic programs and careers. Most videos have been funded with grants to our DO-IT Center. The following UD strategies are routinely applied in the development of DO-IT videos.

- Consider multiple audiences in all phases of the design process.
- Film with captions in mind by presenting only nonessential content at the bottom of the frame so that adding captions will not block key visual content.

- Provide searchable captions in a text-based format.
- Design the video so that key content is spoken as well as visually presented to reduce the need for audio description. For example, have the narrator voice the credits, references to further information, and copyright information at the end of the presentation.
- Provide a version of the video with audio descriptions to ensure individuals who cannot see the screen can access all important content presented in the video.

Besides the design of the video itself, a collection of videos can be made accessible to a broad audience if its media player is universally designed. This is what we do with DO-IT's large collection of videos. First, DO-IT's Videos web page is accessibly designed and offers a printer-friendly version as an option. In addition, DO-IT videos play in a fully accessible media player, Able Player, developed by Terrill Thompson, manager in ATS. Able Player builds on knowledge that users have a variety of needs and preferences, which is the heart of UD.[10] Able Player has been translated into more than a dozen languages and is open source, meaning the original source code is made freely available and may be modified and redistributed.

UD features of the DO-IT collection are articulated on the Videos page, as pictured in figure 4.7, and are described in the following list.[11]

- Closed captions, foreign-language subtitles, and text-based audio descriptions are supported.
- Keyboard-accessible interactive transcripts enable users to jump to any point in a video. Automatic text highlighting is available within a transcript as the media plays.
- The full set of player controls is keyboard-accessible, properly labeled for screen reader users, and controllable by speech recognition software. Each control image is high contrast and scalable.
- The user can control the speed at which a video plays.
- Users can search the text of the closed captions of all videos and begin playing videos at specific start times presented in the search results.
- Users can customize the media player, including how captions are displayed.

The application of UDHE to offer content in multiple ways is exemplified by accompanying DO-IT videos with publications and online resources and by making DO-IT videos available for viewing on DO-IT's website and YouTube channel, by download, and on DVDs.

FIGURE 4.7 DO-IT Videos page

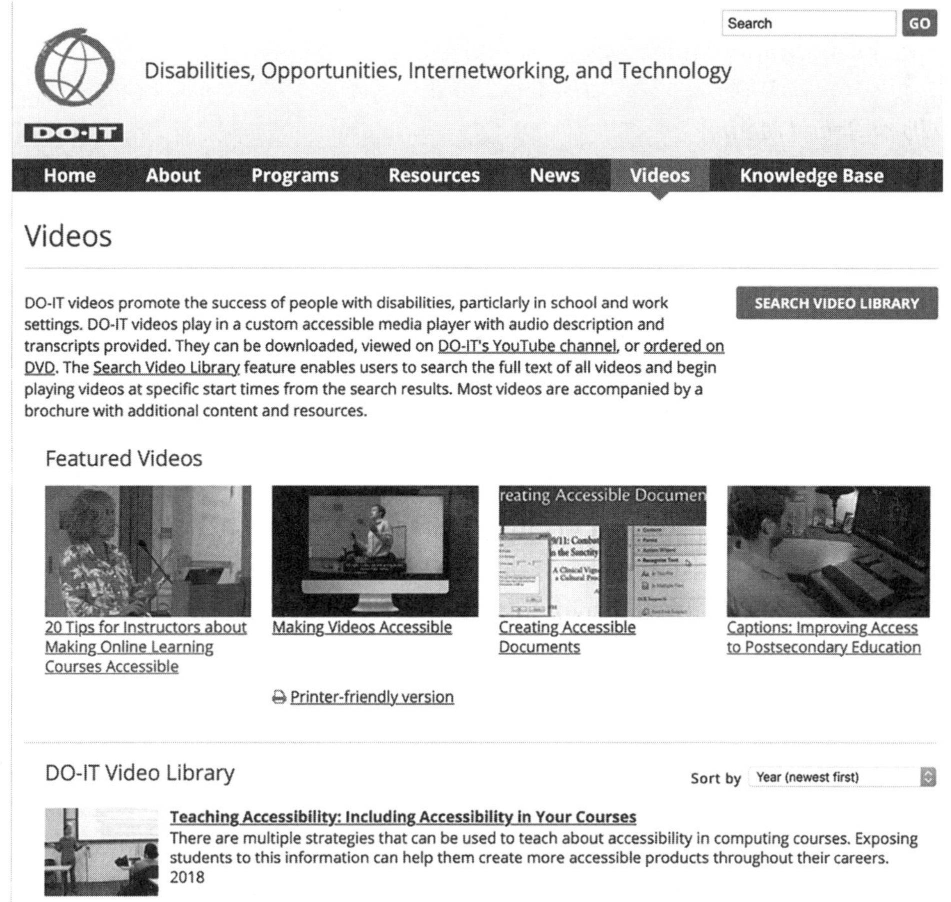

ATS also promotes the accessible design of videos created by other individuals and academic departments at the UW, which is particularly challenging because of the high volume of video creation managed in a distributed manner. Although it is not possible for my group to ensure that UDHE principles are applied to all campus videos, we help units prioritize which videos to caption and audio describe and encourage instructors to proactively caption videos in courses. Of course, central funds through disability services units are always available to caption and audio describe videos for individuals who are deaf or hard of hearing or blind, respectively, and have video remediation as an approved accommodation. Further, ATS secured central funding for captioning high-impact videos (e.g., those of high importance to the UW mission, those used in multiple offerings of courses with large enrollments, those that attract large numbers of viewers). Our team also contributed to establishing a campuswide contract for outside captioning services to make pay-for-service options more affordable.

UD of Social Media

People of all ages and interests are constantly checking their accounts on Facebook, LinkedIn, Twitter, Instagram, and other platforms that enable them to create and share content and otherwise participate in social networking. This phenomenon has created opportunities to spread awareness of what your department, program, or project has to offer. I heard that more than 300 million people with visual impairments use Twitter and Facebook alone; I don't know how accurate this number is, but I do know for sure that the number of people with visual impairments using social media is big. Adding in other disability groups makes this audience too big to ignore (I wish).

Today, most social media platforms include accessibility features and are supported with accessibility teams that regularly roll out accessibility improvements. Arguably, the two most important social media accessibility features are those that allow you to add alt text to images and captions to videos. As with other IT, however, to ensure the accessibility of posts on social media, content creators have to *use* accessibility features and employ other accessibility strategies. Following are a few practices particularly relevant to social media.

- Show respect to members of all groups of people. Avoid, for example, negative phrases that relate to disabilities, like "He's crazy" or "What an insane thing to say."
- Compose hashtags using upper- and lowercase letters. How about #BestVacationEver rather than #bestvacationever? People who have disabilities related to reading or sight are among the beneficiaries of this practice.
- Use emojis sparingly. You can expect a person's screen reader can automatically read aloud descriptions of emojis—among them, "Smiling face with sunglasses," "Winking face with stuck-out tongue," "Nerdy face with thick horn-rimmed glasses," "Smiling face licking lips," "Pouting face"—but being interrupted in your reading with descriptions of a long list of emojis can be at best time consuming.
- Make hyperlink text descriptive of the destination. Doesn't that sound familiar?
- Use plain language. Always a good idea.

In using social media for communication from your department, program, or project, use a social network as just one method of communication to ensure that everyone can access the content. For example, DO-IT projects use Facebook and Twitter but make redundant posts to email discussion lists and websites. Also, consider the accessibility of each service you think of using, especially with respect to inserting alt text for images and captioning videos.

CIVIL RIGHTS REGARDING ACCESSIBLE DESIGN

Did you know?

Section 508 of the Rehabilitation Act of 1973 mandates that IT developed, maintained, procured, or used by federal agencies must be accessible to people with disabilities.

Legal mandates motivate some individuals and institutions to adopt policies to use accessible IT. Almost all institutions of higher education in the United States are covered entities under Section 504 of the Rehabilitation Act of 1973 and the Americans with Disabilities Act of 1990 (ADA) along with its 2008 amendments.[12] These civil rights laws prohibit discrimination on the basis of disability. They do not specifically mention IT but are interpreted by the US Departments of Justice and Education to require that covered entities make offerings that make use of IT accessible to people with disabilities. Similar legislation has been enacted in other countries. Article 9 of the United Nations' Convention on the Rights of Persons with Disabilities, specifically requires participating countries to ensure "persons with disabilities access, on an equal basis with others, to information and communications technologies and systems, and to other facilities and services open or provided to the public."[13]

Some campuses do not adequately address accessible IT issues until they experience a lawsuit or civil rights complaint made through the Civil Rights Division (CRD) of the US Department of Justice or the Office of Civil Rights (OCR) of the US Department of Education regarding the inaccessibility of their IT. The National Federation of the Blind and other organizations along with students with disabilities have registered hundreds of complaints with these federal agencies regarding the inaccessibility of online courses, documents, websites, videos, application software, and other IT at specific postsecondary institutions. The government typically requires that institutions which have received these civil rights complaints conduct accessibility audits of web pages, online courses, documents, video presentations, and other IT; establish accessible IT standards and procedures; monitor compliance; provide training and resources about IT accessibility for faculty and staff; consider accessibility in IT procurement processes; create a procedure for individuals to report the inaccessibility of IT products; and ensure that responses to complaints are timely. It is interesting to note that the definition of "accessible" with respect to IT used in campus resolutions, which follows, is similar to the definition of the UD of IT, but more narrowly focused on people with disabilities rather than all users.

> "Accessible" means a person with a disability is afforded the opportunity to acquire the same information, engage in the same interactions, and enjoy the same services as a person without a disability in an equally effective and equally integrated manner, with substantially equivalent ease of use. The person with a disability must be able to obtain the information as fully, equally, and independently as a person without a disability.[14]

A review of civil rights resolutions that institutions have made with the federal government led EDUCAUSE, the largest professional organization for IT professionals in higher education, to publish *Accessibility Risk Statements and Evidence*. We regularly review the EDUCAUSE document along with new resolutions campuses have reached as we make plans to improve the accessibility of IT on our campus. EDUCAUSE recommends that administrators address the following risks.

1. Failure to allocate sufficient resources and authority to coordinate and implement the Electronic and Information Technology (EIT) Accessibility Policy.
2. Failure to make faculty, staff, and students aware of institutional resources for accommodation and accessibility.
3. Failure to systematically and effectively monitor EIT content and services to ensure accessibility.
4. Failure to provide accurate video captioning.
5. Failure to provide an accessibility policy that demonstrates the campus's commitment to EIT accessibility.
6. Failure to define a technical standard for implementing EIT accessibility (such as WCAG 2 or Section 508).
7. Failure to assign a person or entity to coordinate institution-wide accessibility.
8. Failure to implement a procedure to ensure information obtained, provided, or developed by third parties is accessible.

9. Failure to implement a procedure, which ensures procured EIT is accessible, such as including accessibility requirements in RFPs [requests for proposals] and contractual language.
10. Failure to provide regular ongoing training, instruction, and support at all levels (e.g., administrators, faculty, IT staff, support staff, student employees) appropriate to their roles and responsibilities, regarding the institution's EIT Accessibility Policy and procedures, tools, resources, and techniques to ensure the policy and procedures are effectively and consistently implemented.
11. Failure to implement accessibility solutions for EIT other than web-based, online, or software-based technologies, such as classroom controls, copiers, ATMs [automated teller machines], and digital signage.
12. Failure to provide native EIT accessibility (e.g., relying on second-class EIT alternatives for people with disabilities).
13. Failure to provide a top-level website dedicated to accessibility, which serves as a central repository and includes, but is not limited to, accessibility information, news, tools, and best practices.
14. Failure to provide accessible instructional materials and library resources in a timely manner.
15. Failure to create a culture where accessibility is considered a proactive need, but rather is considered a reactive accommodation need.
16. Failure to provide accessible websites.
17. Failure to provide captioning of announcements and commentary made over public address systems during athletic and other public events.
18. Failure to thoroughly test EIT for accessibility beyond automated testing or VPAT [Voluntary Product Accessibility Template] statements.[15]

Translating a commitment to IT accessibility into action takes substantial effort, especially on campuses with distributed computing environments. Significant results are difficult to achieve without the commitment of the administration along with efforts at all other levels. One place to start is to find out what IT accommodations are most common on your campus and to make reducing the need for them a priority. We are not alone in our two clear "winners": captioning videos and remediating PDF documents. It is not cause for celebration when I hear about the exponential growth in numbers of accommodations in these two areas provided on our campus. It is funny (by funny, I mean horrible) that we don't always react to common barriers with proactive practices to implement workflows so that they are accessible when they are created. Imagine if this were standard practice at our schools?

These are top priorities for IT accessibility efforts at the UW, but fixing systems that create inaccessible products is difficult. Changing practices is difficult. In chapter 8 I propose an Inclusive Campus Model, underpinned by the UDHE Framework, that can be fleshed out into a road map to guide efforts toward more inclusive practices and share an example of applying the model to the procurement, development, and use of accessible IT.

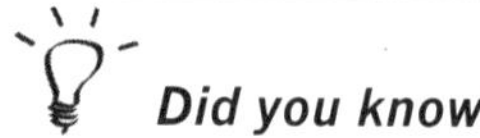

Did you know?

For ongoing engagement regarding AT, accessible IT design, legal mandates, and related policy issues in higher education, join the Access Technology Higher Education Network online community. For details, consult athenpro.org.

THE NEED TO ADVOCATE FOR ACCESSIBLE IT

Many stakeholders can work within their unique positions to promote the procurement, development, and use of accessible IT on campuses. Unfortunately, some people in powerful positions actually inhibit progress in this area.

Administrators and Policy Makers

Campus leaders have the power to set policy and allocate funds, but many do not understand the importance of addressing accessibility issues or do not put the same high priority on accessibility as they do on other IT issues such as security and privacy.

Individuals with Disabilities

As beneficiaries, people with disabilities can push for access to assistive technology and accessibly designed mainstream technology, but most do not self-identify. Many do not ask for accessible IT because of limited awareness or self-advocacy skills or concern about discrimination or inaction should they speak up. People with disabilities also rarely band together to form a powerful voice.

Disability Service Providers

Disability support staff may embrace helping individuals with disabilities registered in their office to gain access to AT and accessibly designed technology, but often they rely only on an accommodation approach that does not result in systemic changes to IT practices and infrastructure.

IT Staff

Technology staff have high technical skills that could be applied to making IT accessible to more people, and they typically work in units that have access to a relatively large pool of funds. However, they may be difficult to convince that accessibility is part of their jobs and that changes in their work flows to address accessibility are justified. My experience working with tech folks is that they are energized by solving problems. So *all we need to do* is get more of them excited about solving accessibility problems!

Procurement Staff

Procurement personnel may be in a position to demand or encourage units to build accessibility into contracts with IT vendors but may not be enthusiastic to add more rules, be told accessibility is a priority by administrators, and be versed on how to evaluate products for accessibility or secure resources to help them do so. In addition, most software and other IT purchased on campuses may be procured directly by departments and not processed through the procurement office.

Faculty

Instructors have a high level of interest in student success overall but may not feel that it is their job to design their courses to be accessible to students with disabilities, but rather that disability services should handle all issues related to students with disabilities. Some claim they do not have time or knowledge to design accessible courses.

Publishing and Technology Companies

Developers of technology, books, and online materials could make the work of postsecondary institutions much easier if they sold and licensed products that are designed to be accessible to individuals with disabilities, but for the most part this is not the case. Many companies are unaware of accessibility requirements at educational institutions, consider the market too small to be concerned about, are not aware of how to design accessible IT, or do not hear enough complaints from customers or potential customers regarding the inaccessibility of their products.

Hmmm . . . this last item suggests that we customers need to speak up. But how can we, as individual schools, promote the availability of more accessible products? I think we should find ways to use our collective purchasing power to increase industry awareness of the importance of IT accessibility and usability by developing procurement policies and procedures that include accessibility considerations. If all institutions did this, the resulting market pressure could significantly increase the availability of accessible products. However, campuses do not often collaborate in an organized way to make this happen. There are notable exceptions. For example, the UW has taken a lead in encouraging Instructure, the developer of Canvas LMS, to prioritize accessibility improvements. A manager within ATS leads a Canvas group that includes over one hundred members nationwide; some represent schools considering its adoption, others are using it already, and a few represent Instructure. In a collegial atmosphere group members identify inaccessible features of Canvas, suggest solutions, and prioritize corrective actions. Some schools have taken the lead in promoting the accessibility of other IT products.

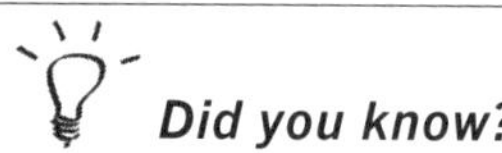

Did you know?

The US Department of Justice and US Department of Education stated, "It is unacceptable for universities to use emerging technology without insisting that this technology be accessible to all students."[16]

What if each large postsecondary campus selected one IT product it uses and led the effort to engage other campuses to report inaccessible features and encourage the publisher of the product to make changes? I think the combined efforts of these groups could efficiently create a sea change toward the availability of more accessible products. Similarly, imagine if all library procurement officers, as they communicated with database vendors, routinely presented to each vendor their commitment to the purchase of products that are accessible to all library users, inquired about current product accessibility features, and asked the company to share their plans for maintaining or improving accessibility in the future. Such efforts would put companies on notice that institutions of higher education expect accessible products to be available and consider accessibility as they make purchasing decisions.

MY GO-TO RESOURCES

Following are some good places to start in your exploration of topics covered in this chapter.

- *Closing the Gap Resource Directory*
  closingthegap.com/resource-directory
- *Accessible Technology*
  uw.edu/accessibility

- *Universal Design of IT*
  uw.edu/doit/programs/center-universal-design-education
- *Web Content Accessibility Guidelines*
  w3.org/WAI/standards-guidelines
- *WebAIM*
  webaim.org
- *Web Accessibility Evaluation Tools List*
  w3.org/WAI/ER/tools
- *Published Books and Articles About Universal Design of Online Learning and Universal Design of Technological Environments*
  uw.edu/doit/programs/center-universal-design-education/resources/published-books-and-articles-about-universal
- *Knowledge Base*
  uw.edu/doit/knowledge-base
- *Universal Design of Technology in Higher Education*[17]

CONCLUSION

Applying UDHE principles to the design of IT tools and resources that support educational opportunities can make the experiences of users with disabilities more like those of others, avoid drawing attention to a disability or other difference, minimize the need for accommodations, and reduce the risk of civil rights complaints. Although established accessible design legislation, principles, guidelines, practices, and resources are readily available, the inaccessible design of IT on postsecondary campuses continues to erect barriers to some users. All stakeholders can contribute to reaching goals for the procurement, development, and use of accessible IT on our campuses. In the next chapter, I present applications of UDHE that make teaching and learning curriculum and activities presented on-site and online more accessible, usable, and inclusive.

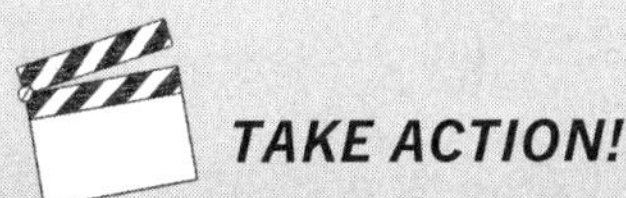

TAKE ACTION!

(REFLECT) Consider your context

Reflect on these questions:

- What message does it send to potential students with disabilities when an institution's website is not accessible to them?

- What resources are available at your institution to help you design accessible websites, documents, and videos?
- How might campus practices for addressing IT security and privacy issues inform those for IT accessibility?
- What new skill could you develop with respect to IT accessibility?

(LEARN) Identify applications of UD, UDL, and WCAG to IT

In a discussion or assignment in an academic course, ask students to share examples of UDHE practices for IT and related spaces and services that apply specific principles of UD, UDL, and WCAG. Have students articulate the importance of all three sets of principles when designing IT applications, particularly at an educational institution.

(LEARN) Make the case for captions

In an academic or professional development course, ask participants to view a short YouTube video that features a woman who is deaf talking in sign language, first without captions and later with captions. The video, "Why We Need Captions," can be found at youtube.com/watch?v=MCm1Emtqo_Q&feature=youtu.be. Then have participants view a video to learn more about the diverse audience that videos benefit, "Captions: Improving Access to Postsecondary Education," at uw.edu/doit/videos/index.php?vid=59. In a group discussion, solicit participant reactions to the two videos, views on who benefits from captions, and opinions about how captioning can be promoted at a postsecondary institution.

(LEARN) Review a Youtube video

For homework in an academic or professional development course, have participants search for a YouTube video related to UD and answer the following questions.

- How accurate and effective is the video in teaching UD?
- Is the video captioned? If so, how accurate are the captions?
- Is the content fully accessible to someone who is blind? Suggestion: Play the video without viewing the screen and then play it while looking at the screen. What did you miss, if anything, the first time you played it?
- How could this video be made more accessible to everyone?

Discuss participant findings in an on-site or online discussion.

(LEARN) Conduct a simulation of web access

An insightful activity is to have students compare the availability of content on a website that is accessible and one that is inaccessible from the perspective of a person with a disability. Conduct a simulation to increase knowledge of assistive technology and accessible web design for people who are blind. Turning off the graphics-loading feature of your browser can simulate the experiences of students who are blind when they access a website, since their screen readers will read only the content presented as text on the screen. Instruct participants to access a website that is understandable in this mode and one that is not.

(LEARN) Identify multiple beneficiaries of accessible web design

Within an online or on-site professional development or academic course where web accessibility practices have been covered, have participants describe a web accessibility strategy that benefits people with very different types of disabilities or other characteristics.

(LEARN) Celebrate benefits of IT accessibility

In an academic or professional development course where IT accessibility practices have been covered, have participants describe a specific accessible IT feature that benefits at least two different groups (e.g., students who are blind and students who are English language learners). Have them elaborate on specific benefits for each group.

(LEARN) Discuss accommodations versus UD

In an academic or professional development course, have participants discuss why the increased use of technology in delivering instruction makes it less effective to employ an accommodations approach (i.e., with little effort toward universal design of mainstream IT) to ensure access to digital materials for people with disabilities.

(APPLY) Teach UD in a computing course

In a computing course, invite a person knowledgeable about assistive technology or accessible technology design to deliver an overview of accessible products that are commercially available. Contact a campus disability services office to help you locate a person on campus who has this expertise.

(APPLY) Teach UD of IT in a web development course

In a course where students create websites, require that they apply one or more of the guidelines included in the Web Content Accessibility Guidelines (WCAG). Under significant time constraints, for example, ask them to include alternate text to describe content within images and use descriptive text for hyperlinks.

(APPLY) Create a poster

Individually or in a group, design a poster that presents general strategies in accessible IT design that can benefit people with a wide variety of disabilities. Print it and post it in an area where IT developers work. To create the poster, participants can consider downloading and editing the posters at github.com/UKHomeOffice/posters/tree/master/accessibility/dos-donts. Produced by a group of researchers and designers who are part of an IT accessibility group in the Home Office, a UK government department, these posters are regularly improved to incorporate user suggestions. A Creative Commons license allows everyone to share, use, and tailor the posters to their needs as long as the posters are used noncommercially and display appropriate attributions.

(APPLY) Promote UD to a vendor

Within an academic or professional development course, ask participants, "How could you convince a representative from an educational software company to make its product more accessible to students with disabilities at your institution?" Have them share their responses in a full-class or small group discussion on-site or an online.

(APPLY) Create an IT accessibility liaisons or advocates group

To extend their impact, IT accessibility staff could recruit an auxiliary group to help promote the development, procurement, and use of accessible IT. Promising practices include those that are top-down—where each department or other unit is required to assign a representative—and those that are bottom-up—where volunteers are recruited to the group. Activities for the group could include engaging in an online community, assisting with developing a website of resources, hosting events, and engaging in and delivering training.

(APPLY) Develop a campus plan

Have members of a campus task force focused on accessible IT review the EDUCAUSE document "IT Accessibility Risk Statements and Evidence" at library.educause.edu/-/media/files/library/2015/7/accessrisk15-pdf.pdf as well as at least one referenced OCR resolution and take notes. Draft broadly described action steps for improving the accessibility of IT campuswide. Then fine-tune and prioritize the steps.

(APPLY) Have some fun!

Conduct a formal or informal challenge or competition campuswide or within your campus unit, perhaps as part of a special day such as the international Global Accessibility Awareness Day, which occurs each spring to get everyone talking, thinking, and learning about digital access for people with different abilities. Incorporate tasks that are readily achievable by individuals without a depth of technology expertise. Individual participants or groups could edit the auto-captions of their YouTube videos; set aside their mice and see if their websites can be fully operated with the keyboard alone and/or report problems; test to see if all of the images on their websites have meaningful alt text and make or recommend corrections; use the accessibility checker in Microsoft Office to check the accessibility of their Word or PowerPoint documents and make improvements; or take an online trivia test related to IT accessibility.

CHAPTER 5

Teaching and Learning Activities

When you plant lettuce, if it does not grow well, you don't blame the lettuce. You look for reasons it is not doing well. It may need fertilizer, or more water, or less sun.

—Thích Nhất Hạnh, Vietnamese Buddhist Monk

LEARNING IS what higher education is all about, making it especially important to get it right! In this chapter I apply the Universal Design in Higher Education (UDHE) Framework to the design of pedagogy, curricula, facilities, and on-site and online activities that are born ready to effectively teach all students. Such Universal Design of Instruction (UDI) practices avoid the creation of learning opportunities that are disabling for some students.

INTRODUCTION

In learning environments, student variability is the norm, not the exception. Learners differ from one another, and an individual learner differs over time. An important step toward creating an inclusive course is to truly value diversity in its many forms—including differences in sensory, physical, and learning abilities—as simply a normal part of the human experience. It is difficult for some faculty to feel this way in part because they perceive that much extra work will be required to fully include a student with a disability. One factor contributing to this perception is that the typical response to the inaccessible design of instructional practices, materials, and facilities is to provide accommodations after a student with a disability enrolls in a course. An alternative approach is for faculty members to proactively design course materials and learning activities for learner variability and thus address the needs and interests of a student body that is increasingly diverse with respect to race, ethnicity, native language, culture, age, gender identity, ability, background knowledge, veteran status, and other characteristics. This approach minimizes the need for individual accommodations when the course is offered. I refer to applications of UDHE in this domain as the Universal Design of Instruction, or UDI.

After you have completed this chapter, you should be able to

- describe the components of a framework for UDI;
- describe how the application of UDI improves learning activities through the use of accessible, usable, and inclusive facilities, materials, technologies, and pedagogy;
- articulate a process for applying UDI to on-site and online teaching and learning activities;
- explain how UDI can enhance practices supported by the science of learning;
- universally design a syllabus, presentations, assessments, and other teaching practices in formal and informal learning settings;
- explain how the application of UDI can minimize the need for academic accommodations;
- give examples of benefits of UDI for students who do *not* have disabilities.

Did you know?

Researchers, developers, and practitioners attending a meeting in 1997 recommended that teachers develop course goals, methods, and materials that are universally designed and that publishers apply UD to instructional materials as well. They suggested that published materials include

- explicit strategies to make clear instructional goals;
- text in digital format;
- captions for all audio and video;
- educationally relevant descriptions for images;
- cognitive supports for content and activities such as summarizing big ideas, providing scaffolding for learning and generalization, and building fluency through practice.[1]

FRAMEWORK, SCOPE, DEFINITION, PRINCIPLES, AND GUIDELINES

Components of the UDHE Framework for any application include scope, definition, principles, guidelines, practices, and process. You can flesh out this framework to build a toolkit for applying UDI. The scope of UDI comprises all facilities, curricula, pedagogies, activities, and technologies used to help students learn. A definition that can be used for the application of the UDHE to instruction, modified from the basic definition of UD, is the design of *teaching and learning* products and environments to be usable by all people, to the greatest extent possible, without the need for adaptation or specialized design.

The principles for UDI, as with other UDHE applications, are the combination of the seven principles of UD for products and environments, the three principles of Universal Design for Learning (UDL) for curriculum and pedagogy, and the four principles of the Web Content Accessibility Guidelines (WCAG) for information technology (IT). Combining these three sets of principles ensures that all aspects of teaching are addressed—curriculum and pedagogy, facilities, and technologies.

I think it is good to know that you do not need to memorize the three sets of principles to effectively practice UDI. Once you begin to intentionally look at teaching materials and practices from the UDI perspective, this behavior will become second nature. Make it a habit to ask these questions:

- Do I offer *multiple ways* for students to *learn* (e.g., via video, reading materials, discussions), *engage* in my course (e.g., in on-site and online discussions), and *demonstrate* what they have learned (e.g., through tests, discussions, projects)? Is each way designed to be accessible (e.g., captioned videos, accessibly designed documents)?
- Does my course design make it more *accessible* to, *usable* by, and *inclusive* of all potential students while minimizing the need for accommodations?

Did you know?

In a course, UDI practices offer students multiple ways to

- learn,
- demonstrate what they have learned, and
- engage.

The process for UDI and examples of UDI practices are shared in the following sections of this chapter.

PROCESS

A process for applying UDI to all aspects of teaching and learning can be adapted from the general process for applying UDHE. Specifically, an instructor can take the following steps, which are also summarized in figure 5.1.

1. *Identify the course and evidence-based teaching practices.* Describe the course, learning objectives, and content. Adopt overall teaching and learning philosophies (e.g., constructivism) and evidence-based practices (e.g., active learning).
2. *Consider the diverse characteristics of potential students.* Describe the population of students eligible to enroll in the course and then consider their potential diverse characteristics—with respect to gender; age; ethnicity; race; native language; learning preferences; size; abilities to see, hear, walk, manipulate objects, read, speak—and the challenges they might encounter in your course.
3. *Integrate UDI with evidence-based teaching practices.* Apply UDI strategies (underpinned by relevant UDHE principles) in concert with evidence-based instructional practices in the choice of teaching methods, curricula, and assessments as well as to all teaching practices and materials to maximize the learning of students with diverse characteristics.
4. *Plan for accommodations.* Learn campus procedures for addressing accommodation requests (e.g., arranging for sign language interpreters) from specific students for whom the course design does not already provide full access. Include information about how students can request accommodations in the syllabus.
5. *Evaluate.* Monitor the effectiveness of instruction through observation and assessments of learning and collect formative feedback from students. Make modifications based on the results. Return to step 3 if your evaluation suggests further improvements to your course should be made.

In integrating UDI with evidence-based teaching practices in step 3, using pedagogical practices supported by the science of learning makes sense. Right? Although UD-inspired approaches to instructional applications are consistent with a common finding in educational research—that learners are highly variable with respect to their abilities and responses to instruction—unfortunately, you will discover two problems when you look for support for UDI in higher education in the vast majority of the studies of teaching practices.

FIGURE 5.1 A process for applying UDI to a course

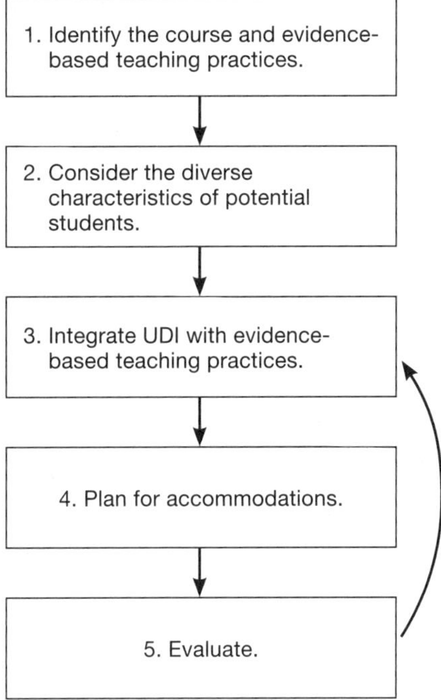

First, although some studies report differences in outcomes based on gender, race, or ethnicity, few specifically collect and report the experiences of participants with a variety of disabilities. This limitation has resulted in the promotion of evidence-based practices that are not even accessible to students with some types of disabilities. The second problem with the current evidence base for instructional practices consistent with UDL principles is that the majority of the studies took place at the precollege level and often with a narrow focus, such as on the development of early reading and writing skills. Because of these issues, some researchers believe a "claim that UDL has been validated through research cannot be substantiated at this time."[2]

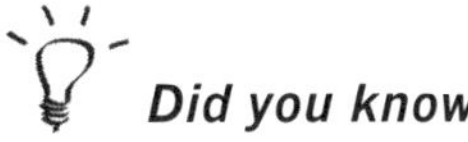

Did you know?

The adoption of more accessible curricula in postsecondary education in the United States has been supported by the US Department of Education's endorsement of a common National Instructional Materials Accessibility Standard (NIMAS). NIMAS is the foundation for a variety of accessible formats for printed materials. However, since NIMAS is not embraced by everyone, educators continue to face challenges in acquiring textbooks in formats accessible to students with disabilities.

UDI and the Science of Learning

Given this state of the science of learning, a good approach for developing inclusive postsecondary instructional practices is to apply UDI principles to practices with some evidence of success to ensure that they meet the needs of a student population with diverse characteristics. This approach is consistent with other applications of UD. For example, UD alone does not ensure the design of a high-quality building. Instead, UD offers a lens through which to view all design decisions to ensure that a facility is accessible, usable, and inclusive. Just as applying UD to a poorly designed building makes the features of a poorly designed building accessible to more people, applying UDI to a poorly designed course makes the poorly designed course accessible to more students. In other words, UDI does not replace but rather complements other teaching philosophies, theories, and evidence-based practices. Instructors who value inclusion argue that all universally designed instruction is not necessarily good instruction, but all good instruction is universally designed.

It is good news to many faculty members that applying UDI does not require that they abandon their adopted teaching and learning philosophies, theories, and practices such as cooperative learning, constructive learning, learner-centered instruction, and "flipped" classrooms. Instead, they can apply UDI to ensure that they employ multiple teaching practices and that each practice is accessible, usable, and inclusive. Examples of how UD might be integrated with teaching practices associated with different teaching and learning philosophies are presented in table 5.1.[3]

The following paragraphs and tables present two examples of how UDI principles can be integrated with established sets of evidence-based principles. UDI principles applied to Chickering and Gamson's guidelines for good practice in undergraduate education result in the practices shared in the second column of table 5.2.[4] They illustrate the value of UDHE as a lens through which to view best practices to ensure that they are inclusive of all learners.[5]

In the second example, UDI principles are integrated with the seven evidence-based principles for how to maximize student learning that were identified by an ambitious study reported by Ambrose, Bridges, DiPietro, Lovett, and Norman in their 2010 book, *How Learning Works: Seven Research-Based Principles for Smart Teaching*.[6] In table 5.3, each principle is paired with an explanation of how UDI can be applied to ensure that a practice supported by the principle is appropriate for all students, including those with disabilities.

TABLE 5.1 UDI applied to practices associated with teaching and learning philosophies

Strategy employed by a specific teaching/learning philosophy	*Example of how UDI might be applied to the strategy*
The differentiated instruction strategy of initial and ongoing assessment of individual student readiness and growth as learning activities unfold and adjustment of practices accordingly.*	Use multiple and accessible assessments (e.g., oral presentations, demonstrations, portfolios, and projects) that take into account the diverse characteristics of potential students, including disabilities.
Computer-assisted self-paced instruction based on behaviorist theory.†	Ensure that content is culturally relevant to a broad audience, that captions or transcriptions are provided for auditory output, and that text descriptions are provided for the content of graphic images.
The constructivist approach for the instructor to serve as a resource to help students access and utilize information resources and share information with peers.‡	Make sure resources and communication options are accessible to all learners, including those for whom English is a second language; those with low-level reading skills; and those who have physical, learning, or sensory disabilities.
The learning-centered instruction focus on the student as learner and the instructor as the facilitator of learning.§	Ensure that learning is defined in such a way that it does not discriminate against any students and is assessed in multiple ways.
The sociocultural approach to teaching and learning based on the notions that learning is situated in contexts, each student has a unique cultural perspective, and communication in the learning process is very important.‖	Ensure that the views of all students are heard, considered, and valued in the classroom.

*Tracey Hall, Ge Vue, Nicole Strangman, and Anne Meyer, *Differentiated Instruction and Implications for UDL Implementation* (Wakefield, MA: National Center for Accessing the General Curriculum, 2003, updated 2014), http://aem.cast.org/about/publications/2003/ncac-differentiated-instruction-udl.html; Carol Anne Tomlinson, *How to Differentiate Instruction in Mixed-Ability Classrooms,* 2nd ed. (Alexandria, VA: Association for Supervision and Curriculum Development, 2001).

†Marilla D. Svinicki, "New Directions in Learning and Motivation," *New Directions for Teaching and Learning*, 80 (1999): 5–27.

‡Catherine Twomey Fosnot, *Constructivism: Theory, Perspectives, and Practice* (New York: Teachers College Press, 1996); Derek Hodson and Julie Hodson, "From Constructivism to Social Constructivism: A Vygotskian Perspective on Teaching and Learning Science," *School Science Review* 79, no. 289 (1998): 33–41; Jonathan F. Osborne, "Beyond Constructivism," *Science Education* 80, no. 1 (1996): 53–82.

§Robert B. Barr and John Tagg, "From Teaching to Learning—A New Paradigm for Undergraduate Education," *Change* 27, no. 6 (1995): 12–25; Elizabeth G. Harrisson, "Working with Faculty Toward Universally Designed Instruction: The Process of Dynamic Course Design," *Journal of Postsecondary Education and Disability* 19, no. 2 (2006): 152–62; Edward J. Kame'enui, Douglas W. Carnine, Robert C. Dixon, Deborah C. Simmons, and Michael D. Coyne, *Effective Teaching Strategies That Accommodate Diverse Learners*, 2nd ed. (Upper Saddle River, NJ: Pearson Prentice Hall, 2002).

‖Michael O'Loughlin, "Rethinking Science Education: Beyond Piagetian Constructivism Toward a Sociocultural Model of Teaching and Learning," *Journal of Research in Science Teaching* 29, no. 8 (1992): 791–820.

TABLE 5.2 UDI applied to Chickering and Gamson's principles of good practice

Principle of good practice in undergraduate education	*Example of how UDI might be applied to the principle*
Encourages contact between students and faculty.	Include a statement on the class syllabus inviting students to meet with the instructor to discuss disability-related and other learning needs.
Develops reciprocity and cooperation among students.	Assign group work in which learners must support each other and that reflects a high value on different skills and roles. Encourage multiple ways for students to interact with each other (e.g., in-class and internet-based communications).
Encourages active learning.	Provide multiple ways for students to participate, ensuring that all students, including those with disabilities, can actively engage.
Gives prompt feedback.	Regularly assess student progress using multiple, accessible methods and tools and adjust instruction accordingly.
Emphasizes time on task.	Ensure all students have adequate time to complete tasks.
Communicates high expectations.	Keep expectations high, including those for students with disabilities, and provide accommodations to level the playing field rather than give unfair advantage.
Respects diverse talents and ways of learning.	Adopt practices that reflect high values with respect to diversity, equity, and inclusiveness.

PRACTICES

All UDI practices are similar when it comes to ensuring students have multiple ways to learn; demonstrate what they have learned; and engage with others using facilities and technology that are accessible, usable, and inclusive. They apply UDI principles and guidelines to

- the overall design of instruction (e.g., using multiple teaching methods),
- specific aspects of learning environments (e.g., to small discussions), and
- the determination of accommodations when universally designed instruction does not fully address the needs of a specific student with a disability (e.g., when a student has an approved accommodation for extended time on a test).

Table 5.4 illustrates the role of accommodations when the UDI Framework is applied. It presents examples of specific teaching practices, UDI practices to

TABLE 5.3 Relevance of UDI to each principle in How Learning Works

Principle based on How Learning Works	*Example of how UDI might be applied to a practice supported by the principle*
Students' prior knowledge can help or hinder learning.	Ensure that all resources provided to help students gain background information are accessible to students with disabilities.
How students organize knowledge influences how they learn and apply what they know.	Explicitly teach students various ways to organize knowledge in the academic area of study.
Students' motivation determines, directs, and sustains what they do to learn.	Present examples and make assignments that may be of interest to individuals with a variety of interests and backgrounds.
To develop mastery, students must acquire component skills, practice integrating them, and know when to apply what they have learned.	Provide multiple ways for students to gain knowledge and skills.
Goal-directed practice coupled with targeted feedback enhances the quality of students' learning.	Make clear the goals for practice and provide specific feedback at key stages of assigned work.
Students' current level of development interacts with the social, emotional, and intellectual climate of the course to impact learning.	Avoid marginalizing students and enforce rules for interaction that demand mutual respect.
To become self-directed learners, students must learn to monitor and adjust their approaches to learning.	Lead exercises that can help students become self-directed learners.

TABLE 5.4 Example of a teaching practice, related UDI practices, and an accommodation that may be needed for a student with a disability

Example of teaching practice	*Example of UDI practices for the teaching practice*	*Example of accommodation for individual student*
Lecture	Use large print, high-contrast visuals; speak aloud visual content; use a microphone if available; repeat questions asked.	A student who is deaf may have an approved accommodation for a sign language interpreter or real-time captioner.
Online timed exam	Design exam in an accessible format with alternate text for images, consistent format for test items, clear instructions, structured headings, etc.	A person who has a specific learning disability may have an approved accommodation for extra time.

make them inclusive, and follow-up accommodations that might be necessary for specific students.

The following subsections describe how UDI principles can be applied to the design of a presentation, a syllabus, and an online course. Then I share how UDI practices can be inspired by an accommodation given to a student with a specific disability or a teaching challenge faced by an instructor. The final subsection shares a comprehensive checklist of practices that apply UDI principles to many types of online and on-site instructional offerings.

Applying UDI to a Presentation

Let me just say one thing out loud: I'M TIRED OF ATTENDING ON-SITE AND ONLINE PRESENTATIONS ABOUT UD THAT USE METHODS THAT ARE NOT UNIVERSALLY DESIGNED!

Thanks. I feel better now.

> ***Did you know?***
>
> People often ask why titles for a specific application of UD sometimes use of (e.g., Universal Design of Instruction) and sometimes use for (e.g., Universal Design for Learning). I prefer of to be consistent with other applications of UD—UD of a website, UD of a building entrance, UD of a microwave oven, where the word or words that follow of tell what product or environment is being universally designed. However, the for in Universal Design for Learning underscores the why of UD—to promote learning. Maybe we should combine the two approaches into Universal Design of Instruction for Learning. Now, there's a mouthful!

You will not find it surprising that I often deliver presentations via webinars and at conferences and postsecondary institutions about UDHE or, more specifically, UDI. In these presentations I model UDI practices, which have simply become habits for me. All videos I use in presentations are captioned and audio described, website resources are universally designed, and handouts are provided in accessible formats. My presentation visuals have large, bold, sans serif fonts on uncluttered backgrounds. I minimize the amount of text per slide, the number of images overall, and the complexity of each one. I make an effort to speak slowly and clearly, describe key content presented visually, avoid unnecessary jargon, and define terms that might be unfamiliar to some attendees. In an on-site presentation, before the audience arrives I arrange chairs so that wheelchair users who might attend have multiple options for positioning themselves in the room; use a microphone; make eye contact with and engage members of the audience; and repeat questions asked by attendees before answering them. For an online presentation, I poll participants as they enter the space to gather information about their backgrounds to help me tailor the talk; mute participants who are not speaking; and tell them how to ask questions or make comments (e.g., using chat and hand-raising functions). Such proactive steps minimize the need for disability-related accommodations. Typically, the only accommodation requested for an online or on-site talk is a sign language interpreter or real-time captioner; such arrangements are made ahead of time with the host of the event. In addition, I encourage the host to film my presentation and make a captioned version available online.

Applying UDI to a Syllabus

A syllabus provides an opportunity for an instructor to tell students what to expect from participation in a course. It also gives students a first impression of the class climate. Examples of UDI principles applied to syllabus design follow.

- UD 1. *Equitable use.* Include information on the syllabus that is useful to students with diverse abilities, backgrounds, interests, technology skills, and other characteristics.
- UD 3. *Simple and intuitive use.* Make the syllabus easy to understand regardless of a student's previous knowledge and language skills, arrange information in a logical order, and use a consistent format.
- UD 4. *Perceptible information.* Provide adequate contrast between text and background in the document.
- UDL 1. *Multiple means of engagement.* Include content to stimulate interest in the course for students with a variety of interests and backgrounds, explain the relevance of the content, and integrate opportunities for choice within the course.
- UDL 2. *Multiple means of representation.* Present content in different ways to support understanding (e.g., provide a printed syllabus along with an accessible online version and a complementary video presentation of you describing the course). Tell students how they can access content (e.g., textbook, web resources, videos) and where they can find background information such as how to operate the learning management system (LMS).
- UDL 3. *Multiple means of action and expression.* Tell students about multiple options they will have to demonstrate what they have learned and engage with their classmates and instructor.
- WCAG. *Accessible technology design.* Present the syllabus in a text-based format, structure headings and lists, provide alternate text for images, and otherwise design the document to be accessible to students with a wide variety of disabilities, including individuals using assistive technologies.

As an example, the syllabus for a graduate course I teach online includes a typical range of topics: Course Name and Number; Credits; Professor Information; Course Description; Target Audience, Accessibility and Accommodations;

Course Learning Objectives; Program Learning Outcomes; Textbook Chapters; Our Online Classroom; Course Requirements and Grading; Schedule for Weekly Topics, Textbook Readings, and Assignments; and Campus Rules and Resources.

I consider it important to include in my syllabus (1) the audience for the course, (2) my commitment to making the course accessible to everyone and invite students to communicate with me about accessibility issues, and (3) information about how to obtain disability-related accommodations from the institution. As an illustration, following is the "Target Audience, Accessibility and Accommodations" section of the syllabus for my course.

Target Audience, Accessibility and Accommodations

The primary audience for this course includes online and on-site instructors, disability services personnel, administrators and other practitioners or future practitioners working to support individuals with disabilities in postsecondary educational settings. It is also appropriate for individuals seeking degrees in disability studies and related fields. Students in the course are expected to be able to use standard applications software (e.g., Word) but will not necessarily have a high level of technical expertise or online experience. Since we will cover the universal design of technology, basic concepts will be presented, but students are not expected to develop high level technical expertise through this course.

This course is designed to be a model of the application of universal design (UD)—I strive to make it welcoming to, accessible to, and usable by all potential students, including those with disabilities. The textbook is available in an accessible format from the publisher. All videos are captioned and most are audio described (in which case, key visual elements are described orally so that individuals who cannot see the screen can better understand the video content). The vast majority of online readings are available in accessible formats. Course materials and activities present a model of the application of UD. If you find any aspect of the course inaccessible to you

> or if you would like to discuss other learning issues, please contact me.
>
> The [institution] is firmly committed to making higher education accessible to students with disabilities by removing architectural barriers and providing programs and support services necessary for them to benefit from the instruction and resources of the University. Early planning is essential for many of the resources and accommodations provided. For further information please see [URL].

UDI adoption requires that instructors give students choices regarding one-on-one communication. Let the students choose communication tools that work best for them, rather than tell them to use the tool you prefer. Here is what I typically say in my syllabus: "Feel free to contact me through [the LMS] or, privately, by email at [email address]. You can also make an appointment with me to communicate real-time using a telephone, [LMS conferencing software], or another synchronous tool."

Applying UDI to an Online Course

It is difficult to find a postsecondary course today that makes no use of IT. Some courses are offered totally online, and many are blended or hybrid courses, where some instruction is on-site and some is online. The past few decades have witnessed dramatic increases in the variety of technologies available for teaching online, the quantity of online courses offered, and the number of students enrolled in them. These trends suggest an urgent need to ensure that delivery tools, pedagogical practices, and teaching materials are designed to be accessible to, usable by, and inclusive of students with disabilities. Most LMSs make it possible to create courses that are accessible to individuals with disabilities but also to create courses that erect barriers. Thus, the accessibility of a course for the most part depends on the choices instructors and designers make with respect to online tools, digital materials, and pedagogy.

Did you know?

Most research reports and other publications about online learning design do not address potential access barriers or solutions for students with disabilities.

A goal for every course I teach is to make it accessible to everyone. "Everyone" includes students with disabilities, but also students with various learning preferences, students whose first language is not the language in which the instruction is delivered, students using a variety of devices and web browsers, and students with slow internet connections. I apply UDI

- to the overall design of the online course (e.g., choosing to employ accessible LMS features),
- to specific course products (e.g., providing alternate text to describe content presented within images),
- to communication methods (e.g., ensuring that course discussions and other communications are accessible to students with all types of disabilities), and
- in the design of specific assignments (e.g., requiring students in small groups to choose a communication method that is accessible to all group members).

In 1993 (at a *very* young age) I cotaught the first online course offered by the University of Washington (UW). My coinstructor was Norm Coombs, a professor at the Rochester Institute of Technology who is blind. The course was about assistive technology for people with disabilities. We set out to make content and interactions in the course fully accessible to Norm as well as to students with other types of disabilities. We mailed to our students a series of VHS tapes (remember those?) created by the Disabilities, Opportunities, Internetworking, and Technology (DO-IT) Center. All of the video presentations, in which high school and college students with a variety of disabilities demonstrated the technology they used, were captioned and audio described. Electronic mail and a text-based distribution list supported all class communications. We used a gopher server to organize the course content (keep in mind, this was before the World Wide Web was fully developed). Our students logged onto websites using Telnet and downloaded online resources using File Transfer Protocol. When Norm and I were asked how many students with disabilities were enrolled in our course offerings, we were proud to say we didn't know. Why proud? Because the course was universally designed, there was never a need for students to disclose their disabilities. You too may make a person's life better in an extraordinary way by simply designing a course to be accessible, but, because UD is built right into the course, you will likely never know about it. How many opportunities do we have to do that as we are engaged in paid employment?

Although the tools used to deliver online learning since Norm and I taught our online class have changed dramatically, principles for ensuring that everyone can participate have not.

I have continued to teach online courses since those early days, ranging from accessible design of online learning as a requirement for a certificate in online learning design to graduate courses about UDHE using LMSs that include eCollege, Blackboard, Canvas, and one that was home-grown at the UW. I routinely

- offer *multiple ways* for students to learn, demonstrate what they have learned, and engage with the course content and each other; and
- ensure that each resource and activity is *accessible, usable*, and *inclusive*.

Did you know?

In one study, online learning environments were reported to be less supportive and less satisfactory by female students with learning disabilities than by females without learning disabilities.[7]

In online components of courses I teach, I format most content within pages provided by the LMS, which present the material using Hypertext Markup Language (HTML). I, for example, present the syllabus on a content page. I also provide my syllabus as an accessible Word document, using Word's Styles formatting function to structure headings and lists. I attach the Word file using the LMS. This version is suitable for printing (yes, in this technological age, some students still prefer to have a printed copy on which to highlight items and make personal notes). Students can tailor the syllabus to include only content most relevant to them and add personal notes, such as a detailed timeline for completing aspects of the course assignments. I also copy and paste into an additional LMS content page one part of the syllabus students are likely to refer to most often—the course schedule of readings, discussions, and assignments. In contrast, many faculty members provide only PDF images of their course syllabus. In this case students who are blind will likely need an accommodation for remediation of the document into an accessible format, students with reading-related disabilities may require an accommodation for an alternative format so text-to-speech systems can read the content aloud, and any student will face a barrier to tailoring the syllabus with extra notes relevant to participation in the course.

Some faculty members report to me that they prefer PDF images for a syllabus to protect their copyrighted content. Really? No one to my knowledge has ever tried to steal the content of my syllabus. (I am a little offended by this, of course.) In any event, anybody wanting to steal your content could do so, no matter what format you use.

No shortage of guidance is available for online course instructors and designers with the desire to make their offerings accessible to individuals with disabilities. After reviewing strategies reported in the literature and considering my own experiences teaching online, I created a list of twenty tips for instructors and designers who wish to get started in making online courses more accessible, usable, and inclusive. For course web pages, documents, images, and videos, I suggest the following.

1. Use clear, consistent layouts and organization schemes for presenting content.
2. Structure headings and lists—using style features built into the LMS, Microsoft Word and PowerPoint (PPt), PDF, etc.—and use built-in designs/layouts (e.g., for PPt slides).
3. Use descriptive wording for hyperlink text (e.g., "DO-IT Knowledge Base" rather than "click here").
4. Avoid creating PDF documents. Post instructor-created course content within LMS content pages (i.e., in HTML) and, if a PDF is desired, link to it only as a secondary source of the information.
5. Provide concise text descriptions of content presented within images.
6. Use large, bold, sans serif fonts on uncluttered pages with plain backgrounds.
7. Use color combinations that are high contrast and can be distinguished by people with color blindness .
8. Caption video and transcribe audio content.
9. Use a small number of IT tools with which all content and navigation can be reached with the keyboard alone and that employ other accessibility practices.

With respect to instructional methods, I suggest the following.

10. Assume students have a wide range of technology skills and

Did you know?

The Quality Matters Rubric includes benchmarks for high-quality online courses. One benchmark is to address accessibility and usability issues in all of the other benchmarks—course overview and introduction, learning objectives, assessment and measurement, instructional materials, course activities and learning interaction and engagement, course technology, and learner support.[8]

provide options for gaining the technology skills needed for course participation.

11. Provide options for learning by presenting content in multiple ways (e.g., in a combination of text, video, audio, and/or image format).
12. Offer options for communicating and collaborating that are accessible to individuals with a variety of disabilities.
13. Provide options for demonstrating learning (e.g., different types of test items, portfolios, presentations, focused discussions)
14. Address a wide range of language skills (e.g., spell acronyms, define terms, avoid or define jargon).
15. Make instructions and expectations clear for activities, projects, discussion questions, and assigned reading.
16. Make examples and assignments relevant to learners with a wide variety of interests and backgrounds.
17. Offer outlines, summaries, graphic organizers, and other scaffolding tools to help students learn.
18. Provide adequate opportunities to practice.
19. Allow adequate time for activities, projects, and tests (e.g., give details of project assignments in the syllabus so that students can start working on them early).
20. Provide feedback on project parts and offer corrective opportunities.[9]

Did you know?

In one online course I taught, small groups were assigned to complete a project and answer specific questions to report their work. The first thing they were told to do was decide which mode of communication they would employ so that all students could attend group meetings online and otherwise fully engage in the collaboration. One group reported back that they used email because one of the participants was deaf and could not easily engage using the synchronous communication modes offered. This is an example of how a UDI practice can be built into an assignment.

Developing UDI Practices Inspired by Accommodations and Teaching Challenges

Requests for accommodations can be used to inspire UDI practices. Most faculty members have received letters from the campus disability services office that state what accommodations have been approved for specific students. They can reflect on these requests by asking if an accommodation might inspire a UD strategy that they can offer to all students. Table 5.5 provides examples illustrating how what could be an accommodation for one student can become a UDI practice offered to all students.

TABLE 5.5 Examples of UDI practices inspired by accommodations

One student	*Example of UDI strategy for the whole class*
cannot hear.	Caption all videos.
has low vision.	On slides, use large, bold fonts on uncluttered backgrounds.
is blind.	Speak aloud all visual content. Provide all materials in accessible electronic formats.
cannot manipulate objects.	Assign group work that ensures the participation of all members but not necessarily in the same ways.
has difficulty following instructions.	Have students repeat directions following teacher explanations. Provide a printed copy.
has difficulty learning new concepts.	Use outlines and other scaffolding tools.
requires much repetition.	Allow ample time for practice.
needs extra time to complete work.	Describe all assignments in the syllabus so that students can work ahead.
has difficulty following a lecture.	Provide an outline. Summarize major points.
learns best visually, orally, or in some other specific way.	Deliver content in multiple ways.
has difficulty organizing large assignments.	Break down large assignments into smaller, more manageable parts with multiple due dates and teach students how to do this themselves.
has difficulty demonstrating what has been learned.	Use multiple methods for assessment (e.g., group work, portfolios, multimedia creation, short/long tests).

Teaching challenges of faculty can also inspire UDI strategies. For example, several years ago a computer science professor asked me if he should offer an alternative assignment to a student for project presentations to be made at the end of the term. He said that, although he had not received an accommodation letter from the disability services office, he informally learned that this student was on the autism spectrum and was convinced this was true since she did not make eye contact, rarely spoke, and fidgeted much of the time. He assumed these behaviors meant that she could not or would not give an oral presentation. I asked what instructions he gave students for their presentations. He said he had told them that everyone had eight minutes to use as they wished to report on their projects. Pointing out that she, along with some other students, might need more direction, I suggested the professor continue to allow students to be creative with their eight minutes but also provide a short outline as an example of how a presentation could be organized (one minute for the title and goal, two minutes to state objectives, etc.). Specific instructions like this are often helpful to students on the autism spectrum (and to other students as well). I saw this professor a few months later, and he was happy to report that this student earned an A on her presentation. She followed his outline to within seconds of the sample time breakdown he provided, and some other students followed the outline too, although not as precisely. This is a great example of how UDI practices (in this case, using a scaffolding tool for the assigned presentation) can benefit many students, without lowering expectations for an assignment and without singling out one student.

The following paragraph presents more examples of how UDI strategies were developed in response to specific challenges faced by students and faculty.

> [A] computer science professor who had received criticism from his students for not providing enough contextual background for his lectures started opening his lectures with an overview of key concepts and their importance. A psychology professor added flexibility in the execution of his final exam by offering students the option of a take-home or in-class exam. And a math/statistics faculty member started distributing copies of overheads to the entire class so that students could use them for reference and review. He also began to deliver his lectures with a greater focus on his audience. The changes he made included making eye contact with students, pausing when appropriate, and being more specific in his descriptions.[10]

When faced with a teaching challenge, instructors who embrace UDI look for a solution that they can offer to all students rather than just as an accommodation for a specific student with a disability. For example, when I began to coteach a seminar in which students met once each week and also engaged online, we identified several challenges. We had difficulty engaging everyone in class because of time constraints and because some students hesitated to speak in class, apparently due to embarrassment about their levels of English language speaking skills.

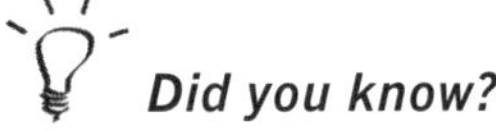

The US Higher Education Opportunity Act (HEOA) of 2008 promotes the practice of UD in postsecondary education. HEOA established the statutory definition for UDL to be a guiding educational practice that provides flexibility in the ways information is presented, in the ways students respond or demonstrate knowledge and skills, and in the ways students are engaged; reduces barriers to instruction; provides appropriate accommodations; and maintains high expectations for all students.[11]

We also wanted to give credit for participation in class that was not simply measured by attendance. Our solution was to place a pile of 3-by-5-inch cards on the front table before course sessions. Students picked up cards as they walked in. By the end of the class session, they wrote their name on one side along with one thing they learned that day. On the back they stated how they would apply that learning or posed a question they hoped would be answered by the end of the term. Students were told they could submit this assignment via email if they preferred. This simple process provided us with an attendance list, created a vehicle for everyone to engage each day, gave us ideas for future content to present, and built in flexibility in how the assignment was submitted so no student needed to request an accommodation. In class we also conducted regular "turn and talk" exercises where individuals discussed a topic with one person. In addition, students were required to answer a question in an online bulletin board and respond to at least one answer a fellow student posted. In the end we engaged students in multiple ways—orally in class, on the 3-by-5-inch cards, and in an online forum. This is UDI in action!

The challenges described in the first column of table 5.6 were presented to me by faculty. There is not just one right answer, but in the second column I offer some of my thoughts about how UDI practices might be applied in each situation. See if you can come up with other solutions that involve the whole class and do *not* single out one student with special instructions or arrangements.

Developing UDI Practices in Response to Potential Barriers to an Assignment

UDI practices can be developed during the process of creating an assignment. As you begin to formulate a design for the assignment, reflect on how it might be inaccessible to students with specific characteristics. For example, in an online course I conceived of an assignment where students would find an image of a space that applied a UD practice but was not labeled as such. Then, in the course discussion board, each student would share the URL or attach the image and state why it is a good example of UD. After that, each student would read the messages posted by classmates and comment on at least one of them. Following is a draft of the assignment.

> Search online for an image that is an example of a feature of a space that is an application of UD but is not labeled as such. On

TABLE 5.6 Examples of UDI practices inspired by accommodations

Challenges reported by instructors	*How UDI practices might be applied*
A student, who has disclosed a disability, raises her hand to answer every question I ask, dominating discussions. Some students in the class are clearly irritated by this. A few are just relieved when they are not called on. How do I correct this situation?	How about announcing that, throughout this class, each student can answer only one question until everyone else has responded? Or, on the spot, you could say, "I want someone who has not spoken yet to answer the next question."
I'm changing my class to all group-based learning. What if a student cannot work well in groups?	Consider writing clear instructions on what you expect from each group, making sure, for example, that everyone has a specific role to play and is engaged in discussions. In group reports, have participants describe and evaluate how well their group worked together and how each member contributed.
Most students are well prepared when it comes to taking notes in class, but each term there are a few who struggle with this. Should I just consider that their problem to solve? Or should I intervene in some way?	Consider giving all students an outline of one of your first lectures. As you deliver that lecture, comment on key points you think they should include in their notes. Consider giving the students a list of notetaking guidelines or a more comprehensive study guide.
I believe that students should have good writing skills before they take my class, but each term a few of them do not. What can I do to help students who struggle with writing assignments without reducing course requirements?	Consider having a greater mix of ways students can demonstrate what they have learned. Post on your website an example of what you consider to be a well-written paper and explain why it is. Research what services are available on your campus or in the community to help students improve their writing skills and share what you learn on the syllabus.
I do not allow students to use mobile devices or other technology in class because some students report it to be distracting. A student with a disability enrolled in my class next term has an approved accommodation to use a mobile device for taking notes in class. How can I allow the accommodation without stigmatizing the student?	To address both courtesy and self-determination issues, consider designating one side of the classroom for students using mobile devices and the other a no-tech zone. A student with a disability using technology will blend in with others doing the same.
I like to introduce class assignments throughout the term as we discuss different topics, but my colleague describes all of hers in detail in the syllabus. Should I do that?	If you ask what is best from the student perspective, you will likely conclude that giving students more time to prepare is best. I vote for putting details about all of the assignments in the syllabus or on a web page.

the course discussion board share the URL or attach the image and state why it is a good example of UD.

Then read the messages posted by your classmates and reply to at least one of them.

To whom might this draft assignment be inaccessible? Clearly, (1) finding and describing the image and (2) accessing the content of images presented by classmates would not be accessible to a student who could not see images, perhaps because of blindness or because of a very slow internet connection. I addressed both of these issues as I created the final assignment described next. I have bolded the text added to address the two potential access issues I identified.

Search online for an image that is an example of a feature of a space that is an application of UD but is not labeled as such. On the course discussion board share the URL or attach the image and state why it is a good example of UD. **Describe the image enough so that someone who cannot see the image can understand the point you are making.**

Alternatively, describe a feature of a space you are aware of that is a good example of UD and explain why it is a good example.

Then read the messages posted by your classmates and reply to at least one of them.

I offered this assignment in five courses by the time this book was published. Although several students have used the alternative assignment, I do not know why. If any of these students were blind, they would not have needed to disclose because all of the materials and methods I use in the courses are fully accessible. What I do know for sure is if I had used the draft version of the assignment, if a student who is blind enrolled in the course, that student would have needed to request an accommodation.

Using the UDI Checklist

For the most part, I view UDI as a way of thinking. Rather than designing for the "typical" or "average" student and then relying on accommodations determined by the disability services office to address the inaccessible features of the course for individual students who are not "typical," instructors who apply UDI anticipate the enrollment of students with diverse abilities and other characteristics and make design decisions accordingly. With this orientation, I was initially reluctant to create a list with examples of UDI practices but eventually did so in response to faculty who wanted concrete examples of UDI practices they could use in their courses.

I selected items for a UDI checklist based on feedback from faculty and administrator collaborators in UDHE initiatives of the DO-IT Center. Over time, I operationalized UDI into a list of examples of promising practices for faculty to consider as they get started in its implementation. Some UDI practices make available to all students what might otherwise be given only to individuals with documented learning disabilities, with sensory differences, on the autism spectrum,[12] or with psychiatric disabilities.[13] UDI strategies on the checklist are clustered around specific aspects of instruction: class climate, interaction, physical environments/products, delivery methods, information resources and technology, feedback and assessment, and accommodations.

Unique among teaching and learning frameworks based on UD, the UDI checklist includes planning for accommodations. As far as "Accommodations," UDI requires that instructors plan for accommodations for students whose needs are not met by their instructional design and have knowledge of how to arrange for accommodations, such as getting materials in alternate formats, providing extra time on exams, and rescheduling courses into accessible classroom locations. The UDI checklist provides a good place for instructors to start as they explore ways to implement UDI in the design of teaching and learning activities for their courses. In contrast to the twenty tips I provided earlier for online courses, this list is more comprehensive and includes suggestions for both on-site and online learning opportunities. The following paragraphs share practices included in the current version of the UDI checklist.[15] Note that each practice is explicitly tied to relevant UD, UDL, and WCAG principles.

Did you know?

A quasi-experimental research study revealed increased grade point averages of students with disabilities in courses taught after faculty were trained in UDI when compared to those of students with disabilities in courses taught by the same faculty before they were trained; this was not the case for students without disabilities in the same courses. In contrast, students with disabilities in a comparison group of untrained faculty did not experience changes in grade point averages over the same period of time.[14]

Class climate. Adopt practices that reflect high values with respect to diversity, equity, and inclusion.

- *Welcome everyone.* Create a welcoming environment for all students. Learn students' names. Build rapport. Encourage the sharing of multiple perspectives. Demonstrate and demand mutual respect. Include a civility statement with behavioral expectations in the syllabus. [UD 1; UDL 3]

- *Avoid stereotyping.* Offer instruction and support based on student performance and requests, not simply on assumptions that members of certain groups (e.g., students with certain types of disabilities or from specific racial or ethnic groups) will automatically do well or poorly or require certain types of assistance. [UD 1]
- *Be approachable and available.* Welcome questions, seek out a student's point of view, and respond patiently. Encourage students to meet with you, maintain regular office hours, and suggest alternatives when student schedules conflict with those hours. [UD 1, 5; UDL 3]
- *Motivate all students.* Use teaching methods and materials that are motivating and relevant to students with diverse characteristics, such as age, gender, cultures, and interests. [UD 1; UDL 3]
- *Address individual needs in an inclusive manner.* Both on the syllabus and in class, invite students to meet with you to discuss disability-related accommodations and other learning needs. On the syllabus, list URLs and other contact information for tutoring and writing centers, disability services, and other campus services that may be helpful. [UD 1, 2; UDL 1]
- *Avoid segregating or stigmatizing any student.* Do not draw undue attention to a difference (e.g., disability) or share private information (e.g., a specific student's accommodation). [UD 1; UDL 2, 3]

Interaction. Encourage regular and effective interactions between students and the instructor, employ multiple communication methods, and ensure that communication methods are accessible to all participants.

- *Offer multiple options for communication and collaboration.* Employ interactive teaching techniques. Use in-person, phone, and multiple electronic communication methods when possible. Make interactions accessible to all participants, including those with disabilities. When meeting on-site, face the class, speak clearly, consider using a microphone, and make eye contact with students. [UD 1, 2, 4, 5; UDL 2, 3; WCAG]
- *Require inclusive cooperative learning.* Assign group work for which learners must engage using a variety of skills and roles. Encourage different ways for group members to interact with each other, insist that all students participate, and facilitate their engagement as needed to

ensure that participants communicate in ways that are accessible to and inclusive of all group members. [UD 1, 2, 4, 5; UDL 3; WCAG]

Physical environments and products. For on-site instruction ensure that facilities, activities, materials, and equipment are physically accessible to and usable by all students and that diverse student characteristics are addressed in safety considerations.

- *Ensure physical access to facilities.* Use classrooms, labs, workspaces, and fieldwork sites that are accessible to individuals with a wide range of physical abilities. [UD 6, 7; UDL 1, 3]
- *Arrange instructional spaces to maximize inclusion and comfort.* Position chairs to encourage participation and give each student a clear line of sight to the instructor and visual aids. Allow room for wheelchairs, personal assistants, sign language interpreters, and captionists. Minimize distractions (e.g., put small groups in quiet work areas). Encourage administrators to routinely apply UD principles in the design of facilities and renovations. [UD 2, 6, 7; UDL 1, 3]
- *Ensure that everyone can use equipment and materials.* Minimize nonessential physical effort. Provide options for operation of equipment, handles, locks, cabinets, and drawers from different heights, with different physical abilities, and by using a right or left hand. Use large print to label controls on lab equipment and other educational aids, using symbols as well as words. Provide straightforward spoken and printed directions for operation. [UD 3–7; UDL 2; WCAG]
- *Ensure safety.* Consider potential issues for people with specific disabilities in emergency situations. Develop procedures for all potential students, including those who are blind, deaf, or wheelchair users. Label safety equipment in simple terms, in large print, and in a location viewable from a variety of angles. Provide spoken and printed safety instructions. [UD 3, 4, 6, 7]

Delivery methods. Use multiple instructional methods that are accessible to all learners.

- *Make content relevant.* Put learning in context. Incorporate multiple examples and perspectives to make specific concepts relevant to individuals with diverse characteristics such as age, ability, gender, ethnicity, race, socioeconomic status, and interests. [UD 1; UDL 1, 3]

- *Select flexible curriculum.* Choose textbooks and other curriculum materials that address the needs of students with diverse abilities, interests, and learning preferences; are well organized; emphasize important points; provide references for gaining background knowledge; include indices and glossaries; and have chapter outlines, study questions, and practice exercises. Consider the use of digital materials that provide feedback, background information, vocabulary, and other supports based on student responses. [UD 2–5; UDL 1, 3; WCAG]
- *Provide cognitive supports.* Summarize major points; give background and contextual information; and deliver effective prompting. Offer outlines, summaries, graphic organizers, and other scaffolding tools to help students learn. Provide options for gaining background information and vocabulary. At the beginning of a lesson, consider posing one or two questions and ask students to answer them at the end of the session. [UD 2–5; UDL 1–3; WCAG]
- *Provide multiple ways to learn.* Use multiple modes to deliver content (e.g., reading, lectures, collaborative learning, small group discussions, hands-on activities, internet simulations, and fieldwork). [UD 2–4; UDL 1, 2; WCAG]
- *Deliver instructions clearly and in multiple ways.* Make instructions clear in the syllabus and follow up with a question-and-answer session. Ask students to summarize instructions to ensure understanding. [UD 3, 4; UDL 1; WCAG]
- *Use large visual and tactile aids.* Use large manipulatives and images to demonstrate content; use a computer to enlarge microscope images. [UD 3, 4; UDL 1; WCAG]
- *Make each teaching method accessible to all students.* Consider a wide range of abilities, interests, learning styles, and experiences when implementing each instructional method to ensure engagement of all students. Describe content presented visually. [UD 2, 4, 5; UDL 1, 2; WCAG]

Information resources and technology. Ensure that course materials, notes, and other information resources are engaging, flexible, and accessible for all students.

- *Select materials early.* Choose materials and prepare a syllabus early to allow students the option of beginning to read materials and work on assignments before the course begins and time to arrange for alternative formats. [UD 4; UDL 1; WCAG]

- *Provide content in accessible, universally designed formats.* Select or create materials (including textbooks, syllabi, lesson pages, presentation materials) that are universally designed. For example, use electronic materials that are text-based, have flexible features, use formatted headings and lists, describe content within images, have consistent layouts and organization schemes whose link text describes its destination, use large sans serif fonts on uncluttered pages with plain backgrounds, and incorporate color combinations that are high contrast and can be distinguished by people with color blindness. Use captioned videos and provide transcriptions for audio presentations. Apply accessibility standards to websites. [UD 4; UDL 1; WCAG]
- *Accommodate a variety of reading and technology skills.* Present content in a logical, straightforward manner and in an order that reflects its importance. Avoid unnecessary jargon and complexity and define new terms when they are presented. Create materials in simple, intuitive formats. Provide options for gaining the technology skills needed for course participation. Share relevant campus resources with students. [UD 3, 4; UDL 1]
- *Ensure the availability of appropriate assistive technology.* If computer or science labs are used, ensure that assistive technology for students with disabilities is available or can be readily acquired. [UD 2, 4, 6, 7; UDL 1, 2; WCAG]

Feedback and assessment. Regularly assess students' progress, provide specific feedback on a regular basis using multiple accessible methods and tools, and adjust instruction accordingly.

- *Set clear expectations.* Keep academic standards consistent for all students, including those who require accommodations. Provide clear statements of expectations for the course, individual assignments, deadlines, and assessment methods. Include straightforward grading rubrics for assignments. [UD 3; UDL 3]
- *Test in the same manner in which you teach.* Ensure that a test measures what students

Did you know?

In 2009, Beckman offered a graduate course in two different ways, teaching one session with lecturing as the primary instructional method and the other "treatment" section with lectures and small group discussions. Although both groups performed at the same level on multiple-choice and fill-in-the-blank test questions, students in the treatment group more often reported that "the instructor was open to a variety of points of view" and performed better on essay exam questions.[16]

have learned and not their ability to adapt to a new format or style of presentation. [UD 3; WCAG]

- *Minimize time constraints when appropriate.* Plan for variety in the ability of students to complete work by describing assignments well in advance of due dates, ideally in the syllabus. Allow extended time on tests, unless speed is an essential course objective. [UD 2, 3]
- *Offer regular feedback and corrective opportunities.* Allow students to turn in parts of large projects for feedback before the final project is due. Give students resubmission options to correct errors in assignments and exams. Arrange for peer feedback when appropriate. [UD 5; UDL 2, 3]
- *Provide multiple ways for students to demonstrate what they have learned.* Assess group and cooperative performance, as well as individual achievement. Consider using traditional tests with a variety of item types (e.g., multiple choice, essay, short answer), group work, demonstrations, portfolios, term papers, and presentations as options for demonstrating knowledge. Provide students choices in assessment methods when appropriate. [UD 2, 4; UDL 3; WCAG]
- *Monitor and adjust.* Regularly assess students' background knowledge and current learning informally (e.g., through class discussions) and formally (e.g., through frequent, short exams), and adjust instructional content and methods accordingly. [UD 5]
- *Provide sample test questions, exemplary work, and study guides.* Consider sharing sample test questions with answers and exemplary work of previous students, discussing how to study for course exams, and providing study guides. [UD 3; UDL 3; WCAG]

Accommodations. Plan for accommodations for students whose needs are not fully met by the instructional content and practices.

- *Know how to arrange for accommodations.* Learn campus protocols for getting materials in alternate formats, captioning videos, and arranging for other accommodations for students with disabilities. [UD 1, 2, 4, 6]
- *Share accommodation information.* Tell how to arrange accommodations on the syllabus. Tell teaching and lab assistants about student accommodations. [UD 1; UDL 2, 3]

The most current version of the UDI checklist is maintained in the online publication *Equal Access: Universal Design of Instruction* in the Center for Universal Design in Education.[17] Educators are encouraged to suggest improvements.

UDHE OF A DEPARTMENT OR PROGRAM

Few institutions have adopted UDHE as a campuswide initiative. However, there are many examples of small pockets of faculty applying a UD approach and of disability services offices and centers for teaching and learning promoting the application of UDHE to campus units. In the subsections that follow, I provide examples of considerations for applying UDHE throughout an academic department and then to a distance learning program.

Did you know?

Further research is needed to test the efficacy of UDI practices in postsecondary courses with students who have a wide range of characteristics. Without a strong research base, practitioners will continue to identify promising practices rather than research-based or evidence-based practices for instruction.

UDHE of an Academic Department

Each item in the following list includes an application area, a general guideline, and an example of a related practice for applying UDHE to an entire academic department of a postsecondary institution. This list provides the structure for a checklist of practices developed through a UDHE initiative of the DO-IT Center that is posted online.[18]

- *Planning, policies, and evaluation.* Consider diversity issues as you plan and evaluate your facilities and programs. For example, include accessibility in the procurement process.
- *Facility and environment.* Ensure physical access, comfort, and safety within an environment that is welcoming to visitors with a variety of abilities, racial and ethnic backgrounds, genders, and ages. For example, include ample high-contrast, large-print directional signs to and throughout departmental labs, administrative offices, classrooms, and other facilities.
- *Support services.* Make sure support staff are prepared to work with all students, faculty, and staff. For example, make sure staff members know how to respond to requests for disability-related accommodations such as sign language interpreters.

- *Information resources.* Ensure that departmental publications and websites welcome a diverse group and that information is accessible to everyone. For example, make sure that pictures in departmental publications and on websites include people with diverse characteristics with respect to race, gender, age, and disability.
- *Courses and faculty.* Ensure that faculty members deliver courses that are accessible to all students and that accommodations are provided in a timely manner. For example, make sure video presentations used in courses or other presentations have captions.
- *Computers, software, and assistive technology.* Make technology in departmental computing facilities accessible to everyone. Begin with a few items and add more later. For example, make available an adjustable-height table for each type of computer workstation in a lab.

UDHE of a Distance Learning Program

There are also guidelines for making entire programs inclusive of individuals with disabilities. For example, representatives from sixteen campuses that were part of DO-IT UDHE initiatives contributed to the list of characteristics of a universally designed online learning program that is documented in table 5.7. It is organized by subcategories defined by stakeholder groups—students and potential students, distance learning designers, distance learning instructors, and program evaluators. Routinely applying these practices can bring us closer to making learning accessible to anyone, anywhere, at any time.[20]

Did you know?

Accessible design recommendations for both technology and learning activities are integrated into the national standards for quality online courses published by the International Association for K–12 Online Learning.[19]

WHAT STUDENTS HAVE TO SAY

Applying UDI requires some work. Is it worth the effort? To answer this question, we need to know what students with disabilities have to say about how teachers teach. I facilitated an informal online discussion with a large group of high school and college students with a wide variety of disabilities. I asked, “What are the qualities of a good teacher?” They said a good teacher is well prepared, is a good role model, makes expectations clear, is approachable, gets to know students, respects students and maintains privacy, does not make

TABLE 5.7 Characteristics of distance learning programs that are inclusive of all potential students

For students and potential students
1. The distance learning home page is accessible to individuals with disabilities (e.g., it adheres to Section 508, World Wide Web Consortium, or institutional accessible-design guidelines/standards).
2. A statement about the distance learning program's commitment to accessible design for all potential students, including those with disabilities, is included prominently in appropriate publications and websites, along with contact information for reporting inaccessible design features.
3. A statement about how distance learning students with disabilities can request accommodations is included in appropriate publications and web pages.
4. A statement about how people can obtain alternate formats of printed materials is included in publications.
5. The online and other course materials of distance learning courses are accessible to individuals with disabilities.
For distance learning designers
6. Publications and web pages for distance learning course designers include ■ a statement of the program's commitment to accessibility, ■ guidelines/standards regarding accessibility, and ■ resources.
7. Accessibility issues are covered in regular course designer training.
For distance learning instructors
8. Publications and web pages for distance learning instructors include ■ a statement of the distance learning program's commitment to accessibility, ■ guidelines/standards regarding accessibility, and ■ resources.
9. Accessibility issues are covered in training sessions for instructors.
For program evaluators
10. A system is in place to monitor the accessibility of courses and, based on this evaluation, the program takes actions to improve the accessibility of specific courses and to update information and training given to potential students, actual students, course designers, and instructors.

assumptions about a student's capabilities, encourages students, is patient, challenges students, helps students apply knowledge, is open to new ideas, is enthusiastic, facilitates the exchange of ideas among students and between teacher and students, and adjusts to the unique needs of students.[21] I found it interesting, but not surprising, that no participant in the discussion specifically mentioned disability. Clearly, good teaching for students with disabilities is good teaching for everyone.

What do students think about being given multiple, accessible ways to *learn*; *engage* with the instructor, fellow students, and the course content; and *demonstrate* what they have learned? Interesting you should ask. I wanted to know the answer to this question too. In my edited book *Universal Design of Higher*

Education: From Principles to Practice, current and past students with disabilities in higher education shared their perspectives about UDI practices.[22] Although they did not always agree, overall, they made it clear that UDI strategies are good teaching practices for everyone and minimize the need for accommodations. They said important considerations include creating an environment that is welcoming and accessible to all students, employing a variety of teaching strategies, ensuring that each strategy is accessible to all students, making effective use of accessible technology, providing course materials in accessible formats, ensuring that facilities are physically accessible and safe for everyone, interacting often with students and in a variety of ways, assessing students in multiple and accessible ways, and being prepared to provide accommodations to make learning activities fully accessible to students with disabilities. Examples of comments by these current and past students about types of UDI practices in various categories of application are as follows.

- *Class climate.* "I don't expect professors to have great knowledge about my disability. I see my role as simply articulating the accommodations I need to do my best work. Even in large classes, when I visit a professor during office hours and she remembers my name and the history of my previous visits, it has impact. It is important for students to recognize their roles in making requests early and otherwise developing positive relationships with faculty by applying skills in self-advocacy and problem-solving."
- *Physical environment and products.* "When safety instructions are provided in electronic format before class, it gives students who rely on computers for access a chance to familiarize themselves with the instructions ahead of time and refer back to them as needed. Quite often, laboratory work includes the use of hazardous materials and substances. For people who are deaf or hard of hearing, it is imperative that oral instructions on safe handling and disposal of materials are also supplemented with instructions in a printed format."
- *Delivery methods.* "It is important that Web-based materials be offered in a format that is accessible, particularly to students who are blind and using text-to-speech technology, which can only access Web content that is in text-based format. The university can benefit students by hiring staff with diverse backgrounds and perspectives so that a college education as a whole can be seen as a mosaic of different and authentic perspectives. I find it very helpful when professors make copies of their PowerPoint slides available to students in electronic and paper format. Supplementing

a lecture with visuals and printed materials, such as a lecture outline, not only benefits a student who is deaf or hard of hearing but also provides a richer experience for all students. Large visual and tactile aids help students with limited vision, as well as those who are visual and tactile learners."

- *Information resources and technology.* "It is important for the faculty to be organized so that students can buy their textbooks and prepare for the class. I have found that even when accessibility standards are applied to departmental Web sites, they are frequently not imposed on course Web sites, which are thrown together during the first week of the quarter."
- *Interaction.* "Several of my professors required a student-instructor meeting. Those who did this tended to develop a strong rapport with their students. Personal connections are an important part of learning for many students. Effective communication is crucial. Most students default to using e-mail, which is an accessible form of communication for most students, including those with disabilities. Phone and in-person meetings are also used to coordinate work between students."
- *Feedback and assessment.* "There is a benefit to group work and collaboratively building on the ideas of your peers, but peer feedback should not reduce the need for faculty to review student work. Professors should encourage discussion and actually incorporate student feedback and comments into their course design and content. I have a great deal of respect for professors who choose written answers over multiple-choice answers. It shows that they are willing to evaluate our unique thoughts, not just what we crammed in the night before. I think choices in assessment methods can work, but grading fairness is a huge issue if several methods are offered. I don't expect a professor to be an expert about my disability; that's my job. What I do expect is that the professor will have a professional conversation with me and facilitate arrangements for my accommodations."[23]

A capacity-building institute DO-IT hosted at the UW engaged a panel of five individuals with disabilities related to mobility, sight, learning, and social interactions. Most of these panelists, each with experience as a student or instructor in online learning, reported practices that contribute to positive experiences in online courses. Their recommendations suggest technology and instructional design practices that are relatively simple to implement can substantially improve the experiences of students and instructors with disabilities in digital learning activities.

- Offer multiple ways to learn, such as through a video paired with printed materials.
- Provide materials accessible to students with disabilities at the same time they are provided to other students.
- Caption videos to benefit a wide variety of students, including English language learners, those in noisy (e.g., airports, buses) or noiseless (e.g., libraries) environments, individuals who want to search content, in addition to people with hearing and learning disabilities.
- Design videos to include audio content for visual elements of a video whenever possible (e.g., have the credits and other information at the end of a video spoken by the narrator) to maximize access for individuals who are blind or otherwise cannot see the screen. Consider adding audio description to describe other key elements of the content presented visually.
- Provide text descriptions for all visuals.
- Use accessibility designed documents.
- Engage with students in multiple ways.
- In online discussions, provide a specific focus to each discussion question, provide guidance in how to answer the question, engage in and guide the discussion, and summarize the group of responses.
- For any on-site components of a course, make sure the facility can be easily maneuvered with a wheelchair.[24]

MY GO-TO RESOURCES

Following are some good places to start in your exploration of topics covered in this chapter.

- *Institute of Education Sciences*
  ies.ed.gov
- *The Faculty Room*
  uw.edu/doit/programs/accesscollege
- *Universal Design of Instruction in Postsecondary Education*
  uw.edu/doit/programs/center-universal-design-education/postsecondary/universal-design-instruction-postsecondary
- *UDL on Campus*
  udloncampus.cast.org/home

- *Published Books and Articles About Universal Design of Instruction*
  uw.edu/doit/programs/center-universal-design-education/resources/published-books-and-articles-about-universal
- *Knowledge Base*
  uw.edu/doit/knowledge-base
- *Universal Design of Instruction in Higher Education*[25]
- *Reach Everyone, Teach Everyone: Universal Design for Learning in Higher Education*[26]
- *Transforming Higher Education Through Universal Design for Learning*[27]

CONCLUSION

UDI holds promise for addressing the needs of a student body that is increasingly diverse with respect to race, ethnicity, gender, native language, culture, age, learning preferences, background knowledge, ability, gender, veteran status, and other characteristics while simultaneously improving learning for many others. UDI practices are applied proactively, make instruction welcoming to all potential students, are accessible to and usable by students with a broad range of characteristics, and are offered to all students in an inclusive on-site or online setting.

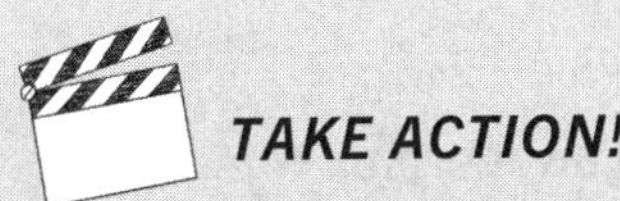

TAKE ACTION!

(REFLECT) Consider your context

Reflect on these questions:

- What motivates you to learn?
- What was a great teaching moment you experienced as a student or a teacher? What made it so?
- What demographic groups do you consider difficult to teach? What UDI practices might benefit these students?
- How could you support students who find it difficult to engage in groups?
- What accommodations typically provided for students with disabilities could also, if offered to everyone, benefit others?

(LEARN) Identify applications of UD, UDL, and WCAG to a learning activity

In a discussion or assignment in an academic course, ask students to share examples of UDI practices for a learning activity that apply specific principles of UD, UDL, and WCAG. Have students articulate the importance of all three sets of principles when designing a learning activity.

(LEARN) Integrate UDI into principles of good practice

For each of the following *Principles of Good Practice in Undergraduate Education,* give an example of how UDI could be applied to the principle to ensure that all students benefit from its application.[28]

Principle of Good Practice in Undergraduate Education	*Example of how UDI might be applied to the principle*
Encourages contact between students and faculty.	
Develops reciprocity and cooperation among students.	
Encourages active learning.	
Gives prompt feedback.	
Emphasizes time on task.	
Communicates high expectations.	
Respects diverse talents and ways of learning.	

(LEARN) Integrate UDI into principles based on how learning works

For each of the following questions from *How Learning Works: Seven Research-Based Principles for Smart Teaching*, tell how UDI is relevant to the question.[29]

Question	*Example of how UDI is relevant to the question*
How does students' prior knowledge affect their learning?	
How does the way students organize knowledge affect their learning?	
What factors motivate students to learn?	
How do students develop mastery?	

Question	*Example of how UDI is relevant to the question*
What kinds of practice and feedback enhance learning?	
Why do student development and course climate matter for student learning?	
How do students become self-directed learners?	

(LEARN) Match practices to UDI principles

In an academic or professional development course, have participants review the UDI principles. Give examples of teaching and learning activities that rest on at least one principle in each of the three sets of principles. Conclude with a discussion of the value of having all three sets of principles inform teaching practices.

(LEARN) Universally design informal learning opportunities

Ask participants in an academic or professional development course to read the article "Promoting the Design of Accessible Informal Science Learning" from the online publication *Universal Design in Higher Education: Promising Practices* at uw.edu/doit/resources/books/universal-design-higher-education-promising-practices. Look for it in "Part 2: Evidence-Based Practices from the Field." In a class discussion, compare UDI practices that can be applied to informal learning activities with those that can be applied to formal learning environments. What are the same? What are differences?

(LEARN) Consider how UD benefits for specific students

In an academic or professional development course, have participants describe one UD strategy made available to all students that is beneficial to a student with a specific type of disability.

(LEARN) Role play perspective of student with a disability

In a group discussion in an academic or professional development course, have participants imagine that they are a student with a disability at a postsecondary institution who is not sure UDI is a good idea, perhaps because of misconceptions. Ask them to describe the person they are pretending to be and state a concern they, as this person, have about the campus embracing UDI.

(LEARN) Role play perspective of faculty

Imagine you are a faculty member at a postsecondary institution who is not a fan of UDI. Describe the person you are pretending to be and state an objection you, as this person, have to embracing UDI in your teaching.

(LEARN) Use case studies for examples of UD applications

Within a professional development or academic course, have a disability services director or counselor give examples of accommodations given to specific students with disabilities. In small groups, have students brainstorm ideas for developing UDI strategies inspired by one or more of these examples of accommodations and describe how the strategies could benefit students who have not disclosed their disabilities, English language learners, or other students.

(LEARN) Identify low-hanging fruit

In an academic or professional development course, have participants describe an accessibility strategy for an online course that is an example of "low-hanging fruit" regarding accessible design of online content—i.e., something that is very easy to do routinely as you develop a course.

[Note: Be sure to describe "low-hanging fruit" since a participant (perhaps from a different culture) might not have heard the expression "low-hanging fruit." This is an example of UDI thinking!]

(APPLY) Add to campus accommodation statement in a syllabus

In an academic or professional development course, draft an "Accessibility and Accommodations" section of a syllabus that you could potentially use if you were teaching the course. Include (1) your personal statement as well as (2) a standard statement that you particularly like that is from your institution or another one (a search at various school websites will yield a good supply to choose from).

(APPLY) Update the faculty handbook

In a task force to update the faculty handbook, edit/add content about what should be included on a syllabus and what file formats are accessible, applying UDI principles to both the content and the format. Look at all other sections of the handbook to determine where disability, UDI, and accommodation content should be included.

(APPLY) Universally design a syllabus

Individually or within a course, universally design a syllabus for a course you are teaching or plan to teach or redesign a syllabus that has been used in a course you have taken. Consider including the course name, number, and credit; information about the professor; a short course description; target audience; accessibility and accommodations statements; learning objectives; textbook; course activities; requirements; grading; schedule of weekly topics and activities/readings/assignments; and relevant campus rules and resources. Describe what UDI strategies are represented in the syllabus.

(APPLY) Universally design instruction

Individually or in an academic or professional development program, have participants access the DO-IT checklist *Equal Access: Universal Design of Instruction* at uw.edu/doit/equal-access-universal-design-instruction. Complete it for an existing or fictitious course or other instructional application. Eliminate checklist items that are not relevant to your application. Check off those items that are already in place. Put a date on tasks you wish to accomplish. Add other UDI issues you would like to address. From this exercise create a planning document that lists specific tasks in order by targeted implementation date, followed by a section of completed items (for positive reinforcement as you see how far you have come). Review the document periodically, revising implementation dates and moving items from the plans section to the accomplishments section. The document could be formatted something like this:

UDI Plans for [name of course(s) or other instructional application]
    Month, year   UDI task #1
    Month, year   UDI task #2 . . .
UDI Accomplishments
    UDI task accomplishment #1
    UDI task accomplishment #2 . . .

(APPLY) Articulate UDI and accommodation strategies for a teaching method

For your own application or as an academic or professional development course assignment for students, select a course you are teaching or an example of one you may teach. List a variety of teaching methods you could employ; for one of these methods, list UDI strategies you could apply to make it more inclusive; for one of these strategies, describe an accommodation that might be needed by a student with a specific type of disability.

(APPLY) Use UDI to solve teaching challenges

In an academic or professional development course, ask faculty or teaching assistants to imagine being faced with each of the following teaching challenges and discuss a solution that you can offer to all students rather than require an accommodation for a specific student or a few students. Be sure they come up with solutions that do not include singling out one student with special instructions.

- A student, who has disclosed a disability, raises her hand to answer every question I ask, dominating discussions. Some students in the class are clearly irritated by this. A few are just relieved that they are not called on. How do I correct this situation?
- I'm changing my class to all project/group-based learning. One student, related to her disability, cannot work well in groups. What can I do?

- Most students are well prepared when it comes to taking notes in class, but each term there are a few who struggle with this. Should I just consider that *their* problem to solve? Or, should I intervene in some way and, if so, how?
- I expect that students should have good writing skills *before* they take my class, but each term a few of them do not. What could I do to help students who struggle with writing assignments without reducing course requirements?
- I like to give out class assignments throughout the term as we discuss different topics, but my colleague describes all of hers in detail in the syllabus. Should I do that?
- Some students whose first language is not English hesitate to contribute to discussions in class. What should I do to help them engage more?

(APPLY) Focus on nontechnical issues

Describe a nontechnical strategy that you could suggest to an online learning instructor for making a course more welcoming or accessible to students with diverse characteristics, including disabilities.

(APPLY) Ask students with disabilities what practices benefit them

To gain insight into what teaching practices best serve students with disabilities, conduct a survey (alternatively, a focus group or panel) of students with disabilities on your campus. Ask them what they consider to be the qualities and practices of good teachers. The campus disability services office may agree to distribute a survey to students registered with this office. Consider implications for practice based on survey results. Consider conducting similar activities to learn what teaching practices benefit other subgroups of students. How are the responses of different groups similar or different? Why do you think this is the case?

(APPLY) Use typical accommodations to identify UD teaching strategies

Think of an accommodation a student with a disability might require. Develop a UDI strategy inspired by the accommodation that an instructor could make available to the whole class.

(APPLY) Proactively adjust an assignment to be accessible to students with disabilities

Give this assignment within a professional development or academic course: Suppose you want to have students search the internet for an image of a universally designed facility. How could you make the assignment and the reports of other students accessible to a student who is blind, thus eliminating a need for an accommodation for a future student who is blind?

(APPLY) Consider benefits of UDI for a specific group

In an academic course that covers UDI, have students read the article "Applying Universal Design to Address the Needs of Postsecondary Students on the Autism

Spectrum," located in the *Journal of Postsecondary Education and Disability* at www.ahead-archive.org/uploads/publications/JPED/jped28_2/JPED28_2_Full%20Document.pdf.[30] After talking about how UDI benefits students on the autism spectrum, ask students to write a similar article, following the organization and using some of the content in the article to create a new paper focusing on how UDI improves the learning environment for another group of students (e.g., students who have dyslexia or who are English language learners).

(APPLY) Incorporate UDI into online course development

Require students in an online learning design course to apply UDI principles to make the courses they design accessible to students with disabilities.

(APPLY) Deliver a universally designed presentation

Require that students in an academic course deliver course presentations that apply UDI principles. Have students evaluate each other using a checklist that they develop as a group.

(APPLY) Incorporate UD in research

Require that students in an academic course address issues related to disability, accessible design, or UDI in their research projects (e.g., in the literature review, problem statement, research design, report of results, limitations of the study, and conclusion).

(APPLY) Universally design an assessment

Individually or within a course, universally design or redesign an assessment for a unit in a course you are teaching or plan to teach.

(APPLY) Universally design a freshman learning community

If your school engages beginning students in freshman learning communities—environments in which freshmen engage in courses and extracurricular activities as a cohort—pull together a group of faculty and staff who are leading these communities and discuss how applying UDI practices might make them more inclusive. For example, you could try to ensure that all aspects of these communities are welcoming, accessible to, and inclusive of a broad audience. As one step toward universally designed learning communities, coordinators can ensure that participating instructors employ UDI in their courses. They can also make sure publications and websites for their communities are welcoming and accessible to a broad audience by including accessible formats, content that explains how to obtain accommodations and other assistance, and pictures of participants with diverse characteristics. In addition, UD can be applied to teaching and learning centers, libraries, computer and science labs, and other places that support student learning.

CHAPTER 6

Teaching and Learning Services

If you want to lift yourself up, lift up someone else.

—Booker T. Washington

MYRIAD CAMPUS SERVICES—among them teaching and learning centers, professional development units, tutoring centers, and career services—play important roles in promoting positive social, academic, and career outcomes for students and in helping faculty deliver effective instruction. This chapter describes how campus services can enhance both on-site and online offerings by applying the principles of Universal Design in Higher Education (UDHE). As campuses become more diverse, the effectiveness of these services for individuals with a wide range of characteristics, including those considered disabilities, increases in importance.

INTRODUCTION

I used to be a mathematics teacher, so of course, I am obligated to impose math problems on anyone nearby—including you, as a reader of this book. Here we go. In an ongoing effort to improve services to faculty, the Teaching and Learning Center director met with nine university students so that they could share their learning experiences in courses in the business school. One of the students requested a sign language interpreter for the meeting. Later, the center accountant looked at the bill for interpreting services and remarked, "Wow, $160 for one student. That's expensive!" The Teaching and Learning Center director said, "No, the cost was only $16 per person." Who did the math right?

When I put on my math teacher hat, I can argue that each answer is correct for a different question. In the context of UDHE, though, exploring what each answer might suggest regarding the thinking of these two individuals is worthwhile. The accountant in this story views sign language interpreting as a service exclusively for the student who is deaf or hard of hearing. In contrast, the director's response embodies a view that the interpreting service is of value to each participant in the group—interpreting what others are saying for the benefit of the student who is deaf and interpreting what that student is saying for the benefit of the other nine participants. The view of the Teaching and Learning Center director is consistent with my experiences giving presentations in countries whose primary language is not English. When I give a talk in Japan, English-Japanese language interpreters are always present. The interpreters are provided so that everyone in the room can engage in a conversation, not just so that I, as the minority voice, can understand the words of participants speaking Japanese. If the UD paradigm were fully embraced, more people would think that sign language interpreters benefit everyone in a group.

Next time you run into someone who asks (or complains) about the cost of sign language interpreters, consider saying what I often say, "Yes, sign language interpreters are expensive for small groups, but not so much for large groups." I usually get a puzzled response like, "Do sign language interpreters charge more for larger groups?" to which I respond, "Oh, no, but the cost per person is lower when interpreting is provided for more people." Be prepared that this line of reasoning might take a little time to explain, but I love the way that it gets at least some people thinking outside of the "accommodations-only" box.

Just an idea.

Campus services support faculty (e.g., a teaching and learning center); staff (e.g., a professional development program); students (e.g., a tutoring center); and everyone (e.g., a library). I think that most service leaders would say that their intention is that everyone who is eligible and desires to use their service can do so comfortably and efficiently. However, in practice, do all potential visitors—including those with a variety of abilities with respect to sight, hearing, and mobility—feel welcome? On campus, can they get to the facility and maneuver within it; communicate effectively with support staff; access the content in printed materials; and fully participate in events and other activities? Online, can they easily locate and secure all services using their electronic devices, including assistive technology; communicate with staff in ways that are most effective for them; access the content within videos, documents, and web pages; and fully engage in learning opportunities?

The UDHE Framework holds promise for guiding the development of inclusive practices within any service unit. By the end of this chapter you should be able to

- list examples of services on a postsecondary campus that can maximize their impact through the adoption of more inclusive practices;
- describe components of the UDHE Framework—definition, principles, guidelines, practices, and processes—with respect to campus services;
- name the three sets of principles that underpin the UDHE Framework;
- apply the process of UDHE to create inclusive on-site and online practices for campus services;
- list UDHE practices for making services more inclusive;
- provide examples of how UDHE can minimize the need for accommodations within a service unit;
- describe how staff can work effectively with the disability services office to accommodate a person with a specific disability in their service unit.

FRAMEWORK, SCOPE, DEFINITION, PRINCIPLES, AND GUIDELINES

Components of the UDHE Framework include scope, definition, principles, guidelines, practices, and process. The scope of applications covered in this chapter comprises all services that directly or indirectly support teaching and learning. A definition that can be used for the application of UDHE to these campus services, modified from the basic definition of UD, is the design of products and environments *that deliver services that support teaching and learning* to be usable by all people, to the greatest extent possible, without the need for adaptation or specialized design. UDHE principles for addressing all facilities, materials, technologies, and training used in the delivery of a service are the combination of the seven principles of UD for products and environments, the three principles of Universal Design for Learning (UDL) for curriculum and pedagogy, and the four principles that underpin the Web Content Accessibility Guidelines (WCAG) for information technology (IT).

PROCESS

Rather than memorizing basic principles, consider focusing more on the definition of UDHE for services, the importance of offering multiple ways to access resources and to interact with personnel, and the basic characteristics of a UD strategy. Get in the habit of asking these questions:

- Do I offer *multiple ways* for service users to *access* information (e.g., consulting a website or communicating with staff) and *engage* in service offerings (e.g., talking with staff in person, by phone, or via email individually or in a group)?
- Is each approach used to deliver a service *accessible* to, *usable* by, and *inclusive* of all potential users and does it minimize the need for accommodations?

The process of applying UDHE to all aspects of a service unit can be adapted from the general process for applying UDHE to any product or environment. A service administrator can follow the process presented here and illustrated in figure 6.1.

FIGURE 6.1 A process for applying UDHE to a campus service

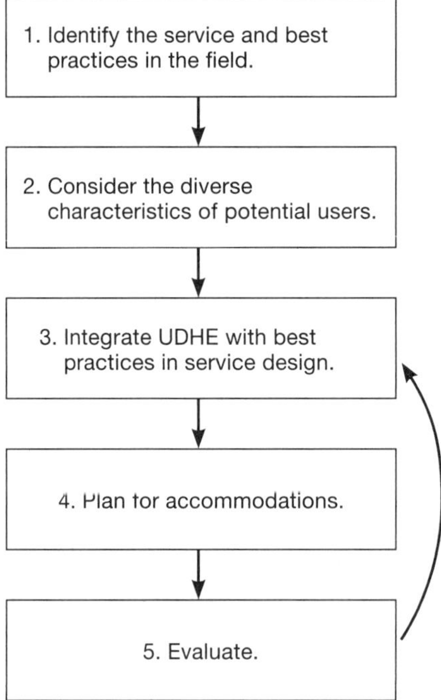

1. *Identify the service and best practices in the field.* Select a campus service (e.g., a library) to which you wish to apply UDHE. Identify best practices for the delivery of this type of service (e.g., for the design of postsecondary campus libraries).
2. *Consider the diverse characteristics of potential users.* Describe the population and then consider the diverse characteristics of those who might potentially use the service—e.g., with respect to gender; age; ethnicity; race; native language; learning preferences; size; abilities to see, hear, walk, manipulate objects, read, speak—and the challenges they might encounter in using the service.
3. *Integrate UDHE with best practices in service design.* Integrate best practices within the field of service delivery (e.g., for the design of libraries) with UDHE practices (underpinned by relevant UD, UDL, and WCAG principles) to maximize benefits of the service to individuals with a wide variety of characteristics.
4. *Plan for accommodations.* Develop processes to address accommodation requests (e.g., arrangements for a sign language interpreter) from individuals for whom the design of the service does not automatically provide access. Promote the process through the service's website, publications, and signage.
5. *Evaluate.* After implementing the service, collect feedback from individuals with diverse characteristics who use the service (e.g., through online surveys, focus groups). Make modifications based on the results. Return to step 3 if evidence from your evaluation suggests improvements for your design.

Examples of practices that result from applying the process to any campus service are shared in the next section of this chapter.

PRACTICES

In UDHE initiatives of the Disabilities, Opportunities, Internetworking, and Technology (DO-IT) Center, representatives from campuses nationwide contributed to the creation of training materials and resources for guiding campus service personnel in being both (1) proactive in designing accessible, usable, and inclusive services and then (2) reactive in providing accommodations for individuals with disabilities. A checklist of questions about UDHE strategies for service units that operationalizes UDHE principles and guidelines into practices relevant to student service units was created, tested on more than twenty campuses, and refined from the results of a nationwide survey of student service personnel.[1]

Categories of UDHE applications that are common to most campus service checklists are planning, policies, and evaluation; physical environments and products; staff; information resources and technology; and events. Following are examples of questions included in the checklist to address when applying UDHE practices to a student service.

Planning, policies, and evaluation. Consider diversity issues as you plan and evaluate services.

- Are people with disabilities, racial and ethnic minorities, students with diverse gender identities and sexual orientations, young and old students, and other groups represented on your staff in numbers proportional to those of the whole campus or community?
- Do you have policies and procedures that ensure access to facilities, printed materials, computers, and electronic resources for people with disabilities?
- Is accessibility considered in the procurement process?
- Do you have a procedure to ensure a timely response to requests for disability-related accommodations?
- Are disability-related access issues addressed in your evaluation practices?

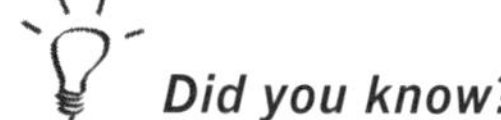

Did you know?

Postsecondary students with disabilities who participated in thirteen focus groups reported incidents where student services staff did not know how to make accommodations for their disabilities and where they felt disrespected. Results of the study suggest a need to increase the knowledge and skills of staff with respect to disabilities, particularly those that are not obvious; the rights and responsibilities of students and institutions; accommodation strategies; issues unique to specific units; and available resources.[2]

Physical environments and products. Ensure physical access, comfort, and safety within an environment that is inclusive of people with a variety of abilities, racial and ethnic backgrounds, gender identities, and ages.

- Are there parking areas, pathways, and entrances to the building that are wheelchair-accessible and clearly identified?
- Are all levels of the facility connected via an accessible route of travel?

- Are there ample high-contrast, large-print directional signs to and throughout the office and to elevators and wheelchair-accessible restrooms?
- Do elevators have auditory, visual, and tactile signals and are elevator controls accessible from a seated position?
- Is at least part of a service counter at a height accessible from a seated position?
- Are aisles kept wide and clear of obstructions for the safety of users who have disabilities related to mobility or sight?
- Are there quiet work or meeting areas where noise and other distractions are minimized or facility rules, such as no phone use, in place to minimize noise?
- Is adequate light available?

Staff. Make sure staff are prepared to work with all students.

- Do staff members know how to respond to requests for disability-related accommodations, such as arranging for a sign language interpreter or providing a document in an alternative format?
- Are all staff members aware of issues related to communicating on-site and online with members of a diverse student body, including those with disabilities?

Information resources and technology. Ensure that computers on-site as well as digital resources are designed to be accessible to individuals with disabilities and that systems are in place for providing accommodations.

- Do pictures in your publications and on your website include people with diverse characteristics with respect to race, gender, age, and disability?
- In key publications and on your website, do you include a statement about your commitment to universal design as well as procedures for requesting disability-related accommodations?
- Is an adjustable-height table available for each type of workstation provided in your center to assist students who use wheelchairs or are small or large in stature?
- Do you provide adequate work space for both left- and right-handed users?
- Are staff members aware of accessibility options (e.g., enlarged text feature) included in computer operating systems and of assistive technology available in the facility or by special request?

- Are printed materials within easy reach from standing and sitting positions in an uncluttered area within the facility?
- Do web pages, adhere to accessibility guidelines or standards adopted by your institution (e.g., the World Wide Web Consortium's Web Content Accessibility Guidelines)?
- Are documents available in an accessible electronic format?
- Are videos used by your service captioned?
- Are procedures in place for a timely response to requests for assistive technology and remediation of inaccessible documents?

Events. Ensure that everyone can participate in on-site and online events sponsored by your organization.

- Is information about how to request disability-related accommodations included in publications and websites promoting events?
- Are on-site events located in wheelchair-accessible facilities? Is the accessible entrance clearly marked? Is accessible transportation available if transportation is arranged for other participants?
- Are online events hosted on accessible conferencing systems, and do support staff know how to present captions and arrange for other accommodations upon request?

As UDHE initiative collaborators field-tested the original checklist for any service unit, personnel on multiple campuses requested checklists that operationalize UD principles into examples of practices for specific units. Checklists available in the Center for Universal Design in Education tailored to specific services include those for

- recruitment and undergraduate admissions,
- libraries,
- registration,
- financial aid,
- advising,
- career services
- housing and residential life,
- tutoring and learning centers,
- computer labs,
- student organizations, and
- teaching and learning centers.

The most current version of the general checklist is in the online publication *Equal Access: Universal Design of Student Services*.[3] This document as well as the more specific checklists can be found on the Center for Universal Design in Education website.[4]

The experiences of participants in UDHE initiatives suggest that measurable change toward the universal design of a service often requires ongoing staff encouragement, training, support, resources, and systematic monitoring. During their many interactions on their campuses, disability service personnel may have opportunities to promote UDHE practices that could benefit more people than those who secure accommodations through their offices. For example, they could encourage the staff employment office to use application forms and processes that are accessible to anyone applying for a job, including those with disabilities. Disability service staff could encourage teaching and learning centers and organizational development units to include UDHE in their training opportunities, perhaps offering to present or copresent this specific content in a session. They could promote the procurement, development, and use of accessible technology campuswide. And, like any other service unit, they can apply UDHE strategies in delivering their offerings to ensure that all individuals feel welcome and can effectively make use of the services offered. In other words, although a typical disability services unit has as its primary function to ensure that students, faculty, staff, and campus visitors with documented disabilities receive reasonable accommodations, they can apply and promote UDHE principles as agents of change.

Did you know?

The UDHE checklists for campus services continue to be updated and maintained by the DO-IT Center. Other campuses are encouraged to use and modify them for their service units as long as the source is acknowledged.

MY GO-TO RESOURCES

Following are some good places to start in your exploration of topics covered in this chapter.

- *The Conference Room*
  uw.edu/doit/programs/accesscollege
- *Universal Design of Student Services*
  uw.edu/doit/programs/center-universal-design-education

- *Published Books and Articles About Universal Design of Services*
  uw.edu/doit/programs/center-universal-design-education/resources/published-books-and-articles-about-universal
- *Knowledge Base*
  uw.edu/doit/knowledge-base
- *Universal Design of Student Services and Physical Spaces in Higher Education*[5]
- *Beyond the Americans with Disabilities Act: Inclusive Policy and Practice for Higher Education*[6]

CONCLUSION

Campus services play important roles in promoting positive social, academic, and career outcomes for students and in helping faculty deliver more effective instruction. Promising practices for the inclusive design of on-site and online services have been developed and implemented on some campuses, but much work remains to be done before UDHE becomes common practice nationwide. In the next chapter, I will segue from applying UDHE to incorporating disability, accessibility, and UD content into the curricula of academic and professional development courses, thereby preparing future professionals to contribute to the design of a more inclusive world.

TAKE ACTION!

(REFLECT) Consider your context

Reflect on these questions:

- What message does it send to potential users of a service when the website is not accessible to them?
- What demographic groups do you find difficult to serve? What UDHE practices might benefit these individuals?
- What training opportunities relevant to improving your service or instruction do you have at your institution? What options are you given for gaining the knowledge taught? Would having more options benefit you and others? Do trainings address accessibility issues for individuals with disabilities? Why is it important to do so?

(LEARN) Identify applications of UD, UDL, and WCAG to a service

In a discussion or assignment in an academic course, ask students to share examples of UDHE practices for a campus service that apply specific principles of UD, UDL, and WCAG. Have students articulate the importance of all three sets of principles when designing a campus service.

(LEARN) Consider potential impact on disability services

Have participants in an academic or professional development course share an example of what the campus as a whole could do that would potentially reduce the accommodation needs of individuals with disabilities who wish to use campus services.

(LEARN) Brainstorm necessary collaborations

In an academic or professional development course, discuss why, compared to applying an accommodation-only approach to provide access for individuals with disabilities, the UDHE approach requires greater collaboration between campus units. Give at least one example of specific units that must work together to effectively promote the application of UDHE within campus services.

(APPLY) Universally design a campus service

In a task force or course, have participants access the checklist "Equal Access: Universal Design of Student Services" at uw.edu/doit/programs/center-universal-design-education/postsecondary/universal-design-student-services/applying. Complete it for a service unit. Eliminate checklist items that are not relevant to the service. Check off those items that are already in place. Put a date on tasks you wish to accomplish. Add other UDHE issues you would like to address. From this exercise create a planning document that lists specific tasks in order by targeted implementation date, followed by a section of completed items (for positive reinforcement as you see how far you have come). Review the document periodically, revising implementation dates and moving items from the plans section to the accomplishments section. The document could be formatted something like this:

UDHE Plans for [name of space]
    Month, year   UDHE task #1
    Month, year   UDHE task #2 . . .
UDHE Accomplishments
    UDHE task accomplishment #1
    UDHE task accomplishment #2 . . .

(APPLY) Universally design a disability services office

In an academic or professional development course, discuss how UDHE could impact the services and operation of a disability services office for students, faculty, staff, or visitors. Start by reviewing the checklist in "Equal Access: Universal

Design of Student Services" at uw.edu/doit/videos/index.php?vid=11. Analyze what makes sense, what needs editing, and what needs to be added to make it appropriate for disability services.

(APPLY) Create a UD checklist

In an academic course, have students review the checklist "Equal Access: Universal Design of Student Services" at uw.edu/doit/programs/center-universal-design-education/postsecondary/universal-design-student-services/applying. Use ideas from that publication to create an accessibility checklist related to a service of interest in the course. For example, for

- a specific student service unit on your campus in a postsecondary student services course,
- a hotel or restaurant as part of a hospitality program,
- a space selected for a project in an architectural course, or
- an informal science learning center studied in a museology program.

(APPLY) Create a checklist

In a course within a hospitality degree program, ask students to adapt checklists for campus services to address issues related to services provided by a hotel or restaurant.

CHAPTER 7

Teaching About UD

Strive for progress, not perfection.

—Unknown

SPECIAL EDUCATION, physical and occupational therapy, rehabilitation engineering, and disability studies are among academic offerings where disability-related topics are center stage. However, reports of how instructors of courses not primarily focused on disability, accessibility, and universal design (UD) integrate these topics into their curriculum illustrate their relevance to many fields of study and practice. In this chapter I share examples of how such content can be included in a variety of academic and professional development courses along with ideas for making this practice more widespread.

INTRODUCTION

Are you hesitant to teach your students about accessibility because your curriculum is already too full, you don't know much about it yourself, it is not covered in your textbook, and students don't seem to have much interest in the topic? Many faculty share these thoughts.

Would you be more motivated to find room in your curriculum for disability, accessibility, or UD topics if you learned that potential employers of graduates in your field put a high value on knowledge about accessible design in reviewing applicants and claim they cannot find enough applicants with this expertise? Are you now wondering on what planet and when this might be the case? Would you believe that in some fields it is this planet and now? Consider Teach Access, a collaboration of major universities and high-tech companies established in 2015 to address what its founders considered to be an urgent need to enhance the skills of college graduates to design mobile and desktop technologies that are "born accessible" by proliferating fundamental skills and concepts of accessible design within mainstream computer science, information technology (IT), and related fields of study. Organizations that founded Teach Access include Adobe, Facebook, Google, Hewlett-Packard, Intuit, LinkedIn, Microsoft, Verizon Media, California State University, Michigan State University, Rochester Institute of Technology, Stanford University, University of Colorado, University of Michigan, and University of Washington (UW). The continual expansion of membership in Teach Access suggests interest in this issue by both the tech sector and higher education.

Earlier chapters of this book are about the application of UD practices to myriad aspects of postsecondary institutions. This chapter addresses how we might increase the practice of UD by future professionals in a wide variety of fields by including relevant topics in curricula. By the end of this chapter, you should be able to

- describe how disability, accessibility, UD, and related topics are relevant to the content of many postsecondary academic and professional development programs;
- explain how disability, accessibility, and UD topics can enrich the curricula in a variety of courses; and
- design disability, accessibility, UD, and related content and activities that can be integrated into an existing or new course.

WHY TEACH ACCESSIBILITY AND UD?

Many innovations for individuals with disabilities have led to mainstream products widely used today, such as personal texting, speech synthesis, voice recognition, and automatic door openers. People with disabilities are not the only beneficiaries of the accessibility features of smartphones, such as changing text and background colors, adjusting brightness, magnifying screen images, adjusting text sizes, zooming in and out, and talking to a digital assistant. It's more than accessible design; it's universal design. Accessible and universal design practices in courses that cover other design approaches are a natural fit.

Some faculty members are motivated to cover such topics by emerging standards in their academic field. For example, ABET—the accreditation board for postsecondary engineering and computing programs—defines engineering design as "the process of devising a system, component, or process to meet desired needs and specifications within constraints. . . . [E]xamples of possible constraints include accessibility, aesthetics, constructability, cost, ergonomics, extensibility, functionality, interoperability, legal considerations, maintainability, manufacturability, marketability, policy, regulations, schedule, standards, sustainability, or usability."[1] In this definition the inclusion of *accessibility, ergonomics, functionality, legal considerations, standards,* and *usability* can motivate some faculty to teach inclusive design topics in their courses.

Other faculty members and administrators are motivated to include accessibility and UD topics in a field of study so that they can attract to their field individuals who are particularly interested in social impact. Still others may wish to expose students to a comprehensive set of design practices, legal mandates regarding accessibility, and ethical issues with respect to the inclusion of underrepresented and underserved populations. Including disability, accessibility, or UD topics in postsecondary programs in design fields can result in positive impacts, which include those that follow.

- Future engineers know how to create commercial products that the elderly and individuals with disabilities can use easily.
- Future webmasters will routinely employ accessible design principles and thus minimize the risk of future employers with respect to civil rights complaints regarding the inaccessibility of their public websites.
- Computer science graduates are prepared to lead the development of future accessibility guidelines and standards for IT.
- Future architects can design homes in which owners can expect to dwell as they age.
- History graduates can articulate issues regarding people with disabilities for various historical periods.
- Technology procurement officers can ensure that US federal agencies meet requirements of Section 508 of the Rehabilitation Act of 1973 to procure, develop, and use IT that is accessible to individuals with disabilities.

- Graduates of computing programs have an advantage over other applicants for positions with companies that seek to hire a workforce with expertise in accessible IT design.
- Software engineers can address accessibility issues in all products they create.
- Graduates of media design programs can help future employers comply with the 21st Century Communications and Video Accessibility Act, which requires providers of advanced communications services to include video captioning for people who are deaf, audio descriptions for individuals who are blind, and access to user guides and menus for people with a variety of disabilities.
- Future museum administrators and designers can make exhibits accessible to visitors with disabilities.
- Students who have completed communication courses will design accessible digital content for future employers.

Disability-related topics integrated into courses not specifically focused on the design of products and environments can lead to more inclusive practices in a wide variety of fields. Outcomes could include the following.

- Graduates of disability study and service courses know how to provide reasonable accommodations but are also prepared to guide others in applying inclusive practices in service and course design.
- Political science graduates understand issues of particular relevance to individuals with disabilities and other underrepresented and underserved groups.
- Graduates of rehabilitation programs who work with individuals who have physical disabilities are skilled at engaging with patients who have additional disabilities as well.
- Hospitality school graduates effectively serve customers with diverse communication methods, behaviors, and access needs.
- Counseling and social work graduates effectively communicate with clients who have disabilities.
- General education teachers fully engage students who have disabilities and are otherwise marginalized.
- International business graduates understand disability-related laws in foreign countries.
- Human resources and counseling staff effectively work with a diverse population.

Did you know?

UD is not the only design framework or approach that promotes the consideration of diverse characteristics of potential users of a product or environment. Search the internet to learn more about the meaning of barrier-free design, accessible design, inclusive design, usable design, human-centered design, ability-based design, user-centered design, user-centered inclusive design, participatory design, design for all, and design for user empowerment.

For any course, complete this sentence: If the students in this class learned about disability, accessibility, or UD, they would be better prepared to . . . For many courses, listing something of value is not difficult. Clearly, faculty and professional developers may choose to teach disability, accessibility, and UD topics in their courses for many reasons. They include reaching students with diverse career interests, responding to civil rights legislation, promoting ethical practices in support of social justice, demonstrating that inclusive design benefits everyone, complying with professional standards or legislative mandates, and responding to the demand from companies for future employees with knowledge and skills in these areas. Teaching about disability, accessibility, and UD may open career opportunities for some students and make all students better prepared for whatever field of employment they pursue.

WHO TEACHES ACCESSIBILITY AND UD?

James J. Pirkl, chair of the Department of Design at Syracuse University, began sensitizing his students to the needs of people who are elderly or who have disabilities in the mid-1970s. In 1985, he pioneered an approach called "transgenerational design," in which products and environments are designed to be compatible with the declining physical and sensory abilities associated with aging.[2] Multiple internet searches suggest to me that including disability, accessibility, or UD topics in mainstream courses is not widely practiced, but that increasing numbers of websites, publications, and conference presentations share examples of how they can be integrated into many types of academic courses and why it is important to do so. An informal review of the literature also suggests that courses that most commonly integrate these topics into their curriculum include those in computing and engineering.

A nationwide survey was recently undertaken to determine who is teaching about accessibility, what barriers faculty see to teaching accessibility, what factors predict who is teaching accessibility, and what resources are needed to encourage faculty members to teach about accessibility.[3] Twenty percent of 1,857 survey respondents reported that they taught about accessibility. The respondents who said they taught about accessibility were more likely to be female, to know someone with a disability, to think accessibility is an important part of computing fields, and to specialize in human-computer interaction. Content they teach includes understanding technology barriers, knowing about models of disability, engaging diverse populations, evaluating web accessibility standards, employing accessible design techniques, and understanding legal regulations. Some respondents considered it particularly important that students develop an awareness of access issues and solutions for IT users with disabilities through research projects that engage people with disabilities, guest speakers, field trips, simulations, and videos of individuals with disabilities interacting with technology.

Survey respondents reported that challenges to incorporating accessibility topics in their courses include that these topics are not a core part of the existing curriculum, that they don't know enough to teach about accessibility, that they cannot find an appropriate textbook covering accessibility topics, that leaders at their institution or academic field do not encourage them to teach about accessibility, and that they perceive little demand for employees with this expertise. Faculty members who responded to the survey reported that to include accessibility topics in their courses they need

- help with making connections with people who have disabilities for students to interact with one-on-one or as part of a panel or presentation in class;
- tools, technologies, guidelines, and problem examples;
- curricular samples for specific courses; and
- training and other opportunities to gain expertise.

HOW TO INTEGRATE UD TOPICS INTO COURSES

I know for sure that there is no shortage of ways for me to integrate disability, accessibility, and UD topics into academic and professional development programs in which I have taught. Many years ago I agreed to teach the introductory course in a new e-learning instructional design certificate program at the UW. One of the reasons I wanted to teach this course was to explore how I could promote the integration of UD practices into the thought patterns and workflows of future online learning designers. More recently, online courses I have taught specifically focus on UD topics—in a short course on accessible design and compliance as part of a certificate program in online learning design and in master's degree courses on applications of Universal Design in Higher Education (UDHE) to student services, physical spaces, IT, instructional practices, and physical spaces. I coteach a hybrid seminar (with both online and on-site components) about disability issues that integrates UD topics. I have also been a guest speaker in online and on-site courses and facilitated panels of people with disabilities to share their experiences related to topics covered in courses of other faculty members. In summary, both online and on-site I have (1) taught entire academic and professional development courses on UD-related issues, (2) integrated these topics within courses with a focus not specifically related to UD, (3) delivered lectures and facilitated panels of people with disabilities in courses led by other instructors, and (4) provided materials and videos in still others.

Disability, accessibility, and UD topics can be included in the curriculum of an academic program in many different ways. They include

- scheduling a specialized program that trains students to become disability-related specialists (e.g., assistive technology designers),
- teaching about accessibility as an isolated topic in a course (e.g., including a panel of students with disabilities sharing their educational experiences with students in a sociology of education course),
- integrating content throughout a course (e.g., addressing disability-related issues throughout a course on diversity),
- offering a single course focused on these topics (e.g., a UDHE course in a program focused on higher education), and
- including accessibility content throughout an entire degree program.

You can find examples of courses that integrate disability, accessibility, or UD topics throughout in the *Published Books and Articles About Teaching About Universal Design* web page referenced in the "My Go-To Resources" section at the end of this chapter. I will share two examples in which high school and college students learn about accessible web design within mainstream web design courses. Both are supported through the *AccessComputing* project at the UW, which is funded by the National Science Foundation. *AccessComputing* is a collaboration of the Disabilities, Opportunities, Internetworking, and Technology (DO-IT) Center; the Paul G. Allen School of Computer Science and Engineering; and the Information School to help students with disabilities successfully pursue computing fields and improve those fields with their experiences and expertise. We also work to increase the capacity of postsecondary institutions to fully include students with disabilities in computing, IT, and information systems (IS) programs.

One curriculum resulted when teachers from a local school district partnered with an IT accessibility specialist in DO-IT to develop a free web design curriculum that includes accessible design along with other web design practices throughout the course. This introductory course, Web Design and Development, continues to be used in high school and college courses around the world. The curriculum includes eight units that cover introductory design and site planning, HTML coding, cascading style sheets, JavaScript, graphic design, site design and management, and web authoring tools. By the end of the course, students design accessible websites for their schools or local organizations. When teachers using the curriculum were surveyed, responses to a request to "describe how disability, accessibility, and/or universal design topics were integrated into your web design or other computing courses" included inviting guest speakers (e.g., webmasters who are knowledgeable about web accessibility and legal mandates), evaluating school websites, tapping into the perspective of students with disabilities regarding accessibility barriers and potential solutions, and using disability simulations (e.g., simulating the experiences of individuals with visual differences).

DO-IT's IT accessibility staff also worked with three instructors who teach a web design course in the UW's Information School to integrate accessible design practices throughout their course. These two course examples illustrate one effective way for computing and IT instructors to efficiently integrate accessibility topics in their courses—collaborate with someone who has this expertise.

Disability awareness activities can be incorporated into almost any course. For example, you could invite a panel of individuals with disabilities to share challenges they have faced using products, engaging in environments, or navigating social structures and how their designs could be improved. To recruit panelists, compose a short recruiting email message providing information about the panel and contact information and, ideally, offer a small stipend for participation. Ask staff at your disability services office to distribute the invitation to students registered in this unit. Individual presentations, simulations, and demonstrations can help students become aware of disability-related challenges and potential solutions. Disability awareness activities can also make participants more comfortable engaging with individuals with disabilities in academic activities, research, and the workplace, as reflected in figure 7.1.

FIGURE 7.1 Disability awareness activities can promote engagement between individuals with and without disabilities in academic, research, and workplace activities

Review the "TAKE ACTION!" activities at the end of the preceding chapters in this book to stimulate ideas for integrating disability, accessibility, or UD topics into an academic or a professional development course. Clearly, disability, accessibility, and UD can enrich the curriculum of many courses and ultimately contribute to a more inclusive world through the future practices of professionals in your field.

STAKEHOLDER ROLES

Multiple stakeholders in higher education, professional organizations, and industry can promote the inclusion of UD-related topics in academic and professional development courses. For example, in job listings, companies can post required or preferred knowledge of accessibility issues and encourage faculty members to teach related topics in their courses. K–12 teachers can teach their students about UD. People with disabilities and their allies can also advocate for UD content. Technology vendors can create more accessible products. Funding agencies can require that applicants for grants develop technological innovations and pedagogical practices that are accessible, usable, and inclusive of people with disabilities. Figure 7.2 illustrates how these and other stakeholders might play roles in ensuring that students in computing and information science programs graduate with knowledge in disability, accessibility, and UD.

The role industry can play in promoting UD is illustrated in the Teach Access initiative supported by academia, industry, and people with disabilities and their allies. Useful resources provided on the Teach Access website include those related to why it is important that students study accessibility, accessibility fundamental concepts and skills, a tutorial, slides for delivering a presentation accessible design, and posters for spreading the word. Are you a member of a professional group that might want to take on the charge of promoting the teaching of disability, accessibility, or UD content in your field of study and application? If so, check out resources listed in the next section.

FIGURE 7.2 Stakeholder roles in ensuring computing/IS students are trained in accessible technology design

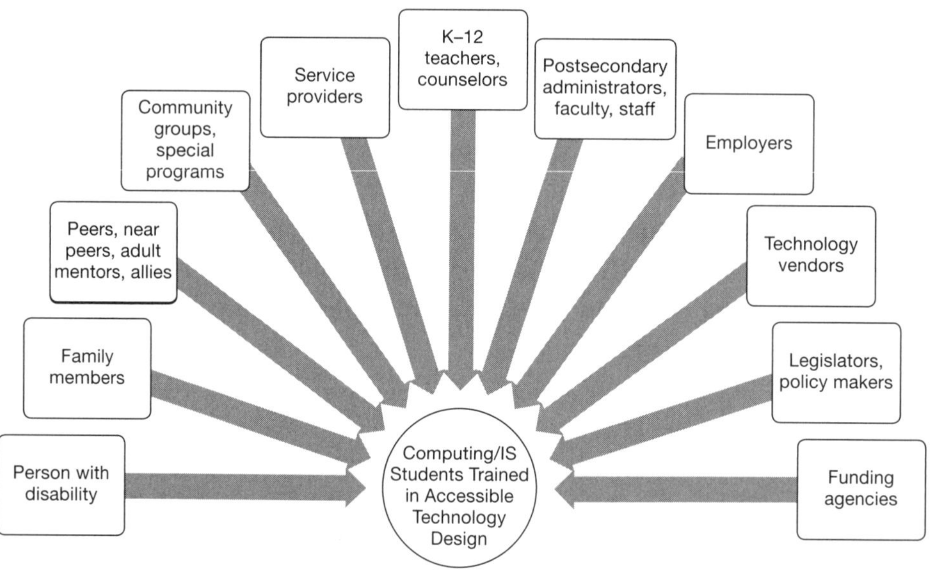

MY GO-TO RESOURCES

Following are some good places to explore how UD-related topics can be included in a course.

- *Published Books and Articles About Teaching About Universal Design*
  uw.edu/doit/programs/center-universal-design-education/resources/published-books-and-articles-about-universal
- *Knowledge Base*
  uw.edu/doit/knowledge-base
- *Web Design and Development*
  uw.edu/accesscomputing/webd2
- *Teach Access*
  teachaccess.org

CONCLUSION

This chapter should leave you with no shortage of ideas regarding how disability, accessibility, and UD content can enrich almost any course and of how multiple stakeholders can promote this practice. Beneficiaries of such practices are students who are better prepared for their careers and, ultimately, people with diverse characteristics who find themselves in a more inclusive world. In the next chapter, I propose a model underpinned by the UDHE Framework that can be fleshed out to create a road map that can contribute to developing practices that make an institution more inclusive.

TAKE ACTION!

(REFLECT) Consider your context

Reflect on these questions:

- How could disability, accessibility, or UD topics have been covered in a course you have taken or taught?
- Are disability-related topics generally covered in diversity-focused academic or professional development courses offered at your institution? Why or why not?

- In a course teaching design skills, what might be the response of students with a disabilities or their allies if practices taught result in products that are *not* accessible to people with disabilities?

(LEARN) Integrate UD topics in curriculum

In a community of practice, have participants describe an academic or professional development course they have taken, taught, or would consider taking or teaching and tell how disability, accessibility, or UD topics could be integrated into the course and how including this content would benefit students enrolled in the course.

(LEARN) Gather ideas for teaching about UD in a course

In a community of practice or academic or professional development course, have participants look through the articles presented on the *Published Books and Articles About Teaching About Universal Design* web page at uw.edu/doit/programs/center-universal-design-education/resources/published-books-and-articles-about-universal or search online for other articles on this topic. Ask participants to report answers to the following questions:

- What is the title, author, publication year, and journal/book/website in which the article was published?
- What are some ideas for teaching disability, accessibility, or UD content in a specific course that you gained by reading this article?
- How would teaching these topics benefit students as they pursue careers in the field?

(LEARN) Identify Applications of UD, UDL, and WCAG

In a discussion or assignment in an academic course, ask students to share examples of UDHE practices for an application that apply specific principles of UD, UDL, and WCAG. Have students articulate the importance of all three sets of principles in this application area.

(APPLY) Research proactive design terminology

In an academic course, have students research design approaches and frameworks that promote the consideration of diverse characteristics of potential users, compare and contrast their (sometimes multiple) meanings, and discuss which are most relevant to the course's focus. Be sure barrier-free design, accessible design, inclusive design, usable design, human-centered design, ability-based design, user-centered design, user-centered inclusive design, universal design, participatory design, design for all, and design for user empowerment are on the list.

(APPLY) Articulate benefits of learning about accessibility and UD

As an initial activity of an individual faculty member or within a group working on curriculum revisions for a department, select relevant courses, and for each, complete the following sentence: If the students in this class learned about disability, accessibility, or UD, they would be better prepared to . . .

(APPLY) identify roles for stakeholder groups

In a task force undertaking an effort to infuse disability, accessibility, and UD topics into an academic program, identify key stakeholder roles for promoting and implementing these changes.

(APPLY) Develop activities for your course

Use this book as a resource for developing disability, accessibility, and UD activities appropriate for your course. For example, chapter 1 shares suggestions for disability awareness activities that include demonstrations, simulations, and panels. TAKE ACTION! items at the end of chapters throughout the book also suggest in-course activities.

(APPLY) Conduct a survey

In an academic course, have students survey other students in their field of study about how disability, accessibility, or UD topics are or are not relevant to careers to this field or study or practice. Conduct a class discussion about their findings.

(APPLY) Universally design posters to present research

In an academic course, require that students universally design posters that present their research (e.g., use a large sans serif font, avoid color combinations that are difficult for people with color blindness to distinguish, use a plain background that has a high contrast with the text, make the organization of the content easy to follow with subheadings, be concise).

CHAPTER 8

A Model for an Inclusive Campus

The way to get started is to quit talking and begin doing.

—Walt Disney

WE HAVE EXPLORED how applying Universal Design in Higher Education (UDHE) can contribute to making physical spaces, technology, teaching and learning activities, and services more accessible, usable, and inclusive. My UDHE Framework can be used to create a toolkit for applying UDHE in each of these areas or to the campus as a whole. So you have a toolkit, but for systemic change, you need more than a toolkit—you need a road map. In this chapter we take the next step, the creation of a step-by-step Inclusive Campus Model, underpinned by the UDHE Framework, and begin to flesh it out into a road map for any institution seeking a paradigm shift toward a more inclusive campus.

INTRODUCTION

Many years ago I played a small part in a much larger effort to make a paradigm shift toward a more welcoming climate for female students at the University of Washington (UW). I was on what was affectionately called the "potty parity committee," charged with investigating complaints that the Business School, College of Engineering, Department of Computing Science, and some other academic units traditionally dominated by men had more available locations for men than for women to do you-know-what. In information technology (IT) management at the time, let's just say I had the ladies room all to myself! Some argued that there were simply more men in those locations, so the distribution of these facilities made sense. But for those who wanted to be more proactive on many fronts, it was a chicken-and-egg situation: to shift toward increased engagement of women in these fields, we needed to make them more welcoming to women in large *and small* ways. I imagine that the vast majority of people on campus today expect potty parity in the design of new buildings and probably don't give this issue much thought. I am proud to have contributed to this paradigm shift at the UW!

There are likely efforts on your campus that promote a paradigm shift toward more inclusive practices with respect to gender, race, and ethnicity. Consider integrating them with UDHE strategies presented in this book. An outcome will be a change in the way the school addresses the needs of individuals with disabilities—from primarily a reactive accommodations approach to a proactive approach where UDHE practices are employed, while still being responsive in providing accommodations for individuals with disabilities.

By the end of this chapter, you will be able to

- describe indicators of a paradigm shift toward a more inclusive campus,
- list key steps in the Inclusive Campus Model and how they can contribute toward making a campus more inclusive,
- list stakeholders and their potential roles in promoting UDHE practices campuswide,
- give examples of promoters and inhibitors with respect to the institutionalization of UDHE, and
- apply promising practices for institutionalizing UDHE practices.

A UNIVERSALLY DESIGNED CAMPUS

As TV's Dr. Phil says, "The best predictor of future behavior is past behavior." Changing habitual behavior is difficult even if institutional change to more inclusive design practices may make sense to many people. Without such changes, UDHE will join many other good ideas that are largely unimplemented. It is encouraging to remember that many people in the 1970s thought this would be the case with sidewalk curb cuts, which are arguably the most successful widespread application of UD. Today including curb cuts is an accepted and expected practice for everyone who installs sidewalks anywhere. Think of them as a readily available reminder that infusing a UDHE mindset campuswide just might be possible.

Let's consider what behaviors might indicate that a campus has made a paradigm shift—when the collection of values or the dominant system of thought changes—from an accommodations approach to the UDHE Framework for dealing with access issues. What might be the first response of a professor when a student who is quadriplegic enrolls in her mechanical engineering class on your campus? Would she look forward to the unique perspective this student brings to her field? Would she be eager to observe how well he maneuvers his wheelchair in her lab and accesses online content using assistive technology and then solicit suggestions from him for improving the design of on-site and online components of her course? Would she hope that working with this student might reinforce for her and her students how important it is for mechanical engineers to consider accessibility barriers and employ accessible design practices in all of their research and practice? Would the tone and content of her communication with this student make it clear that he is welcome? I would say that if most faculty on a campus answered "yes" to questions like these, the paradigm embraced on that campus has high values with respect to diversity, equity, and inclusiveness, which are characteristics of a UDHE approach.

What are other indicators of a universally designed campus, especially with respect to students with disabilities? This question was tackled by disability leaders from postsecondary institutions who participated in one of the UDHE initiatives hosted by the Disabilities, Opportunities, Internetworking, and Technology (DO-IT) Center at the UW. They engaged in an iterative process to develop a short list of campus accessibility indicators that together describe high-level practices of an institution that fully includes people with disabilities. Table 8.1 shares what they came up with.[1]

These indicators provide a starting point as campus leaders identify high-level issues for developing an institution that is more inclusive of individuals with disabilities and other underrepresented and underserved groups.

STAKEHOLDER ROLES

Think about the many stakeholders that can contribute to the design of more inclusive campuses in our country. Following is the beginning of a list of those

TABLE 8.1 Campus accessibility indicators

Campus conversations
■ The campus-level mission statement is inclusive of everyone, including people with disabilities. ■ Disability is included in discussions of diversity and special populations on campus.
Administrative empowerments
■ Policies, procedures, and practices are regularly reviewed for barrier removal and inclusivity. ■ Administrators, staff, faculty, and student leaders are trained, encouraged, and empowered to take action around universal design issues. ■ People with a wide variety of identities, including disabilities, are visible on campus, including in positions of power and authority.
Infusion of UD for all campus offerings
■ Budgeting reflects the reality of the cost of universal design and of accommodating current and prospective employees, students, and visitors with disabilities. ■ Measures of student success are the same for all student populations; institutional data collection and research include data on all groups, including students with disabilities. ■ Campus marketing and publications are accessibly designed and include images of individuals with diverse characteristics, including disabilities. ■ Campus websites, videos, and documents, including those in online courses, meet established accessibility standards. ■ Disability access issues are addressed in curricula, and relevant universal/inclusive design content is included in courses. ■ All campus facilities are universally designed.

who can contribute and what they can do. You can likely think of other stakeholders to add to the list.

Industry

Industry can promote UD in a variety of ways. Companies can hire a diverse workforce, engage consumers with a wide range of abilities and perspectives in product design and usability testing, make accessibility features readily apparent and promote them in advertising, and tell marketing staff and sales representatives to share universally designed product features with potential customers. Publishers can design textbooks and online learning materials that are fully accessible to students and instructors with disabilities or make them available in alternate, accessible formats.

Professional Organizations

Professional organizations can further the cause by publishing UDHE articles in their journals, making their meetings and websites accessible to all potential participants, offering presentations and exhibits on UDHE topics at conferences, encouraging members to adopt UDHE practices, and promoting the inclusion of UD topics within academic courses at all levels. Professional organizations can also promote consideration of the needs of students with diverse characteristics in the evaluation of educational entities overall and of specific fields of study and practice.

Consumers

Consumers of higher education offerings can affect the adoption of UDHE through advocacy groups and individual input to various campus units. Students with disabilities who advocate for accommodations as they need them could become UD advocates by also providing suggestions to the institution for how more inclusive practices could reduce the need for these accommodations and benefit many other students in the future. For example, students who cannot access the content of a video in a course because it is not captioned could get their accommodation needs addressed and also advocate for the routine captioning of videos campuswide. Individuals with disabilities can further the adoption of UDHE by learning about access issues and solutions for their peers with different types of disabilities, as is done in the DO-IT Scholars program. This knowledge could lead to advocacy that goes beyond the specific needs of individuals with disabilities like their own. Similar efforts can make a more welcoming campus for other underrepresented groups as well.

Government

To promote UDHE, government agencies can fund projects to apply UDHE, disseminate information about UDHE, develop and enforce legislation and standards, and use accessible products and processes in their own agencies. For example, governments could provide tax breaks to encourage companies to develop universally designed products and make accessible products more affordable. As an example of one federal effort to promote UDHE, the Office of Postsecondary Education of the US Department of Education provided funding for more than ten years to support successful postsecondary outcomes for students with disabilities, primarily through the professional development of faculty and administrators. These funds supported several of DO-IT's UDHE initiatives that led to the creation and support of the Center for Universal Design in Education, which shares information and resources about applications of UD to instruction, services, technology, and physical spaces.[2]

Institutions of Higher Education

To achieve a paradigm shift to a UDHE approach requires that campus leadership and individual units embrace the idea that addressing disability-related issues is not the exclusive territory of personnel assigned to services for people with disabilities. Administrators can promote the adoption of UDHE practices by setting up a new unit to take on leadership in this area or redefining the role of an existing unit to include assisting faculty and staff in applying UDHE in their respective areas of responsibility. I was recently encouraged by a campus that is beginning this transformation by changing the name of an office to Student Accessibility and Accommodation to reflect its proactive and reactive roles, respectively. Efforts should be made to engage units throughout the institution (e.g., faculty, physical plant, libraries, centers for teaching and learning, student services, IT units). Potential efforts include disseminating UDHE guidelines customized to specific audiences (e.g., webmasters, administrators, faculty), publishing articles on UD in campus periodicals, and delivering presentations on UDHE. All stakeholders should have access to training that is tailored to their specific application areas. Specifically, campus leadership could, perhaps with incentives, encourage faculty to design their courses to be more accessible and to voice accessibility concerns to textbook publishers, use accessible technologies, employ inclusive teaching practices, and teach UD content in their courses. Administrators can also adopt procurement policies that promote the purchase of universally designed products.

When I deliver presentations, I often use an engagement activity that reinforces the idea that a paradigm shift from an accommodations approach to the UDHE Framework for dealing with access issues requires change at both individual and institutional levels. In this activity, I give participants two sticky notes that are different with respect to color, shape, and size. I ask participants to write on the sticky notes:

YELLOW rectangle: Things you will do to make your course, service, facility, technology, or resource more inclusive.
PINK square: Things administrators should do to make the institution more inclusive.

At the end of the presentation, participants attach their sticky notes to walls beside the exit doors. They can also send their responses via email. I point out that the exercise itself provides two examples of universal design practices: the two sticky notes are different with respect to shape and size to ensure everyone can distinguish between them, and participants are given the option to send responses via email in case the sticky note activity does not work for them. When the session is over, the hosting school collects the sticky notes into two piles and creates bulleted lists to share with attendees and decision makers to guide next steps for individuals and the institution. I like using the larger rectangular sticky notes for recording what they can *personally* do to apply the UDHE Framework in their areas of practice and influence to reinforce the point that, although institutional change is desirable, no one needs to wait for that to happen to apply UDHE principles right now no matter where they are on the org chart.

Depending on their positions, people can work top-down, bottom-up, or middle-out; efforts at all levels are important. What I know for sure is everyone can have a role in making a campus better if they choose to and don't worry about who gets the credit. "Lead, follow, or get out of the way!" Each role is important. You can stay in your own lane and still have an impact beyond it. I know for sure that I can be most productive when I focus on what I can accomplish in *my* role, but from my position I can still be a cheerleader for inclusive practices campuswide. I avoid being the lone ranger in my work. I find allies (or coconspirators?), and we work together. In the words of Robert Fulghum in one of my favorite books, *All I Really Need to Know I Learned in Kindergarten*, "When you go out into the world, watch out for traffic, hold hands, and stick together."[3]

Researchers

Efforts to get UDHE on the research agendas of disciplines such as technical communications, computer and information sciences, education, engineering, communications, and user interface design can contribute to its adoption in higher education. Researchers can examine the impact, efficacy, and cost of UDHE. There is also a need to further develop and validate guidelines and checklists to measure levels of application of UDHE to specific products and environments and to share best practices. Dissemination of research results tailored to specific audiences can encourage effective applications of UDHE. Industry and consumers can participate in the research agenda with the goal of creating more economically viable and inclusive products and environments in higher education.

A specific example of how researchers can work toward positive change is the work of a collaborative group in DO-IT's *AccessCyberlearning* initiative. Multiple projects funded by the National Science Foundation (NSF) have served to improve access to future digital learning opportunities—called cyberlearning by NSF—for students with disabilities. Project partners came to the conclusion that current cyberlearning research is leading to many engaging technologies with potential to *reduce* barriers to students with disabilities but, instead, are creating many more. Participants considered whether new design principles are needed but concluded that the issue is less about new principles and more about ensuring that the technologies of the future apply today's principles and best practices in mind. To promote changes in cyberlearning research practices, project partners created recommendations for researchers as they develop new technologies and pedagogy for learning experiences that employ IT. Here, the recommendations are organized into two groups: actions that should be taken immediately and those that will require more time to implement.

Recommendations for immediate actions. Immediately, cyberlearning researchers should:

- become familiar with the UD, UDL [Universal Design for learning], and WCAG [Web Content Accessibility Guidelines] principles and established guidelines and practices they support as they apply to the design of inclusive cyberlearning tools and pedagogy;
- explore how cyberlearning practices supported by the science of learning can be overlaid with UD, UDL, and WCAG principles to make them inclusive of individuals with disabilities;
- invite someone with IT accessibility knowledge to be a member of their research teams;
- ensure project staff are trained on basic accessibility principles and standards-compliant coding practices;
- establish internal policies and guidelines for accessibility within their projects, and, if relevant, their departments or institution;
- consider a broad range of learning styles and disability types during the earliest phases of conceiving and designing a project;
- analyze the experiences of participants with different types of disabilities along with other demographic groups when reporting research results; and
- when reporting limitations of their studies, include accessibility limitations.

Recommendations for future actions. In the future—both in near-term (i.e., 1–3 years) and longer term (3–5 years) time frames—cyberlearning researchers should develop and promote practices related to the following suggestions that fully embrace disability-related considerations into their research workflows. They should:

- implement an agile, iterative design process that involves users with a wide variety of disabilities and other human characteristics in all phases of the research and design process;

- actively participate in collaboration and communication among academia and industry on issues pertaining to the accessible design of cyberlearning;
- contribute to the development and sharing of guidelines for accessible design of cyberlearning tools and pedagogy;
- avoid being deterred by cost. Low-cost interventions can provide great benefits to users. On the other hand, early designs of innovative technologies may be quite expensive, but long term, if widely adopted and/or if adjustments are made to the design, the cost per user can drop significantly;
- articulate the broad characteristics of potential users in the design of a tool or pedagogy being developed or studied, and specify how the characteristics of various groups of individuals with disabilities will be addressed in the research design;
- resist generalizing all people who share a specific disability when designing technology to improve access for a population—for example, designing something to improve access for people who are blind should consider that not all people who identify as "blind" have the same vision capabilities or personal preferences for learning. Technology design should allow the user to customize their experience;
- if instructor guidelines will be created as part of the study, share information about accessibility issues for students with disabilities, including how some activities/products developed in the project may not be accessible to certain groups (e.g., students who are blind) along with suggested accommodations that might be provided (e.g., working with a sighted person); and
- integrate accessibility recommendations into existing project management practices to keep them on the forefront, rather than being an afterthought. Doing so will allow accessibility to be addressed as an integrated part of the project.[4]

AN INCLUSIVE CAMPUS MODEL UNDERPINNED BY THE UDHE FRAMEWORK

Previously we fleshed out the UDHE Framework to create a toolkit for applying UDHE practices to physical spaces, technology, instruction, and services. But, by itself, a toolkit does not provide a road map for managing change toward a more inclusive campus. The model for implementation presented in this chapter resulted from undertaking an exercise similar to that commonly used in grant writing—the development of a "logic model." A logic model is a graphic depiction that presents relationships between vision, goals, objectives, activities, outputs, outcomes, and impacts, and other relevant aspects of a project or initiative. Using this approach, I created the Inclusive Campus Model, underpinned by the UDHE Framework, to guide UDHE efforts in all offerings of a campus, in an academic department or other campus unit, or in a particular application such as online learning. The model is illustrated in figure 8.1 and described in the subsections that follow.

Vision and Values

In applying the Inclusive Campus Model, a leadership team that includes multiple stakeholder groups could begin by viewing existing institutional vision and value statements to determine whether they reflect values such as diversity, equity, inclusion, and compliance or if they should work through appropriate channels to adjust them to do so. Where will you likely find vision and value statements? Begin with the president's office and other high-level offices on your campus.

Framework

The framework for UDHE begins with the scope which, for applications covered in this book, is all products and environments that support teaching and learning. The definition is a modification of the UD definition established by the Center for Universal Design: the design of products and environments *that support postsecondary teaching and learning* to be usable by all people, to the greatest extent possible, without the need for adaptation or specialized design. The principles in the model are the UDHE principles, a combination of the seven principles of UD, the three principles of Universal Design for Learning (UDL), and the four principles that support the Web Content Accessibility Guidelines (WCAG). Guidelines apply UDHE principles to each application area along with best practices in the field. Exemplary practices for each application area build on the UD, UDL, and WCAG guidelines. The process is to identify best practices in the field, consider the diverse characteristics of potential users,

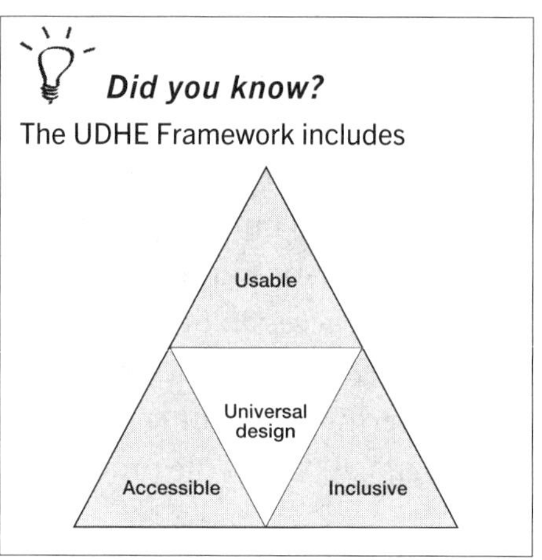

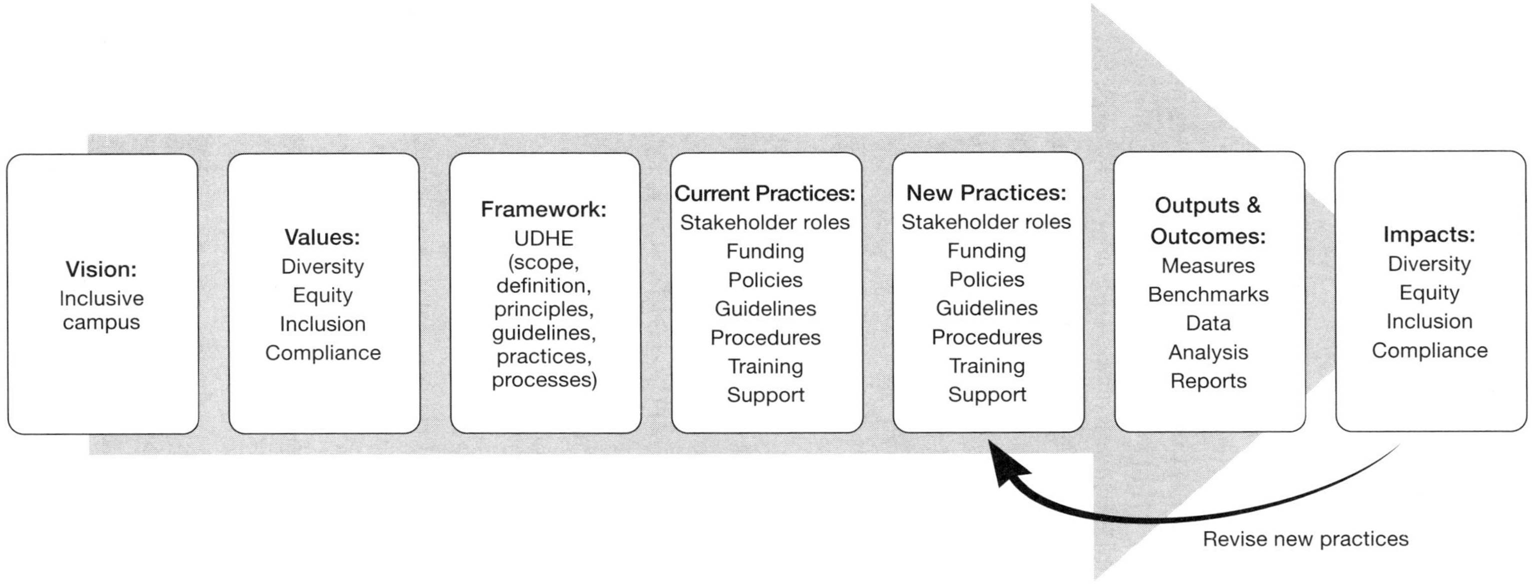

FIGURE 8.1 Inclusive Campus Model built upon the UDHE Framework

integrate UDHE practices with the best practices, plan for accommodations, and evaluate. Flesh out the framework with content related to your school and application area on your campus.

Current Practices and New Practices

The next two steps in applying the Inclusive Campus Model are for leaders to identify current practices—e.g., stakeholder roles, funding, policies, guidelines, procedures, training, support—and then redesign old practices and create new ones that are consistent with the UDHE Framework. Detailing these steps in the model will likely take a significant amount of focused effort from multiple stakeholder groups. One approach is to identify key campus units and create a task force for each unit that could flesh out the current and new practice sections of the Inclusive Campus Model for that unit, summarizing their work in a spreadsheet listing the current and evolving practices along with timelines and implementation progress. These task forces could meet periodically to learn from each other and join together as similar human resource, professional development, and other needs are identified.

Outputs and Outcomes

Before new practices are implemented, it is good for leaders to agree on measures of success. Once the measures are articulated, plans can be made for the collection of data, production of reports, and analysis of results with respect to outputs (e.g., numbers of people trained, specific web resources created) and outcomes (e.g., what participants in training sessions learned and how they planned to or actually applied it).

Impacts

From all the output and outcome data collected, UDHE leaders can assess impact with respect to established campus and unit visions and values. Leaders implementing the model can ensure continuous improvements with the initiative by fine-tuning practices based on their measures of outputs, outcomes, and impact, and then repeating the outputs, outcomes, and impact steps in an iterative process.

Applying and Adapting the Inclusive Campus Model

The logic of this approach is revealed in the following short description of the efforts of a fictitious institution—FirstRateUniversity—that applies the Inclusive Campus Model.

> Our FirstRateUniversity's vision of an inclusive campus culture reflects our values that include diversity, equity, inclusion, as well as compliance with all relevant legislation and policies. Underpinning our model for change is the UDHE Framework, which we fleshed out into a toolkit tailored to our campus; we assigned stakeholder roles; secured funding; developed policies, guidelines, and procedures; engaged in training tailored to stakeholder groups; created resources; and made structural changes. Throughout these activities, we updated old practices and created new ones that more closely align with our vision, values, and the UDHE Framework. We regularly measure outputs, outcomes, and impacts from these efforts and, from lessons learned, revise our practices to ensure continual project improvements. There is clear evidence that our efforts are gradually leading to a paradigm shift toward a more inclusive campus that better reflects our vision and values.

To apply the Inclusive Campus Model or similar model tailored to your campus, create a working document and begin to flesh out key components of your model by answering the following questions.

- *Vision*: What is our vision for an inclusive campus?
- *Values*: What campus values (e.g., diversity, equity, inclusion, compliance) are most relevant to making our campus more inclusive?
- *Framework*: What framework (e.g., the UDHE Framework along with principles, guidelines, practices, and processes) reflects our vision and values and can be fleshed out to help us work toward making our campus more inclusive?
- *Current Practices*: What are our current practices with respect to stakeholder roles, funding, policies, guidelines, procedures, training, support, and other relevant issues?
- *New Practices*: What existing practices should we modify and which new practices should we develop to be more consistent with our vision, values, and framework?
- *Outputs and Outcomes*: What measures should be identified, what benchmarks should be set, what data should be collected and analyzed, and what reports should be made?
- *Impact*: What evidence suggests a positive impact of our efforts with respect to a more inclusive campus that better reflects our campus vision and values?

Aspects of the Inclusive Campus Model can be fleshed out with practices promoted by business leaders. There is no shortage of books on change management. For example, John P. Kotter, in his international best seller *Leading Change*, suggests eight key practices to include in the change process.[5] Each of these practices can be integrated in the Inclusive Campus Model for promoting the procurement, development, and use of accessible IT, as suggested in table 8.2.

The Inclusive Campus Model can be easily adapted to focus on a specific application of UDHE. For example, you can modify the Inclusive Campus Model to apply to online learning, student services, or IT. In the next section I share how I adapted the model on our campus to guide efforts with respect to the procurement, development, and use of accessible IT, including its many applications for offering instruction, services, and resources.

CASE STUDY: APPLICATION OF THE INCLUSIVE CAMPUS MODEL TO IT

The UW strives to ensure that people with disabilities have access to the same opportunities that are available to people without disabilities, including those offered through the use of IT. My unit, Accessible Technology Services (ATS), promotes the accessibility of IT products (e.g., websites, documents, videos, application software) and environments (e.g., library spaces for student computer use) that benefit everyone in our campus community. As our practices continue to evolve over time, elements of the Inclusive Campus Model have been applied to develop processes for making it a common practice to develop, procure, and use accessible IT. So how is this approach working for us? I am not alone in feeling generally satisfied with our basic approaches, the leadership groups and support systems we have put in place, and the choices we have made in using funds allocated to us, but we have not secured all of the online tools and personnel we need to accomplish all of the tasks ATS staff consider necessary for a paradigm shift to a UDHE way of thinking with respect to IT. Sound familiar?

For schools that are just starting the promotion of accessible IT, I always recommend settling on a vision followed by continually working on policies, procedures, organizational structures, a framework, and a road map. Promote the development of a campuswide policy regarding accessible IT, but don't stubbornly choose that as a hill to die on; without a formal policy, build a foundation for your case for IT accessibility on Section 504 and the ADA. There is no reason to wait until a policy and high-level support are in place to begin addressing priority issues and develop online resources. If you are in

TABLE 8.2 The integration of UDHE with a change process

Steps in Kotter's change process	*Example of how change steps might be integrated into the inclusive campus model*
Establish a sense of urgency.	How about to avoid joining the growing group of hundreds of postsecondary institutions that have had to resolve expensive civil rights complaints about the inaccessibility of their IT, online learning courses, or other offerings?
Create the guiding coalition.	How about setting up a task force sponsored by high-level administrators and charged with taking actions regarding the institutionalization of UDHE practices as well as making recommendations to its sponsors?
Develop a vision and strategy.	Determine your goal, objectives, and steps for reaching them.
Communicate the change vision.	Use websites, newsletter articles, and other media to share your motivations, plans, and progress.
Empower employees for broad-based action.	How about establishing a UDHE liaisons or advocates group to continually increase in skills and take actions within their areas of influence?
Generate short-term wins.	Keep track of accomplishments and share them in reports, newsletters, and on a campus website.
Consolidate gains and produce more change.	Evaluate progress and develop plans for the future that build on your success.
Anchor new approaches in the culture.	Tie actions to your campus vision and values.

this situation, consider hiring a person or reassigning an existing staff member to gain expertise and begin working on improving the accessibility of high-impact documents, websites, and videos. As far as an organizational structure and services, look at how other issues related to IT are addressed on your campus; we pattern our approach after how the UW handles security issues with respect to IT.

History

When I came to the UW in 1984, I considered ensuring access to technology for individuals with disabilities just a part of the mission of the Microcomputer Support Group I was hired to lead—to serve *all* students, faculty, and staff. As far as specific mandates to justify efforts in this regard, I pointed to our legal obligation to comply with Section 504 of the Rehabilitation Act of 1973 and, later, the Americans with Disabilities Act of 1990. Without specific funding for IT accessibility efforts, I simply built into the job description for the next general consultant within my group the requirement that the person hired would be responsible for assisting with efforts to ensure that faculty, staff, and students with disabilities had access to IT. I did not require experience in this area because I assumed we would not be able to find someone with it, and that was the case when I reviewed our pool of applicants. The person I hired was eager to learn, so we were able to begin to integrate this focus within our consulting group. For details about our long journey in promoting access to technology for individuals with disabilities, consult our IT Accessibility website listed in the "My Go-To Resources" section at the end of this chapter and select "Progress and Plans."

Fast forward to today. As the director of ATS, I lead two teams within the central IT organization known as UW-IT: the DO-IT Team, which includes the DO-IT Center, and the IT Accessibility Team (ITAT), which includes the Access Technology Center. As part of my role with ITAT, I am the campus IT Accessibility Coordinator, which includes leadership of campuswide IT accessibility efforts toward meeting federal, state, and UW mandates. The ITAT unit is charged with undertaking IT accessibility efforts in promoting and supporting the proactive design of videos, documents, websites, software, and other IT to improve access to computing resources and to minimize the need for accommodations with respect to IT. The ITAT works closely with other units on campus, in particular those responsible for providing accommodations to students, faculty, and staff with disabilities.

Policy and Resources

Formal IT accessibility policy at the UW came into being in 2016 when the state of Washington published Policy #188 on IT accessibility for which the UW is a covered entity. We share the following aspirational statement on our website:

> The University of Washington (UW) strives to ensure that people with disabilities have access to the same services and content that are available to people without disabilities, including services and content made available through the use of information technology (IT). IT procured, developed, maintained, and used by the UW should provide substantially similar functionality, experience, and information access to individuals with disabilities as it provides to others. Examples of IT covered by this policy include web sites, software systems, electronic documents, videos, and electronic equipment such as information kiosks, telephones, and digital signs.
>
> Our efforts in this regard align with:
>
> - the UW's vision to educate a diverse student body and its values of diversity, excellence, collaboration, innovation and respect.

- Section 504 of the Rehabilitation Act of 1973 and the Americans with Disability Act of 1990 together with its 2008 Amendments.
- Washington State Policy #188—Accessibility.
- UW Executive Order 31—Nondiscrimination and Affirmative Action and UW Administrative Policy Statement 2.3—Information Technology, Telecommunications and Networking Projects and Acquisitions.

Over time we expanded resources to help individuals and units understand and meet their obligations. The UW's Accessible Technology website includes topics that are described here.

- UW Policy to procure, develop, and use accessible IT.
- IT Accessibility Guidelines, with our purpose, definition, scope, standards, progress and plans, and resources.
- An IT Accessibility Checklist and Tutorial to guide webmasters at the UW and IT companies who wish to sell IT products or services to the UW.
- IT Accessibility Leadership, which shares our organizational structure.
- Progress and Plan, which documents both work done and work planned.
- Getting Started, with suggested first steps.
- Specific sections with guidelines and practices for the design of documents, videos, websites, and online courses.
- Procuring IT, with guidelines for purchasing IT projects and services that are accessible to individuals with disabilities.
- Managing for Accessibility, with guidance for academic departments and other campus units.
- Getting Help, with descriptions of resources related to disability and IT.
- Events and Collaboration, for ways to get engaged now.
- Laws, Policies and Standards, with a summary of legislative mandates and what can be learned from resolutions of postsecondary campuses with the federal government with respect to civil rights complaints about the inaccessibility of their IT.
- Accessible Technology Blog, with articles about campus efforts and how faculty, students, and staff can engage in them.

Our website content makes it clear that everyone shares responsibility for IT accessibility at the UW. In other words, it is the responsibility of the person who creates websites, videos, or electronic documents to do so in an accessible manner. Likewise, those who purchase technology that others will use should ensure that they address accessibility issues in their procurement process. This view is consistent with how IT security is handled: there are central resources with in-depth expertise and responsibility regarding the security of our IT, but even end users know they should not post a list of their passwords on their computer monitor or share them with their kids.

The definition we use for what it means for IT to be accessible can be found in resolution agreements between postsecondary institutions and the federal government regarding civil rights complaints about the inaccessibility of their IT.

> "Accessible" means a person with a disability is "afforded the opportunity to acquire the same information, engage in the same interactions, and enjoy the same services as a person without a disability in an equally effective and equally integrated manner, with substantially equivalent ease of use. The person with a disability must be able to obtain the information as fully, equally, and independently as a person without a disability."[6]

The standard we adopted for IT accessibility is stated in Policy #188, which is, at the time this book was published, WCAG 2.1 Level II, which is consistent with most other institutions of higher education that have standards in the United States. Besides looking to WCAG for guidance, when we work with campus units on the accessibility of spaces that include IT, we embrace the seven principles of UD and the three principles for the Universal Design for Learning when IT is used to deliver learning activities (e.g., in online academic or professional development courses).

Leadership

As the campus IT Accessibility Coordinator, I lead the IT Accessibility Task Force. The task force, founded in 2012, is charged by the UW Vice President and Chief Information Officer and the Vice President, Office of External Affairs, to develop and implement plans for promoting IT accessibility and establishing best practices campuswide. Its members

- take steps toward the procurement, development, and use of accessible websites, documents, videos, commercial software, and other IT and institutionalize cooperative relationships between key stakeholder groups at the UW;
- develop strategies that can be applied campuswide, such as accessibility audits and the availability of training and IT accessibility tools; and
- recommend steps toward a more comprehensive and coordinated campuswide effort in promoting the development, procurement, and use of accessible IT.

The task force submits annual reports of progress, future plans, and recommendations to our sponsors. The current members represent campus units that include University Marketing and Communications, UW-IT, Disability Resources Office of Human Resources, Disability Resources for Students of Student Services, Compliance Services, UW Procurement Services, Center for Teaching and Learning, Faculty, Continuum College, UW Libraries, UW Tacoma branch campus, and UW Bothell branch campus.

The ITAT manages the Access Technology Center, which includes a showroom of AT for consultation and testing. Most of the work of the ITAT, however, centers around promoting and supporting the proactive design and remediation of videos, documents, websites, commercial software, and other IT. ITAT productivity is enhanced through its leadership of more than one hundred IT accessibility liaisons. These individuals represent work units, large and small, in a tri-campus movement to promote the procurement, development, and use of accessible IT. The liaisons

- communicate via an online discussion list and also meet as a group one morning, three times per year;
- continue to learn about how IT used on campus can be made more accessible; and
- collect information from and spread the word within their units about federal mandates and state-level accessibility policy and otherwise promote IT accessibility.

Did you know?

People often ask me what role paid outside services play in our accessible IT efforts at the UW. We purchase accessibility testing and document remediation tools and developed a contract for a discounted rate for captioning videos campuswide. In the rare circumstances when we use outside consultants, we make sure their contribution results in measurable positive outcomes. For example, we would not hire a consultant to just tell us about the inaccessible IT on our campus (we already know), though we have used consultants as part of pilot projects where we work with a large campus unit to develop workflows for creating accessible documents and train their staff. We employ outside consultants to remediate existing inaccessible documents the unit considers important to include on their website. Using consultants in this way gives them a positive boost toward the goal of document accessibility and allows them to focus their efforts on changes to workflows for future documents. By reducing the burden of routine work, consultants in this role make it possible for my staff to focus on systemic change.

Practices

Our specific practices and priorities are informed by the agreements some campuses have reached with the Office of Civil Rights and the Department of Justice to resolve complaints about inaccessible IT on their campuses and the related EDUCAUSE document of risk statements. ATS services include training, consulting, funding for captioning high-impact videos, assisting in procuring accessible IT, and maintaining the website on accessible IT. We identify groups for whom to provide enhanced support (e.g., for remediating PDFs and captioning videos).We use electronic tools to check our progress in high-impact areas such as public-facing videos, websites, and PDFs. Although these efforts have resulted in more inclusive IT, the most expensive accommodations provided by our disability services offices with respect to IT continue to be remediating inaccessible PDFs and captioning videos. Our goal continues to be that these accommodations will someday no longer be required because our websites, documents, and videos are all universally designed. I am not concerned about having to make a career change after reaching this goal anytime soon, but we always know where we are headed.

PROMOTERS AND INHIBITORS OF CHANGE

It is good to periodically reflect on the importance of engaging multiple stakeholders and identifying their unique roles in moving inclusive design from the back to the front burner campuswide. A common inhibitor to the acceptance of UDHE is adherence to "the way we have always done things" (e.g., reactively providing accommodations for students with disabilities rather than employing proactive measures). More than once I have encountered resistance to a change on my campus that seems perfectly logical to me. I apply the ADKAR model for promoting and sustaining change to avoid roadblocks to making change. The four steps in implementing the ADKAR model are as follows.[7]

- ***A**wareness of the need to change.* Help stakeholders understand why changes toward a more inclusive campus are needed.
- ***D**esire to participate and support change.* Motivate stakeholders to promote and apply UDHE through training, events, encouragement, examples, and positive results.
- ***K**nowledge of how to change.* Share strategies for implementing UDHE in specific areas (e.g., to instruction, recreational facilities).
- ***A**bility to implement the change on a day-to-day basis.* Provide engagement, resources, and professional development to support stakeholders as they create change in their respective areas.

- *Reinforcement to keep the change in place.* Engage with stakeholders to sustain change efforts.

These steps have been helpful to me as I promote accessible IT design on campuses and work with others who do the same at their institutions. Through all of these steps, it is important to tailor change strategies according to the culture of the institution and to the priorities of leadership and other stakeholders. Here are examples of some of the problems I have observed on our campus and others when encouraging webmasters to integrate accessible design into their work flows.

- *Awareness of the need to change.* Webmasters may not understand why changes are needed (e.g., compliance with legal mandates, reduction of accommodation needs, responsiveness to student demographic changes).
- *Desire to participate and support change.* Webmasters may not be motivated because they do not understand what needs to be done and are not encouraged by their superiors to change their practices toward inclusive design.
- *Knowledge of how to change.* Webmasters may not know about guidelines (e.g., WCAG), tools, and specific strategies for designing accessible websites.
- *Ability to implement the change on a day-to-day basis.* Adequate training, resources, and staff time may not be provided by the unit or institution to prepare them to deploy accessible websites.
- *Reinforcement to keep the change in place.* Engagement of webmasters is not adequate for sustaining efforts toward more accessible websites.

It may be helpful to consider specific factors that might inhibit or promote change toward widespread application of UDHE on a specific campus. They may include vision, championship, legislation and litigation, awareness, attitudes, diversity efforts, equity, time and cost, and research. Each area is discussed next.[8]

Vision

Lack of a shared vision, or the presence of a shared vision that embraces an accommodations-only approach to access for people with disabilities, can interfere with widespread implementation of UDHE. Taking steps to promote a shared vision that values diversity, equity, and inclusion and embraces the social model of disability can further UDHE practices. Encourage all stakeholders to celebrate all types of diversity and take steps to ensure that all academic products and environments are usable by everyone, to the greatest extent possible or reasonable, without the need for adaptation or specialized design so individuals with diverse characteristics can experience the campus fully through the same venues, with little need for special accommodations.

Championship

Championship is often identified as an important predictor of change. Champions for UDHE campuswide and for specific applications can come from many areas of a campus, such as the disability services office, faculty, IT services, student services, facilities, and student groups. Without champions, it is difficult for an idea like UDHE to spread. It is particularly helpful when champions who influence key areas of application in the institution emerge. For example, when a teaching and learning center champions UDHE as an approach to help faculty address diversity within their classes, there is a potential to reach faculty members campuswide. A person well placed in IT leadership can also make a big impact with respect to the application of UDHE. UDHE champions can maximize their impact by banding together through task forces, standing committees, advisory groups, and focused gatherings.

Legislation and Litigation

Campuses that ignore their responsibilities specified by civil rights legislation impede the widespread application of UDHE. The practice of UDHE is also inhibited when institutions focus only on meeting minimum mandates for nondiscrimination, such as those that result in "ADA-compliant" physical spaces. Instead, UDHE can be more easily promoted when institutions routinely look beyond minimal legal mandates and focus instead on the spirit of civil rights legislation as well as institutional values and goals that value diversity and support equity and inclusion. Avoiding legal and civil rights complaints can also motivate campuses to be more inclusive.

Awareness

Lack of awareness of accessibility issues and solutions on the part of stakeholders can impede the adoption of UD. Many campus leaders do not understand that accommodations alone cannot ensure the full inclusion of individuals with disabilities. With increased knowledge and resources, these individuals could become promoters of UDHE. Awareness of successful practices at other institutions can also promote the application of UDHE at an institution. When faculty include UD content in their courses, they increase the likelihood that their students will practice UD within the context of their future careers.

Attitudes

Discriminatory attitudes such as ableism—characterizing all people with disabilities as inferior to those without disabilities—can perpetuate inequality and inhibit the acceptance of UDHE as a way to level the playing field. The attitude of some faculty and staff that students with disabilities are an extra burden also inhibits the adoption of UDHE, as does a "survival of the fittest" attitude about students in general. Negative attitudes are often reflected in the use of nominally positive terms that marginalize groups of people (e.g., labeling people as "inspiring" or "special" just because they have disabilities) or that label an aspect of the disability experience as negative (e.g., saying someone "suffers" from a disability). To promote the UDHE paradigm, encourage people to use language that, if they find it to mention disability at all, focuses on function, such as "the student uses a wheelchair" rather than "the student is confined to a wheelchair." As we recognize the implicit ableism in some commonly used terminology and as more individuals with diverse characteristics succeed in academic programs and careers, attitudes should become more positive.

Diversity Efforts

On many campuses disability is not included in the definition of diversity. Instead, they may focus only on gender, race, and ethnic issues. Institutions with such a narrow vision of diversity are unlikely to embrace UDHE. In contrast, institutions that have expanded their definition of diversity to encompass such characteristics as sexual orientation, religion, age, socioeconomic status, nationality, and disability are fertile ground for the promotion of the UDHE paradigm. UDHE advocates can point out that the full participation of members of all of these groups can be achieved in part through the adoption of UDHE practices. For example, including students with a wide range of abilities on a design committee for a new construction or renovation can further the adoption of UDHE. Positioning UDHE as an approach that upholds the principles of nondiscrimination and equal opportunity may promote its application. Helping stakeholders develop "cultural competence"—an ability to interact effectively with people of different cultural, socioeconomic, and other backgrounds—can lead to discussions of disability-related barriers and the application of UDHE.

Some proponents of gender, racial, and ethnic equity think bringing in disability issues complicates things. You bet it does. But equity is equity. A way to begin collaborating with other diversity programs is to encourage leaders of programs focused on gender, race, ethnicity, or other underrepresented or underserved groups to address the needs of students in their target group who have disabilities and then help them do it .

Equity

An inhibitor of UDHE is stakeholder concerns that accommodations or accessible design reduces standards or gives unfair advantage to individuals with disabilities. To level the playing field, however, students who, for example, require course materials in electronic formats so that they can use screen reader software to read aloud the text should have access to the content at the same time that other students have access, thus encouraging faculty members to proactively produce accessible course materials. Not recognizing inequities created when students with disabilities do not have the same access to course content in a timely manner may hinder the adoption of UDHE practices in favor of an accommodation-only approach.

Time and Cost

The expected time and cost to implement UDHE practices are commonly reported as inhibitors to their widespread application. Redesigning products and environments that were not originally designed to be accessible often results in greater expense and effort for the institutions than the initial additional cost of creating them to be accessible during the design process. For example, designing an online learning course to be fully accessible to individuals using assistive technologies may ultimately cost less and result in fewer legal challenges than providing accommodations to every student for whom the online course is inaccessible. Initially, extra time and resources may be required to redesign inaccessible products and environments and to train and support staff in the practice of UDHE. However, UDHE practices can be applied on an incremental basis. For example, administrators of an online learning program may employ UDHE practices whenever a new course is developed or an existing course is updated.

Research

An inhibitor to the adoption of UDHE is lack of research on the effectiveness of UDHE practices in general and specifically with respect to individuals with specific, diverse characteristics. Traditional educational research that analyzes specific outcomes for students with disabilities and other subgroups could promote UDHE. Researchers should ensure that multiple stakeholder groups are represented in studies. For example, in researching the effectiveness of an online learning course, researchers should be sure to gain perspectives from individuals who are blind, deaf, or have other disabilities. It is also important in UDHE research to make sure that diversity is defined broadly. It is easy to find individuals promoting a UDHE practice that benefits students with learning disabilities but does not address making the practice accessible to students with learning disabilities who are also blind.

MY GO-TO RESOURCES

Following are some good places to start in your exploration of topics covered in this chapter.

- *Published Books and Articles About Faculty Development Regarding Universal Design of Instruction*
  uw.edu/doit/programs/center-universal-design-education/resources/published-books-and-articles-about-universal
- *Accessibility and Policy*
  udloncampus.cast.org/page/policy_landing
- *Knowledge Base*
  uw.edu/doit/knowledge-base
- *Promotion and Institutionalization of Universal Design*[9]

CONCLUSION

UDHE practices alone cannot dismantle all institutional inequities, but they can contribute to a powerful movement toward change when combined with other diversity efforts on a campus. In this chapter I brought together all that we've covered in the book into an Inclusive Campus Model that is underpinned by the UDHE Framework. Use the framework to build your toolkit and then use that and campus specifics to flesh out the model to create a road map for implementation of UDHE for your institution. Applying the model can contribute to making a paradigm shift to a more inclusive campus if you tailor it to your institution, engage key stakeholders in the process, and address factors that can promote or inhibit the widespread practice of inclusive practices.

TAKE ACTION!

(REFLECT) Consider your context

Reflect on these questions:

- What are demographic trends in your institution? What, if any, changes have you observed in institutional practices as a result of these changes?
- What practices on your campus do/don't make it welcoming to everyone? What improvements could be made?
- What specific stakeholders at your institution or in your unit need to work together to promote change toward a more inclusive campus or unit, respectively?
- What are barriers to change toward more inclusive practices at your institution?

(LEARN) Identify stakeholders

In an academic or professional development course, have participants identify and discuss what stakeholders need to be engaged to promote the UDHE paradigm on your campus or on campuses nationwide. Consider beginning with a list that includes industry, institutions of higher education, professional organizations, researchers, consumers, and government, and then add other groups that should be involved.

(LEARN) Describe an inclusive campus

In an academic or professional development course, discuss what characteristics are required of an "inclusive campus." For which does everyone agree?

(LEARN) Identify top promoter and inhibitor

In an academic or professional development course or community of practice, have participants describe what they think is the number-one promoter and the number-one inhibitor for the widespread adoption of UDHE on postsecondary campuses in general or on your campus in particular? Why do you believe this to be true?

(APPLY) Create a vision for your campus

In a task force, have participants think about your institution's characteristics with respect to inclusion. To start your creative juices flowing, begin by choosing/editing/deleting items on the list within the document *Self-Examination: How Inclusive Is Your Campus?* at uw.edu/doit/self-examination-how-inclusive-your-campus. Add additional items relevant to diversity issues other than disability.

(APPLY) Brainstorm how to apply UDHE

In a professional development session or academic course on UDHE, give each participant two sticky notes, each a different color and size or shape. On one sticky note, direct participants to write things *they* will do to make your course, service, or resource more inclusive, and on the other, things the *institution* should do to be more inclusive. At the next meeting share the two lists of submissions and discuss how some of these ideas might be promoted and implemented at a postsecondary campus or within an academic department or service unit. Encourage participants to share additional ideas in this regard.

(APPLY) Develop a road map for making your campus more inclusive

Individually or within a community of practice or task force, adapt for your institution the Inclusive Campus Model presented here to create an Inclusive Instruction Model. Begin with a search of the campus high-level web pages to find institutional statements about vision and values and incorporate those into your model.

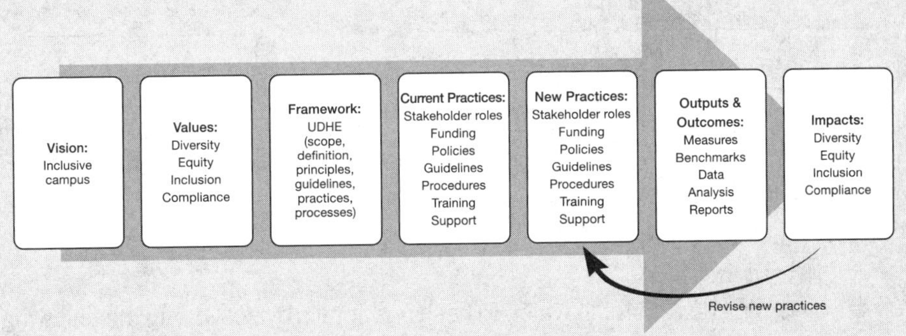

Create a working document that details answers to the following questions about your campus to begin fleshing out your model into a road map toward a more inclusive campus. Record your work in a document that you regularly update.

- *Vision*: What is your vision for an inclusive campus?
- *Values*: What campus values (e.g., diversity, equity, inclusion, compliance) are most relevant to making your campus more inclusive?
- *Framework*: What framework (e.g., UDHE Framework that includes its scope, definition, principles, guidelines, practices, and processes) reflects your vision and values and helps you work toward a more inclusive campus?
- *Current Practices*: What are your current practices with respect to stakeholder roles, funding, policies, guidelines, procedures, training, support, and other relevant issues?
- *New Practices*: How can current practices be modified and new practices be developed to be more consistent with your vision, values, and framework?

- *Outputs and Outcomes*: What measures should be identified, benchmarks should be set, data should be collected and analyzed, and reports should be made regarding outputs and outcomes from your new practices?
- *Impact*: What evidence suggests a positive impact of your efforts with respect to a more inclusive campus that better reflects your campus vision and values?

Keep the working document you create handy as you further refine your road map. Incorporate new insights, particularly with respect to the "New Practices" section.

(APPLY) Build a model for inclusive teaching and learning practices

Individually or within a community of practice or task force, adapt for your institution the Inclusive Campus Model presented here, but more narrowly focused on courses. Begin with a search of the campus high-level web pages to find statements about vision and values with respect to academic courses and incorporate those into your model.

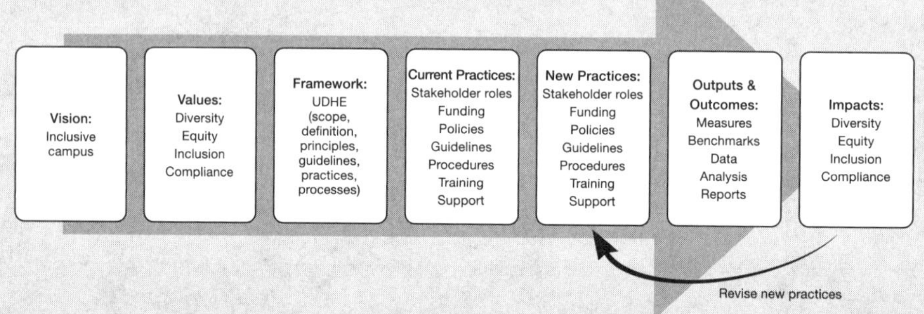

Create a working document in which to flesh out details by answering the following questions.

- *Vision*: What is your vision for inclusive instruction on your campus?
- *Values*: What campus values (e.g., diversity, equity, inclusion, compliance) are most relevant to inclusive instruction?
- *Framework*: What framework (e.g., UDI Framework that includes its scope, definition, principles, guidelines, practices, and processes) reflects your vision and values and helps you work toward more inclusive teaching and learning campuswide?
- *Current Practices*: What are current practices with respect to stakeholder roles, funding, policies, guidelines, procedures, training, support, and other relevant issues?
- *New Practices*: How can current practices be modified and new practices be developed to be more consistent with your vision, values, and framework?
- *Outputs and Outcomes*: What measures should be identified, benchmarks should be set, data should be collected and analyzed, and reports should be made regarding outputs and outcomes from your new practices?

- *Impact*: What evidence suggests a positive impact with respect to your journey toward more inclusive teaching and learning?

Keep the working document you create handy as you further refine your model. Incorporate new insights, particularly with respect to the "New Practices" section.

Consider conducting this exercise for some other aspect of campus life, such as a student service, an IT service, or an online learning program.

(APPLY) Develop an ADKAR process of change for a unit/campus

In a task force or academic or professional development course, have participants describe how each issue of the ADKAR model could be addressed for a unit or the whole campus when implementing change toward a more inclusive campus.

- *Awareness of the need to change.* Who are the stakeholders and how can you help them understand why changes are needed?
- *Desire to participate and support change.* What might motivate stakeholders through knowledge, engagement, encouragement, examples, and results?
- *Knowledge of how to change.* What basic strategies could be employed to implement UDHE in specific areas or campuswide?
- *Ability to implement the change on a day-to-day basis.* How could you provide for engagement, resources, and professional development to support stakeholders as they create change in their respective areas?
- *Reinforcement to keep the change in place.* How can you engage stakeholders to sustain efforts to change?

(APPLY) Institutionalize

In an organization where you work or otherwise engage, make a recommendation for at least three concrete steps this organization could take to be more welcoming and accessible to people with disabilities or other underrepresented or underserved groups.

(APPLY) Develop a leadership team

Set up or encourage someone else to set up a campuswide UDHE or Diversity, Equity, and Inclusion Leadership Team with members representing a diverse group of stakeholders. Work through this book and other materials to develop common knowledge and use that knowledge to develop a plan for stimulating a sea change toward a more inclusive campus. Consider how other groups, such as accessibility advocates or liaisons, might take on roles in making specific aspects of campus life more inclusive.

(APPLY) Categorize current policies and practices

Within a task force or advisory group, review a body of campus policies and practices that address access issues for students with disabilities. Identify each one as primarily an accommodation approach, a universal design approach, or both.

Brainstorm ways to increase the inclusion of universal design approaches within this body of campus policies and practices.

(APPLY) Flesh out a process for change

Read John P. Kotter's international best seller *Leading Change* (1996). Work within a task force or community of practice to flesh out the eight-stage process of change toward the creation of a more inclusive practice.

- Establish a sense of urgency.
- Create the guiding coalition.
- Develop a vision and strategy.
- Communicate the change vision.
- Empower employees for broad-based action.
- Generate short-term wins.
- Consolidate gains and produce more change.
- Anchor new approaches in the culture.

(APPLY) Develop plans for individUal and institutional change toward UDHE

In a UDHE training session, give participants two sticky notes that are different with respect to both color and shape. Ask participants to write on the sticky notes:

- *YELLOW rectangle*: Things you will do to make your course, service, facility, technology, or resource more inclusive.
- *PINK square*: Things administrators should do to make the institution more inclusive.

At the end of the presentation, ask participants to attach their sticky notes on walls beside the exit doors or send their responses via email. Point out that the exercise itself provides two examples of universal design practices: the two sticky notes are different with respect to shape and size to ensure everyone can distinguish between them, and participants are given the option to send responses via email in case the sticky notes activity does not work for them. When the session is over, collect the sticky notes into two piles and create bulleted lists to guide next steps for individuals and the institution in moving toward a more inclusive campus.

(APPLY) Review action items

Review TAKE ACTION! activities at the end of the preceding chapters and develop them into activities that can impact systemic change toward a more inclusive campus.

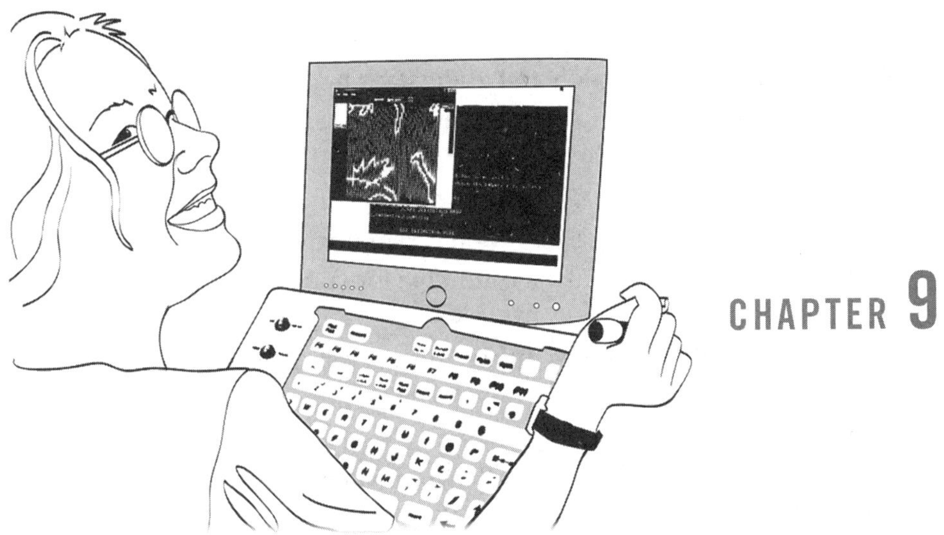

CHAPTER 9

What I Know for Sure

Your journey begins with a choice to get up, step out, and live fully.

—Oprah Winfrey

THE YEAR WAS 1998. Gene Siskel, the *Chicago Tribune* film critic, was interviewing Oprah Winfrey about the movie *Beloved*. The interview was uneventful until the very end. "Tell me," he asked, "what do you know for sure?" Uncharacteristically, Oprah was at a loss for words. "Uhhhh, about the movie?" she stammered, knowing full well that he was after something bigger, deeper, more complex, but trying to stall until she could come up with a semi-coherent response. "No," he said. "You know what I mean—about you, your life, anything, everything . . . " to which she replied, "Uhhhh I know for sure . . . uhhh . . . I know for sure, I need time to think about that some more. . . ."

And she did take that time. Siskel's question became a central one of her life and the topic of a column in each issue of *O* magazine. So, what does Oprah know for sure? Here are ten things she reports in her book, *What I Know for Sure*.

- You are the single biggest influence in your life.

- Extend a hand of connection and understanding, and offer three of the most important words any of us can ever receive: "I hear you." I know for sure your relationship will be the better for it.
- I don't want to live a shut-down life—desensitized to feeling and seeing. I want every day to be a fresh start on expanding what is possible.
- If you're holding anyone else accountable for your happiness, you're wasting your time.
- If you can get paid for doing what you love, every paycheck is a bonus.
- [Y]our deepest struggle can, if you're willing and open, produce your greatest strength.
- [T]here is no strength without challenge, adversity, resistance, and often pain.
- [T]his very moment is the only one you know you have for sure.
- [H]ow you spend your time defines who you are.
- [T]here's no them, there's only us.[1]

Oprah's answers to this question inspired me to ask myself, at the end of the day, what do I know absolutely—in my heart and in my head and beyond a shadow of a doubt—for sure? I've found that just asking this question helps me sort out what is important in personal and professional situations that seem complicated, at least at first glance. Thanks, Oprah.

But what about Universal Design in Higher Education (UDHE)? There is so much to do in the workspace discussed in this book, hard work. A paradigm shift to the UDHE Framework may require no less than a different way of thinking about every campus offering to nudge a campus toward the ideal of UDHE. It may be worth the time for members of a task force or community of practice to periodically step back and reflect on what, as a group, they know for sure. Can they at least agree that UDHE is a good idea? Here are a few things I think a group like this might agree that they know for sure. And at least one of us agrees with each statement. Maybe even both of us?

- When it comes to human beings, variability (in culture, in abilities, in opinions, in everything) is not the exception; it is the norm. That's a good thing.
- Every student has a right to access all that we have to offer.
- UD has a simple, honorable goal: to design products and environments for everybody, thus minimizing the need for accommodations.
- One size does not fit all. Universal designs build in flexibility to meet the needs of a diverse group.

- Every field, every project, every initiative can benefit from the engagement of people with diverse expertise and experiences, including those with disabilities.
- We don't need to all agree; we just need to create safe places in which to disagree.
- UDHE can make a useful service even better, an excellent course even better, a well-conceived facility even better, an informative website even better.
- Everyone has a role to play in making a campus more inclusive, but it takes strong leadership to draw them together and identify ways for everyone to contribute.
- What is "possible" and "reasonable" with respect to a design will be different tomorrow than it is today.
- It is good to celebrate progress, no matter how small and no matter how much remains to be done.
- Promoting inclusive practices is the right thing to do!

My passion for inclusion is rooted in personal, academic, and professional experiences as well as simple observations about how the world works . . . or doesn't. If this is all new but makes sense to you, reflect on how you can make your debut as a UDHE advocate. Think small. Universally design something in a course, at your worksite, in your home, or in your community, or share the idea with someone who will! If you just look for them, you will see UD opportunities everywhere. Take incremental steps toward the ideal. And, as you witness how inaccessible something is, build your capacity for outrage; then use that energy to promote change. Aristotle's insight on this matter is worth considering: "Anyone can get angry, but to do this to the right person, to the right extent, at the right time, with the right motive, and in the right way, that is not for everyone, nor is it easy."

This concludes our discussion of UDHE. But, oh, one more thing: I promised you in the preface of this book I would tell you the conclusion of my quest to become a Patrol Boy. Recall that my elementary school would not even consider my application because, well, I am not a boy. When my son Travis was in elementary school, he too wanted to take on this leadership position (genetic, I guess), long after its title had been changed to "Crossing Guard" and girls filled at least half of the positions. His application was accepted. I told him about how I wanted that job, but girls were not allowed. Toward the end of the school year, when it was time for the fifth graders to go on a five-day trip to camp, he was excited to tell me that the Crossing Guards who would be away that week needed to find someone to replace them. You guessed it: Travis offered the job to me. I accepted, of course, and enjoyed feeling his pleasure in making my dream come true. Morals of this story? (1) Something you *really* wanted may not be as much fun as you thought it would be; (2) sometimes our kids do really sweet things; and (3) once programs become more inclusive, maybe the next generation will not be able to imagine it any other way.

NOTES

PREFACE

1. Sheryl Burgstahler, *Critical Junctures Towards STEM Careers* (Seattle, WA: University of Washington, 2011).
2. Molly Follette Story, "The Principles of Universal Design," in *Universal Design Handbook*, 2nd ed., eds. Wolfgang F. E. Preiser and Korydon H. Smith (Chicago: McGraw-Hill Professional, 2011), 43.
3. Sheryl Burgstahler, ed., *Universal Design in Higher Education: From Principles to Practice*, 2nd ed. (Cambridge, MA: Harvard Education Press, 2015).

CHAPTER 1

1. Americans with Disabilities Act of 1990, 42 U.S.C.A. § 12101 *et seq.*; Americans with Disabilities Act Amendments Act of 2008, 42 U.S.C.A. § 12102 note (2011).
2. Edward Griffin and David Pollak, "Student Experiences of Neurodiversity in Higher Education: Insights from the BRAINHE Project," *Dyslexia*, 15, no. 1 (2009): 23–41.
3. Sheryl Burgstahler and Tanis Doe, "Disability-Related Simulations: If, When, and How to Use Them in Professional Development," *Review of Disability Studies: An International Journal* 1, no. 2 (2004): 4–17.
4. David Pfeiffer, "Disability Simulation Using a Wheelchair Exercise," *Journal of Postsecondary Education and Disability* 7, no. 2 (1989): 53–60.
5. Disability Justice, "The Americans with Disabilities Act (ADA) of 1990," https://disabilityjustice.org/the-americans-with-disabilities-act-ada-of-1990/.
6. United Nations, "Article 9 of the Convention on the Rights of Persons with Disabilities," http://un.org/development/desa/disabilities/convention-on-the-rights-of-persons-with-disabilities/article-9-accessibility.html.

CHAPTER 2

1. Jacques Carelman, *Catalogue D'objets Introuvables* (Paris: Cherche Midi Editeur, 1989).
2. Pat Moore and Charles Paul Conn, *Disguised: A True Story* (Waco, TX: World Books, 1984).
3. The Center for Universal Design, North Carolina State University, http://projects.ncsu.edu/ncsu/design/cud/about_ud/about_ud.htm.
4. The Centre for Excellence in Universal Design, "10 Things to Know About UD," National

Disability Authority, http://universaldesign.ie/what-is-universal-design/the-10-things-to-know-about-ud/10-things-to-know-about-ud.html.
5. DO-IT, "The Center for Universal Design in Education," University of Washington, http://uw.edu/doit/programs/center-universal-design-education.
6. Molly Follette Story, James L. Mueller, and Ronald L. Mace, "The Principles of Universal Design and Their Application," in *The Universal Design File: Designing for People of All Ages and Abilities* (Raleigh, NC: Center for Universal Design, 1998), 32–36.
7. Moore and Conn, *Disguised.*
8. World Wide Web Consortium, "Web Content Accessibility Guidelines (WCAG) Overview," Web Accessibility Initiative, updated June 22, 2018, http://w3.org/WAI/standards-guidelines/wcag/.
9. Frank G. Bowe, *Universal Design in Education: Teaching Nontraditional Students* (Westport, CT: Bergin and Garvey, 2000).
10. Sally S. Scott and Joan M. McGuire, "A Case Study Approach to Promote Practical Applications of Universal Design for Instruction," in *Universal Design in Higher Education: From Principles to Practice*, ed. Sheryl Burgstahler (Cambridge, MA: Harvard Education Press, 2015), 315–24.
11. Jenna W. Gravel, Laura A. Edwards, Christopher J. Buttimer, and David H. Rose, "Universal Design for Learning in Postsecondary Education: Reflections on Principles and Their Application," in *Universal Design in Higher Education: From Principles to Practice*, ed. Sheryl Burgstahler (Cambridge, MA: Harvard Education Press, 2015), 81–100.
12. Scott and McGuire, "A Case Study Approach to Promote Practical Applications," 318.
13. CAST, "Universal Design for Learning Guidelines version 2.2," 2018, http://udlguidelines.cast.org/search?query=checkpoint+2.5.
14. Sheryl Burgstahler, ed., *Universal Design in Higher Education: From Principles to Practice*, 2nd ed. (Cambridge, MA: Harvard Education Press, 2015).
15. Sheryl Burgstahler, "Universal Design in Higher Education," in *Universal Design in Higher Education: From Principles to Practice*, 2nd ed., ed. Sheryl Burgstahler (Cambridge, MA: Harvard Education Press, 2015), 22.
16. *Merriam-Webster's Collegiate Dictionary*, 11th ed. (Chicago: Encyclopedia Britannica Company) s.v. "paradigm."
17. Bowe, *Universal Design in Education*, 4.
18. Burgstahler, "Universal Design in Higher Education," 1–28.
19. The Center for Universal Design, North Carolina State University, http://projects.ncsu.edu/ncsu/design/cud/about_ud/about_ud.htm.

CHAPTER 3

1. American Association of Retired Persons, "The Room-by-Room HomeFit Tour," February 2015, https://aarp.org/livable-communities/info-2014/what-is-universal-design.html.
2. Sheryl Burgstahler, *Equal Access: Universal Design of Physical Spaces* (Seattle: University of Washington, 2020), http://uw.edu/doit/equal-access-universal-design-physical-spaces.
3. AccessEngineering, *Making a Makerspace? Guidelines for Accessibility and Universal Design* (Seattle: University of Washington, 2015), http://uw.edu/doit/making-makerspace-guidelines-accessibility-and-universal-design.
4. Katheryne Staeger-Wilson and Douglas H. Sampson, "Infusing JUST Design in Campus Recreation," *Journal of Postsecondary Education and Disability* 25, no. 3 (2012): 247–52, files.eric.ed.gov/fulltext/EJ994289.pdf.

5. Community Resources for Independent Living and Disability Action Network, "Universal Design: Home for All Ages," http://crilhayward.org/policies-advocacy/docs/UD-Brochure-2.pdf.
6. Sheryl Burgstahler, "Universal Design of Student Services and Physical Spaces in Higher Education," in *Universal Design in Higher Education: From Principles to Practice*, 2nd ed., ed. Sheryl Burgstahler (Cambridge, MA: Harvard Education Press, 2015), 177–228.

CHAPTER 4

1. Andrew S. Tanenbaum, *Computer Networks*, 2nd ed. (Upper Saddle River, NJ: Prentice Hall, 1988), 254.
2. Cynthia D. Waddell, "The Growing Digital Divide in Access for People with Disabilities: Overcoming Barriers to Participation in the Digital Economy" (paper presented at the Understanding the Digital Economy Conference, Washington, DC, May 25–26, 1999).
3. Sheryl Burgstahler, "Web-Based Distance Learning and the Second Digital Divide," in *Encyclopedia of Information Science and Information Technology*, ed. Mehdi Khosrow-Pour (Hershey, PA: Idea Group Inc, 2005), 3079–84.
4. Gregg C. Vanderheiden and Katherine R. Vanderheiden, *Accessible Design of Consumer Products: Guidelines for the Design of Consumer Products to Increase Their Accessibility to People with Disabilities or Who Are Aging* (Madison: University of Wisconsin Trace Research and Development Center, 1992), https://trace.umd.edu/publications/consumer_product_guidelines.
5. Tim Berners-Lee, "W3C Web Accessibility Initiative," World Wide Web Consortium, www.w3.org/WAI.
6. Andrew Kirkpatrick, Joshue O. Connor, Alastair Campbell, and Michael Cooper, eds. "Web Content Accessibility Guidelines (WCAG) 2.1," World Wide Web Consortium, June 5, 2018, http://w3.org/TR/WCAG21/.
7. Plain Language Action and Information Network (PLAIN), *Federal Plain Language Guidelines* (Washington, DC: US General Services Administration, 2011), http://plainlanguage.gov/guidelines/.
8. US Department of Justice, "A Guide to Disability Rights Laws," US Department of Justice, Civil Rights Division, February 2020, http://ada.gov/cguide.htm.
9. Web Accessibility Initiative, "Complex Images," World Wide Web Consortium, updated July 27, 2019, http://w3.org/WAI/tutorials/images/complex/.
10. Terrill Thompson, "Video for All: Accessibility of Video Content and Universal Design of a Media Player," in *Universal Design in Higher Education: From Principles to Practice*, 2nd ed., ed. Sheryl Burgstahler (Cambridge, MA: Harvard Education Press, 2015), 259–73.
11. DO-IT, "Videos," University of Washington, http://uw.edu/doit/do-it-videos.
12. Rehabilitation Act of 1973, § 504, 29 U.S.C. § 794 *et seq* (2012); Americans with Disabilities Act of 1990, 42 U.S.C.A. § 12101 *et seq*; Americans with Disabilities Act Amendments Act of 2008, 42 U.S.C.A. § 12102 note (2011).
13. United Nations, "Article 9 of the Convention on the Rights of Persons with Disabilities," http://un.org/development/desa/disabilities/convention-on-the-rights-of-persons-with-disabilities/article-9-accessibility.html.
14. Office of Civil Rights, University of Montana-Missoula Resolution Agreement, Reference No. 10122118, March 10, 2014, www2.ed.gov/about/offices/list/ocr/docs/investigations/more/10122118-b.pdf.
15. EDUCAUSE IT Accessibility Constituent Group, "IT Accessibility Risk Statements and

Evidence," EDUCAUSE, 2015, http://library.educause.edu/-/media/files/library/2015/7/accessrisk15-pdf.pdf.

16. US Department of Justice and US Department of Education, "Joint 'Dear Colleague' Letter: Electronic Book Readers," June 29, 2010, https://www2.ed.gov/about/offices/list/ocr/letters/colleague-20100629.html.
17. Sheryl Burgstahler, "Universal Design of Technology in Higher Education," in *Universal Design in Higher Education: From Principles to Practice*, 2nd ed., ed. Sheryl Burgstahler (Cambridge, MA: Harvard Education Press, 2015), 229–84.

CHAPTER 5

1. Raymond Orkwis and Kathleen McLane, *A Curriculum Every Student Can Use: Design Principles for Student Access*, ERIC/OSEP Topical Brief. (Reston, VA: ERIC/OSEP Special Project, ERIC Document Reproduction Service No. ED423654, 1998), eric.ed.gov/fulltext/ED423654.pdf.
2. Dave L. Edyburn, "Would You Recognize Universal Design for Learning if You Saw It? Ten Propositions for New Directions for the Second Decade of UDL," *Learning Disability Quarterly* 33, no. 1 (2010): 33–41.
3. Sheryl Burgstahler, "Universal Design of Instruction in Higher Education," in *Universal Design in Higher Education: From Principles to Practice*, 2nd ed., ed. Sheryl Burgstahler (Cambridge, MA: Harvard Education Press, 2015), 45.
4. Arthur W. Chickering and Zelda F. Gamson, *Seven Principles for Good Practice in Undergraduate Education* (Washington, DC: American Association for Higher Education, ERIC Document Reproduction Service No. ED282491, 1987).
5. Burgstahler, "Universal Design of Instruction," 45.
6. Susan A. Ambrose, Michael W. Bridges, Michele DiPietro, Marsha C. Lovett, and Marie K. Norman, *How Learning Works: Seven Research-Based Principles for Smart Teaching* (San Francisco: John Wiley & Sons, Inc., 2010).
7. Tali Heiman, "Females with Learning Disabilities Taking On-Line Courses: Perceptions of the Learning Environments, Coping and Well-Being," *Journal of Postsecondary Education and Disability* 21, no. 1 (2008): 4–14.
8. Quality Matters, "Course Design Rubric Standards," 6th ed., http://qualitymatters.org/qa-resources/rubric-standards/higher-ed-rubric.
9. Sheryl Burgstahler, "20 Tips for Teaching an Accessible Online Course," DO-IT, University of Washington, 2020, http://uw.edu/doit/20-tips-teaching-accessible-online-course.
10. Robbin Zeff, "Universal Design Across the Curriculum," *New Directions for Higher Education* 137 (2007): 27–44.
11. David Gordon, Jenna W. Gravel, and Laura A. Schifter, *A Policy Reader in Universal Design for Learning* (Cambridge, MA: Harvard Education Press, 2009).
12. Sheryl Burgstahler and Rosalie J. Russo-Gleicher, "Applying Universal Design to Address the Needs of Postsecondary Students on the Autism Spectrum," *Journal of Postsecondary Education and Disability* 28, no. 2 (2015): 199–212. ahead-archive.org/uploads/publications/JPED/jped28_2/JPED28_2_Full%20Document.pdf
13. Al Souma and Deb Casey, "The Benefits of Universal Design for Students with Psychiatric Disabilities," in *Universal Design in Higher Education: From Principles to Practice*, 2nd ed., ed. Sheryl Burgstahler (Cambridge, MA: Harvard Education Press, 2015), 131–38.
14. Sheryl Burgstahler and Elizabeth Moore, "Impact of Faculty Training in UDI on the Grades of Students with Disabilities," in *Universal Design in Higher Education: Promising*

Practices (Seattle: DO-IT, University of Washington, 2015).

15. Sheryl Burgstahler, *Equal Access: Universal Design of Instruction* (Seattle: University of Washington, 2020), http://uw.edu/doit/equal-access-universal-design-instruction.
16. Paul Beckman, "Universal Design for Learning: A Field Experiment Comparing Specific Classroom Actions," in *The Americas Conference on Information Systems Proceedings* (2009), aisel.aisnet.org/amcis2009/10.
17. Burgstahler, *Equal Access: Universal Design of Instruction*, http://uw.edu/doit/equal-access-universal-design-instruction.
18. Sheryl Burgstahler, *Equal Access: Universal Design of an Academic Department* (Seattle: University of Washington, 2020), http://uw.edu/doit/equal-access-universal-design-academic-department.
19. International Association for K–12 Online Learning, *Version Two National Standards for Quality Online Courses* (Vienna, VA: Author, 2011).
20. Sheryl Burgstahler, "The Development of Accessibility Indicators for Distance Learning Programs," *Association for Learning Technology Journal* 14, no. 1 (2006): 79–102.
21. Burgstahler, "Universal Design of Instruction," 49.
22. Burgstahler, *Universal Design in Higher Education: From Principles to Practice*, 2nd ed., ed. Sheryl Burgstahler (Cambridge, MA: Harvard Education Press, 2015).
23. Imke Durre, Michael Richardson, Carson Smith, Jessie Amelia Shulman, and Sarah Steele, "Universal Design of Instruction: Reflections of Students," in *Universal Design in Higher Education: From Principles to Practice*, ed. Sheryl Burgstahler (Cambridge, MA: Harvard Education Press, 2015), 117–130.
24. *AccessCyberlearning 2.0*, "AccessCyberlearning 2.0 Capacity Building Institute," University of Washington, January 18, 2019, http://uw.edu/doit/accesscyberlearning-20-capacity-building-institute-2019.
25. Burgstahler, *Universal Design in Higher Education*, 29–175.
26. Thomas J. Tobin and Kirsten T. Behling, *Reach Everyone, Teach Everyone: Universal Design for Learning in Higher Education* (Morgantown, VA: West Virginia University Press, 2018).
27. Sean Bracken and Katie Novak, *Transforming Higher Education Through Universal Design for Learning* (London: Routledge, 2019).
28. Arthur W. Chickering and Zelda F. Gamson, *Seven Principles for Good Practice in Undergraduate Education* (Washington, DC: American Association for Higher Education, ERIC Document Reproduction Service No. ED282491, 1987).
29. Ambrose, Bridges, DiPietro, Lovett, and Norman, *How Learning Works*.
30. Burgstahler and Russo-Gleicher, "Applying Universal Design to Address the Needs," 199–212. ahead-archive.org/uploads/publications/JPED/jped28_2/JPED28_2_Full%20 Document.pdf

CHAPTER 6

1. Sheryl Burgstahler and Elizabeth Moore, "Development of a UD Checklist for Postsecondary Student Services," in *Universal Design in Higher Education: Promising Practices* (Seattle: DO-IT, University of Washington, 2013).
2. Sheryl Burgstahler and Elizabeth Moore, "Making Student Services Welcoming and Accessible Through Accommodations and Universal Design," *Journal of Postsecondary Education and Disabilities* 21, no. 3 (2009): 155–74.
3. Sheryl Burgstahler, *Equal Access: Universal Design of Student Services* (Seattle: University of Washington, 2020), http://uw.edu/doit/equal-access-universal-design-student-services.

4. DO-IT, "The Center for Universal Design in Education," University of Washington, http://uw.edu/doit/programs/center-universal-design-education.
5. Sheryl Burgstahler, "Universal Design of Student Services and Physical Spaces in Higher Education," in *Universal Design in Higher Education: From Principles to Practice*, 2nd ed., ed. Sheryl Burgstahler (Cambridge, MA: Harvard Education Press, 2015), 177–228.
6. Neal E Lipsitz, Kaela Parks, and Mary Lee Vance, *Beyond the Americans with Disabilities Act: Inclusive Policy and Practice for Higher Education* (Washington, DC: National Association of Student Personnel Administrators, 2014).

CHAPTER 7

1. ABET, "Criteria for Accrediting Engineering Programs, 2019–2020," https://www.abet.org/accreditation/accreditation-criteria/criteria-for-accrediting-engineering-programs-2019-2020/#definitions.
2. James J. Pirkl, *Transgenerational Design: Products for Aging Population* (Hoboken, NJ: Wiley, 1994).
3. Kristen Shinohara, Saba Kawas, Amy J. Ko, and Richard E. Ladner, "Who Teaches Accessibility?: A Survey of US Computing Faculty," *49th ACM Technical Symposium on Computer Science Education Proceedings*, February 2018, 197–202, http://faculty.washington.edu/ajko/papers/Shinohara2018AccessComputingSurvey.pdf.

CHAPTER 8

1. DO-IT, *Self-Examination: How Accessible Is Your Campus?* (Seattle: University of Washington, 2015), http://uw.edu/doit/self-examination-how-inclusive-your-campus.
2. DO-IT, "The Center for Universal Design in Education," University of Washington. http://uw.edu/doit/programs/center-universal-design-education.
3. Robert Fulghum, *All I Really Need to Know I Learned in Kindergarten* (New York: Random House Publishing Group, 1986).
4. Sheryl Burgstahler and Terrill Thompson, *Accessible Cyberlearning: A Community Report of the Current State and Recommendations for the Future* (Seattle: University of Washington, 2019), 7–8, http://circlcenter.org/events/synthesis-design-workshops.
5. John P. Kotter, *Leading Change* (Boston: Harvard Business School Press, 1996).
6. South Carolina Technical College System and US Department of Education, Office for Civil Rights, *Resolution Agreement South Carolina Technical College System OCR Compliance Review No. 11-11-6002* (February 2013), http://www2.ed.gov/about/offices/list/ocr/docs/investigations/11116002-b.pdf.
7. Jeffrey Haitt, *ADKAR: A Model for Change in Business, Government and Our Community* (Loveland, CO: Prosci, 2006).
8. Sheryl Burgstahler, "Promoters and Inhibitors of Universal Design in Higher Education," in *Universal Design in Higher Education: From Principles to Practice*, 2nd ed., ed. Sheryl Burgstahler (Cambridge, MA: Harvard Education Press, 2015), 288–93.
9. Sheryl Burgstahler, "Promotion and Institutionalization of Universal Design," in *Universal Design in Higher Education: From Principles to Practice*, 2nd ed., ed. Sheryl Burgstahler (Cambridge, MA: Harvard Education Press, 2015), 285–346.

CHAPTER 9

1. Oprah Winfrey, *What I Know for Sure* (New York: The Oprah Magazine, 2000).

ABOUT THE AUTHOR

Sheryl Burgstahler

I was born and raised in Seattle. My brother and I shared memorable times on my dad's used car lot, which to us was a large extension of our front yard, well positioned on a busy street. I learned from a young age what a family business was all about. As a little girl, even I had a job sorting nails, screws, bolts, and washers into little glass jars; the mechanics praised me and now I know why—who wants to sort nails, screws, bolts, and washers into little glass jars? Doing things that need to be done and that others do not want to do has been an asset in my career. I learned other lessons from my dad—don't try to sell something to people until you know what they're looking for and they trust you; build your business on return customers (at the time I didn't know these were not characteristics of a stereotypical used car dealer)—that apply to my career as well. In selling an idea, like Universal Design in Higher Education (UDHE), we need to tailor the message to the audience and provide trusted resources for continued support and future growth.

I earned a master's degree in mathematics and education. I have been a teacher and administrator in a mix of settings, taught various topics to students, and worked at multiple educational levels—high school and college courses at a military installation in South Korea for the Department of Defense; mathematics in middle and high school; and computer programming, mathematics, teacher training, educational applications of technology, and disability studies at college and university levels. I earned my PhD in policy, governance, and administration of higher education with a focus on access and use of computer technology by postsecondary students with disabilities.

In 1984 I left a faculty position at St. Martin's College to manage the new Microcomputer Support Group at the University of Washington (UW). My group was charged with helping faculty, staff, and students gain access to and effectively use desktop computers. After I grew that group into the comprehensive Desktop Computing Services, in 1992 the leader of IT at the UW presented me with a challenge—to "dabble" in grant writing to secure funds to demonstrate the value of technology, especially in K–12 schools. I took the challenge. My dabbling has brought in consistent funding, mostly from the National Science Foundation and US Department of Education, and led to the founding of the DO-IT (Disabilities, Opportunities, Internetworking, and Technology) Center. Our projects have demonstrated transformative changes in the lives of people with disabilities once technology access and other interventions are employed and how institutions can create inclusive offerings. Outcomes from our projects have earned many awards, including the Professional Recognition Award for the Association on Higher Education and Disability, the National Information Infrastructure Award in Education, the President's Award for Mentoring, the Golden Apple Award in Education, the Harry J. Murphy Catalyst Award, the Economic Opportunity Award, the Susan M. Daniels Disability Mentoring Hall of Fame, a featured program of the Council for Exceptional Children, and the Diversity in Technology Leadership Award from the National Alliance for Partnerships in Equity. Most of my research, publications, teaching, and presentations focus on the successful transition of students with disabilities to college, graduate school, and careers and on the application of UDHE to technology and learning activities.

I live in Seattle with my husband, Dave, who is an accounting professor at the UW. Our son, Travis, and his family live nearby. We all enjoy hanging out with family and friends at our beach house on Hood Canal and taking on fun projects that include a kid retreat in the attic, a tree house, a man-made sandy beach, and the relocation of my childhood playhouse from my parents' home in Seattle to the Canal. My motto—if the kids are happy, everybody's happy!

INDEX

AARP (American Association of Retired Persons), 61
ability level, continuum of, 2–3
ableism, 199
Able Player, 96
AccessCollege (DO-IT Center), xvi
AccessComputing, 169
AccessCyberlearning, 183
accessibility of content, 41–42, 46, 81–82, 85–94. *see also* Web Content Accessibility Guidelines (WCAG)
Accessibility Risk Statements and Evidence (EDUCAUSE), 100–101, 108
accessible design, 30–31, 33–34
accessible IT. *see also* Information Technology (IT), universal design of
  civil rights regarding, 99–102
  history of, 75–77, 81
Accessible Technology Services (ATS), xii, 93, 96–97, 104, 190
AccessSTEM project (DO-IT Center), xii-xiii
Access Technology Higher Education Network (ATHEN), 102
accommodations
  compared with UDHE, 49–50
  definition, 17
  inspiring UDHE practices, 18–19
  inspiring UDI practices, 125–129, 146, 148
  for instruction, 112–113, 116–117, 131, 136–137
  for IT, 80–81, 84–85
  in K-12 compared with higher education, 15–16
  limitations of, 17–19
  for physical spaces, 63, 66–67
  "reasonable" criteria for, 15–16
  securing, process for students, 17–18
  for services, 154–155
  within UDHE, 48
ADA. *see* Americans with Disabilities Act
ADHD as a Difference in Cognition, Not a Disorder (TEDx talk), 24
adjustable-height furnishings, 64–65, 138, 157
ADKAR model, 196–197, 205
aging population, 61, 67
American Association of Retired Persons (AARP), 61
Americans with Disabilities Act (ADA) (1990)
  2008 amendments, 3, 13, 99
  applicability to higher education, 13–16, 194
  Checklist for Readily Achievable Barrier Removal, 33, 52, 68, 69
  complaint resolutions, 99–100, 194, 195–196
  definition of disability in, 3–4
appearance of physical spaces, 44, 63
application areas
  best practices for. *see* best practices in the field
  identifying, as part of UDHE process, 47–48, 56
  instruction. *see* Universal Design of Instruction (UDI)
  list of, 44
  physical spaces. *see* physical spaces, universal design of
  specified by scope, 36
  technology. *see* Information Technology (IT), universal design of
"Applying Universal Design to Address the Needs of Postsecondary Students on the Autism Spectrum" (*Journal of Postsecondary Education and Disability*), 148–149
Architectural Barriers Act (1968), 13
assessment and feedback, 44, 46, 135–136, 141

assistive technology (AT)
examples of, 77–80
history of, 75–77, 81
legislation regarding, 80
practices for, 85–89
usability of, 85
Association for Higher Education and Disability, 19
asynchronous communication, 88–89
AT. *see* assistive technology
ATHEN (Access Technology Higher Education Network), 102
ATS (Accessible Technology Services), xii, 93, 190
attention differences, 9
audio descriptions, 88, 96, 142, 166
autism spectrum disorder, 5–6, 7, 126–127, 131, 148–149
awareness about disabilities, 9–13. *see also* teaching about disabilities

barrier-free design, 30, 167. *see also Checklist for Readily Achievable Barrier Removal*
behaviorist theory, 115
best practices in the field
identifying, 47–48
for instruction, 113–114. *see also* evidence-based teaching practices
for physical spaces, 66–67
for student services, 154–155
for technology, 84
Beyond the Americans with Disabilities Act (Lipsitz, Parks, and Vance), 159
Blackboard, 123
Bowe, Frank, 51
braille, 8–9, 78
Brown v. Board of Education of Topeka (1954), 14
Burgstahler, Sheryl (author)
about, xi, 207–210, 217–218
Universal Design in Higher Education: From Principles to Practice, xvii, 52, 68, 105, 143, 160

campus accessibility indicators, 179–180
campus services, universal design of. *see* universal design of services
Canvas, 104, 123
captions
beneficiaries of, 50–51, 88–89, 95, 106
practices for, 95–99
for public announcements, 101
quality of video content with, 47
real-time, for conferences and lectures, 88–89, 117, 118
CAST (Center for Applied Special Technology), 42
CCVA (21st Century Communications and Video Accessibility Act), 166
CDC. *see* Centers for Disease Control and Prevention
Center for Applied Special Technology (CAST), 42
Center for Excellence in Universal Design, 32, 37
Center for Universal Design (CUD), 61
Center for Universal Design in Education (CUDE), xv, 36–37, 52
Centers for Disease Control and Prevention (CDC), 19
change, models for. *see also* Inclusive Campus Model
ADKAR model, 196–197, 205
logic model, 186
Checklist for Readily Achievable Barrier Removal (ADA), 33, 52, 68, 69
Chickering and Gamson's principles of good practice, 114, 116, 144
civil rights, 13–16, 42, 80, 99–102, 194–196, 198
class climate, 44, 131–132, 140
classroom design. *see* physical spaces, universal design of
Closing the Gap (CTG), 104
Coffeepot for Masochists (Carelman), 27–28
college campuses. *see* higher education; physical spaces, universal design of
communication
asynchronous, 88–89
terminology, 2–5
tips for, 10–11, 21
communication differences, 7
compatibility in technology, 44, 46, 82
computer-assisted self-paced instruction, 115
constructivist approach to teaching, 115
consumers, role of, 181
content, accessibility of, 41–42, 46, 81–82, 85–94. *see also* documents, universal design of; images, text descriptions for; videos
Convention on the Rights of Persons with Disabilities, 14, 59, 99
courses, universal design of. *see* Universal Course Design (UCD); Universal Design of Instruction (UDI)
CTG (Closing the Gap), 104
CUD. *see* Center for Universal Design
CUDE. *see* Center for Universal Design in Education
curb cuts, 39–41, 179

deaf or hard of hearing
captions benefitting. *see* captions
communication differences including, 7
sign language interpreters benefitting, 16, 48, 118–119, 152
terminology for, 4
deficit or medical view of disabilities, 17–18, 29, 74
delivery methods, 44, 46, 133–134, 140–141
demonstrations, 11–12, 21–22
Department of Education, U.S.
Office of Postsecondary Education, 181
Students with Disabilities Preparing for Postsecondary Education, 19
design for all, 30. *see also* universal design (UD)
differentiated instruction, 115
digital content, guidelines for, 85–94, 123–124
digital divide, 74–75
digital technology. *see* Information Technology (IT), universal design of
disabilities. *see also* students with disabilities
awareness about, increasing, 9–13
civil rights regarding, 13–16, 42, 80, 99–102, 194–196, 198
deficit or medical view of, 17–18, 29, 74
definition, 3–4
as diversity issue, 2, 24
invisible (not obvious), 6, 12, 156
prevalence of people with, 5–7
self-disclosure of, 6, 18, 33, 122
simulations of, 12–13, 23
terminology used for, 2–5
types of, 7–9, 77–79
Disabilities, Opportunities, Internetworking, and Technology (DO-IT) Center
AccessCollege, xvi
AccessSTEM project, xii-xiii
Center for Universal Design in Education (CUDE), 36–37
communication tips, 21
The Conference Room, 159
Equal Access: Universal Design of Computer Labs, 70
Equal Access: Universal Design of Engineering Labs, 70
Equal Access: Universal Design of Instruction, 147
Equal Access: Universal Design of Physical Spaces, 70
Equal Access: Universal Design of Student Services, 161
Equal Access: Universal Design of Your Engineering Research Center, 70
Facilitating Accessibility Reviews of Informal Science Education Facilities and Programs, 70
The Faculty Room, 142
Knowledge Base, xv, 20, 105, 143, 160
Making a Makerspace? Guidelines for Accessibility and Universal Design, 70
overview, xv-xvi, xix-xxi
Published Books and Articles About Universal Design in Higher Education, 52, 68, 105, 143, 160
Scholars program, 15, 18, 181
STEM Lab, 68
Universal Design in Higher Education: Promising Practices, 145
Universal Design of Instruction in PostSecondary Education, 142
Universal Design of IT, 105
Universal Design of Physical Spaces, 68
Universal Design of Student Services, 159
videos by, 11, 22
Disability and Health Overview (CDC), 19
Disguised: A True Story (Moore), 29
diversity
components of, 1–2
disability as a diversity issue, 2, 24, 29, 49
documents, universal design of, 85–94, 123–124
DO-IT Center. *see* Disabilities, Opportunities, Internetworking, and Technology Center
dyscalculia, 3
dysgraphia, 3
dyslexia, 3
dyspraxia, 3

eCollege, 123
EDUCAUSE, 100–101, 108
EIT (Electronic and Information Technology), 100–101. *see also* Information Technology (IT), universal design of
e-learning. *see* online courses, universal design of
Electronic and Information Technology (EIT), 100–101. *see also* Information Technology (IT), universal design of
email. *see* asynchronous communication
entrances and routes of travel, 44, 46, 60, 63
Equal Access: Universal Design of Computer Labs (DO-IT Center), 70
Equal Access: Universal Design of Engineering Labs (DO-IT Center), 70

Equal Access: Universal Design of Instruction (DO-IT Center), 136–137, 147
Equal Access: Universal Design of Physical Spaces (DO-IT Center), 63, 70
Equal Access: Universal Design of Student Services (DO-IT Center), 159, 161
Equal Access: Universal Design of Your Engineering Research Center (DO-IT Center), 70
equity
as goal of universal design, xiv-xv, 35, 65
perceptions regarding, as inhibitor, 200
as UDHE principle, 37–38, 45, 119
in vision and value statements, 186–189
evaluation of universal design. *see* planning, policies, and evaluation
events, universal design of, 44, 158
evidence-based teaching practices, 47, 112–117, 137, 145

Facilitating Accessibility Reviews of Informal Science Education Facilities and Programs (DO-IT Center), 70
faculty development. *see* professional development
Federal Plain Language Guidelines (PLAIN), 85
feedback and assessment, 44, 46, 135–136, 141
fixtures and furniture, 63
framework for UDHE
components of, 35–36
definition component, 36
for physical spaces, 59–68
practices, 44–47
principles and guidelines, 36–43
process, 47–49
scope, 36
for services, 153–159
for technology, 83–99
for UDI, 111–137

Go-To Resources. *see* resources
government, role of, 181. *see also* civil rights

handicap, as term, 4
hard of hearing. *see* deaf or hard of hearing
Harrison, Marc, 37
Hawking, Stephen, 5–6
hearing differences. *see* communication differences; deaf or hard of hearing
HEOA (Higher Education Opportunity Act) (2008), 127
higher education
practices of, compared with K-12, 14–15
students' transition to, 15–16, 20, 25
universal design for. *see* Universal Design in Higher Education (UDHE)
higher education institutions, role of, 181–183
Higher Education Opportunity Act (HEOA) (2008), 127
How Learning Works (Ambrose, Bridges, DiPietro, Lovett, and Norman), 114, 117, 144–145
HTML (Hypertext Markup Language), 90–93, 123–124
Hypertext Markup Language (HTML), 90–93, 123–124

IDEA. *see* Individuals with Disabilities Education Act
IDL (Inclusive Design for Learning), 42
images, text descriptions for, 45, 86–88, 90–91, 94, 115, 124, 142
I'm Not Your Inspiration, Thank You Very Much. (TEDx talk), 22
impacts, of model for inclusive campuses, 52–53, 187–188, 189
impairment, 3–4
inclusion, 15, 24
Inclusive Campus Model
campus accessibility indicators, 179–180
case study using, 190–196
components of, 185–190
factors promoting or inhibiting, 197–201
overview, 51–53, 177–178
resources for, 201
stakeholder roles, 179–185, 196–197
inclusive design, 15, 30–31, 33–34. *see also* universal design (UD)
Inclusive Design for Learning (IDL), 42
Individuals with Disabilities Education Act (IDEA), 14–15
industry, role of, 180
information resources and technology, 44, 63, 134–135, 138, 141, 157–158
Information Technology (IT), universal design of
accessibility testers for, 94–95
accommodations approach to, 80–81
advocating for, 102–104
assistive technology for, 75–80
barriers to, 76–79, 88–89

civil rights regarding, 42, 80, 99–102
compared with accommodation approach, 107
complaints and resolutions regarding, 99–100
definition, 73–74, 83
digital content, guidelines for, 85–94, 123–124
digital divide and, 74–75
framework for, 83–99
history of, 75–77, 81
practices for, 85–99, 134–135, 157–158
principles and guidelines of, 81–83, 85. *see also* Web Content Accessibility Guidelines (WCAG)
processes for, 84–85
resources for, 104–105
scope, 83
stakeholder roles in, 102–104
Institute of Education Sciences, 142
institutionalization of UDHE, 191, 201
instruction, universal design for. *see* Universal Design of Instruction (UDI)
interaction, 44, 46, 132–133, 141
invisible (not obvious) disabilities, 6, 12, 156
IT, universal design of. *see* Information Technology, universal design of

K-12 education
practices for students with disabilities, 14–15
students' transition to higher education, 15–16, 20, 25
Knowledge Base, xv
Kotter, John P., 190–191, 206

learning activities. *see* Universal Design of Instruction (UDI)
learning-centered instruction, 115
learning differences, 8
learning management system (LMS), 73–74, 121, 123
learning services. *see* universal design of services
lectures, universal design of, 117, 127, 129, 135
legal issues. *see* civil rights
LMS. *see* learning management system

Mace, Ronald, 30, 36, 37–39
major life activity, 3–4
makerspaces, universal design of, 58, 62–65
Making a Makerspace? Guidelines for Accessibility and Universal Design (DO-IT Center), 70
media players, 95–96
mental health, affecting major life activities, 2–3, 13–14. *see also* attention differences; learning differences
mobility or dexterity impairments, 7, 39, 46, 60, 64, 88
model for inclusive campuses. *see* Inclusive Campus Model
models for change
ADKAR model, 196–197, 205
logic model, 186
models for disability, 17. *see also* deficit or medical view of disabilities

nametag design example, 31–32
National Center for College Students with Disabilities (NCCSD), 19
National Instructional Materials Accessibility Standard (NIMAS), 113
National Science Foundation (NSF), xv, 183
navigation
entrances and routes of travel, 44, 46, 60, 63
user interface and navigation, 44, 82–83, 124. *see also* assistive technology (AT)
NCCSD (National Center for College Students with Disabilities), 19
neuroatypical, 5
neurodiversity, 5
neurotypical, 5
NIMAS (National Instructional Materials Accessibility Standard), 113
"Nothing About Us Without Us" slogan, 24
NSF. *see* National Science Foundation

Office of Postsecondary Education (OPE), 181
online courses, universal design of, 121–125
online timed exams, universal design of, 117
OPE (Office of Postsecondary Education), 181
outputs and outcomes, in model for inclusive campuses, 52–53, 187–188, 189, 204

panels, 11–12, 21–22
paradigm shift, 51–52, 178–179, 181–182, 201, 208–209
participatory design, 30
PDF (portable document format) documents, universal design of, 89–93, 123–124, 196
pedagogy. *see* evidence-based teaching practices; Universal Design for Learning (UDL)

people with disabilities. *see also* students with disabilities
accommodations for. *see* accommodations
awareness about, increasing, 9–13
challenges faced by, 77–79
civil rights of, 13–16
communicating with, 10–11
panels or demonstrations by, 11–12, 21–22
prevalence of, 5–7
terminology used by and for, 2–5
types of challenges faced by, 7–9
philosophies of learning (learning philosophies), 112, 114–115
physical differences, 7
physical environments and products, 44, 133, 156–157
physical spaces, universal design of
AARP recommendations for, 61
areas of consideration for, 62–64
CUD recommendations for, 61
definition, 59
framework for, 59–68
practices for, 59–65, 133, 156–157
principles and guidelines for, 59, 63–64, 70
processes for, 65–68
resources for, 68, 70
PLAIN (Plain Language Action and Information Network), 85
Plain Language Action and Information Network (PLAIN), 85
planning, policies, and evaluation
for physical spaces, 63, 66–67
for services, 154–155, 156
for teaching and learning, 112–113, 137
for technology, 84–85
in UDHE framework, 44, 48–49
policies. *see* planning, policies, and evaluation
portable document format (PDF) documents, universal design of, 89–93, 123–124, 196
postsecondary education. *see* higher education
PowerPoint documents, universal design of, 91–93, 124, 140
Preamble of the Convention on the Rights of Persons with Disabilities (United Nations), 14
presentations, universal design of, 118–119
proactive approaches to design
accessible design, 30–31, 33–34
barrier-free design, 30
inclusive design, 15, 30–31, 33–34
in instructional practices. *see* Universal Design of Instruction (UDI)
universal design. *see* universal design (UD); Universal Design in Higher Education (UDHE)
usable design, 30–31, 33–34
professional development. *see also* teaching about UDHE; Universal Design of Instruction (UDI)
about UDHE. *see* teaching about UDHE; Universal Design of Instruction (UDI)
campus services providing, 152
communication with people with disabilities, 9–13
disability awareness, 9–13
professional organizations, role of, 180–181
Published Books and Articles About Universal Design in Higher Education (DO-IT Center), 52, 68, 105, 143, 160

Quality Matters Rubric, 124

Reach Everyone, Teach Everyone (Tobin and Behling), 143
real-time captions, 88–89, 117, 118
"reasonable" criteria for accommodations, 15–16
Rehabilitation Act (1973), Section 504, 13–14
Rehabilitation Act (1973), Section 508, 80, 99
researchers, role of, 183–185
resources
communication with people with disabilities, 21
disabilities and higher education, general, 19–20
model for inclusive campuses, 201
physical spaces, 68, 70
simulations, 23
for student services, 159–160
technology, 104–105
TEDx talks. *see* TEDx talks
UD and UDHE framework, 52
Universal Design of Instruction (UDI), 142–143, 145, 148–149
restrooms, universal design of, 18–19, 46, 177–178
routes of travel and entrances, 44, 46, 60, 63
rubrics. *see* feedback and assessment; Quality Matters Rubric

safety, 44, 63, 133, 140, 156–157
Scholars program, DO-IT Center, 15, 18, 181

science of learning. *see* evidence-based teaching practices
screen reader, 11–12, 22, 77, 83, 85, 90–92, 94
Section 504, Rehabilitation Act (1973), 13–14
Section 508, Rehabilitation Act (1973), 80
sign language interpreters, 16, 48, 118–119, 152
social networking, accessibility of, 98–99
sociocultural approach to teaching, 115
staff
  for physical spaces, 64
  in services, 46, 157
  of student services, 157
  in technology, 103
stakeholder roles
  consumers, 181
  government, 181
  higher education institutions, 181–183
  industry, 180
  list of, xiv
  professional organizations, 180–181
  researchers, 183–185
  in universal design of IT, 102–104
stereotypes, avoiding, 4–5
student services, universal design of. *see* universal design of services
students with disabilities
  accommodations for. *see* accommodations
  awareness about, increasing, 9–13
  challenges faced by, 7–9, 77–79
  civil rights of, 13–16
  communicating with, 10–11
  communication with instructor, 121
  interactions with, 132–133, 141
  practices for, K-12 compared with higher education, 14–15
  prevalence of, 5–7
  responses to UDI applications, 138–142
  securing accommodations, process for, 17–18
  self-disclosure of disabilities by, 6, 18, 33, 122
  services for. *see* universal design of services
  terminology used by and for, 2–5
Students with Disabilities Preparing for Postsecondary Education (US Department of Education), 19
syllabi, universal design of, 119–121
synchronous communication, 88–89

teaching about disabilities
  panels or demonstrations, 11–12, 21–22
  simulations, 12–13, 23
teaching about UDHE
  practices for, 168–171
  prevalence of, 167–168
  reasons for, 164–167
  stakeholder roles, 171–172
teaching and learning activities. *see* Universal Design of Instruction (UDI)
teaching and learning services. *see* universal design of services
technology. *see* Information Technology (IT), universal design of
TEDx talks
  ADHD as a Difference in Cognition, Not a Disorder, 24
  I'm Not Your Inspiration, Thank You Very Much., 22
  The Myth of Average, 20
terminology used for disabilities, 2–5
textbooks, universal design of, 94, 113, 120, 134–135, 180
The Conference Room (DO-IT Center), 159
The Faculty Room (DO-IT Center), 142
The Myth of Average (TEDx talk), 20
transcripts, 78, 96, 115, 135
Transforming Higher Education Through Universal Design for Learning (Bracken and Novak), 143
21st Century Communications and Video Accessibility Act (CCVA), 166

UCD (Universal Course Design), 42
UD. *see* universal design
UDHE. *see* Universal Design in Higher Education
UDI. *see* Universal Design of Instruction
UDL. *see* Universal Design for Learning
UDL on Campus, 52, 142
UDT. *see* Universally Designed Teaching
UID. *see* Universal Instructional Design
United Nations, Convention on the Rights of Persons with Disabilities, 14, 59, 99
Universal Course Design (UCD), 42
universal design (UD)
  characteristics of, 30–32
  checklist incorporating, 131–136
  compared with other approaches, 30, 33–34
  definition, xiv-xv, 29–35
  history of, 30–31
  principles and guidelines of, 37–41
Universal Design in Higher Education (UDHE)
  for academic departments, 137–138
  application areas of, 44, 46

Universal Design in Higher Education (UDHE), *continued*
of assessments, 44, 46, 135–136, 141
characteristics of, 30–31
compared with accommodation approach, 49–50
definition, 32–36
for distance learning programs, 138–139
of documents, 85–94, 123–124
of events, 44, 158
framework for. *see* framework for UDHE
history of, 36–43
of instruction. *see* Universal Design of Instruction (UDI)
of IT. *see* Information Technology (IT), universal design of
of media players, 95–96
model for. *see* Inclusive Campus Model
of online courses, 121–125
paradigm shift required for, 178–179, 181–182, 201, 208–209
of physical spaces. *see* physical spaces, universal design of
of presentations, 118–119
principles of, 43, 45
processes for, 47–49
promoters and inhibitors of, 196–201
research base, 43
of social media, 98–99
stakeholder roles, 49–51
of student services. *see* universal design of services
of syllabi, 119–121
of teaching and learning. *see* Universal Design of Instruction (UDI)
transitioning to, 49–52
of videos. *see* videos
of websites, 85–94, 123–124
Universal Design in Higher Education: From Principles to Practice (Burgstahler), xvii, 52, 68, 105, 143, 160
Universal Design in Higher Education: Promising Practices (DO-IT Center), xxi, 145
Universal Design of Instruction (UDI)
accommodations within, 136–137
definition, 109–111
evaluating, 112, 139
evidence-based teaching practices with, 112–115
framework for, 111–137
inspired by accommodations, 125–129
practices for, 44–47, 116–137
practices for, checklist of, 130–138, 142, 147
practices for academic departments, 137–138
practices for class climate, 131–132, 140
practices for delivery methods, 133–134, 140–141
practices for distance learning programs, 138–139
practices for feedback and assessment, 135–136, 141
practices for interaction with and between students, 132–133, 141
practices for online courses, 121–125
practices for physical spaces and products, 133, 140
practices for presentations, 118–119
practices for syllabi, 119–121
practices for technology and resources, 134–135, 141
principles and guidelines of, 111, 114–116
processes for, 112–114
resources for, 142–143, 145, 148–149
scope, 111
student communication with instructor, 121
students' response to, 138–142
Universal Design for Learning (UDL), 42–43, 45, 119, 131–136
Universal Design of Instruction in PostSecondary Education (DO-IT Center), 142
Universal Design of IT. *see* Information Technology (IT), universal design of
Universal Design of Physical Spaces (DO-IT Center), 68
universal design of services
checklists for, 158–159, 161–162
definition, 151–153
framework for, 153–159
practices for, 155–159
principles and guidelines of, 153
processes for, 154–155
resources, 161–162
resources for, 159–160
scope, 153
Universal Design of Student Services (DO-IT Center), 159
Universal Instructional Design (UID), 42
Universally Designed Teaching (UDT), 42
usable design, 30–31, 33–34
U.S. Department of Education, *Students with Disabilities Preparing for Postsecondary Education*, 19
user interface and navigation, 44, 82–83, 124. *see also* assistive technology (AT)

values, in model for inclusive campuses, 51–53, 179, 186–187, 189
videos. *see also* TEDx talks; YouTube
  audio descriptions for, 88, 96, 142, 166
  captions on, 47, 50–51, 88–89, 95–99, 106
vision
  in Kotter's change process, 191
  in model for inclusive campuses, 52–53, 186–187, 189, 197–198, 202
visual differences, 7–8

W3C. *see* World Wide Web Consortium
WAI. *see* Web Accessibility Initiative
WCAG. *see* Web Content Accessibility Guidelines
Web Accessibility Evaluation Tools List, 105
Web Accessibility Initiative (WAI), 41, 81–82
WebAIM, 105
Web Content Accessibility Guidelines (WCAG)
  checklist incorporating, 131–136
  levels of compliance with, 42, 194
  practices using, 45, 119
  principles and guidelines of, 41–42, 81–82
  resources for, 105
website content, guidelines for, 85–94, 123–124
website resources. *see* resources
Why We Need Captions (video), 106
Winfrey, Oprah, 207–208
World Wide Web Consortium (W3C), 41, 81–82

YouTube. *see also* TEDx talks
  captions created by, 22, 95
  disability and accessibility topics, 11, 20, 22
  Why We Need Captions, 106